A Captive Lion

By the same author

NOVELS
The Circle
The Amberstone Exit
The Glass Alembic
Children of the Rose
The Ecstasy of Dr Miriam Garner
The Shadow Master
The Survivors
The Border

BIOGRAPHICAL ESSAY
Bessie Smith

SHORT STORIES
The Silent Areas

POEMS
In a Green Eye
The Celebrants
The Magic Apple Tree
Some Unease and Angels
Badlands

(TRANSLATIONS)
The Selected Poems of Marina Tsvetayeva
Three Russian Poets

A Captive Lion

The Life of Marina Tsvetayeva

Elaine Feinstein

Hutchinson
London Melbourne Auckland Johannesburg

Copyright © Elaine Feinstein 1987

All rights reserved

First published in Great Britain in 1987 by Century Hutchinson Ltd
Brookmount House, 62–65 Chandos Place, Covent Garden, London
WC2N 4NW

Century Hutchinson Australia Pty Ltd
PO Box 496, 16–22 Church Street, Hawthorn, Victoria 3122, Australia

Century Hutchinson New Zealand Ltd
PO Box 40–086, Glenfield, Auckland 10, New Zealand

Century Hutchinson Group South Africa Pty Ltd
PO Box 337, Bergvlei 2012, South Africa

Set in Linotron Bembo 12 on 13 pt by Input Typesetting Ltd, London
SW19 8DR

Printed in Great Britain by Redwood Burn Ltd, Trowbridge, Wiltshire
and bound by W. B. C. Bookbinders Ltd., Maesteg, Mid-Glamorgan

ISBN 0 09 165900 0

Contents

Acknowledgements   vii

Introduction   15

PART I: Russia

1 'Childhood is the history of my truths': 1892–1907 23
2 'The sweetest of ailments . . .': 1907–1912 43
3 'I could not love anyone else . . .': 1912–1916 58

PART II: Civil War

4 'Loyalty held us, firm as an anchor': 1917–1920 79
5 'I think of him day and night': 1920–1922 97

PART III: Emigration: Berlin and Prague

6 'You are not a child': 1922 117
7 'To have someone loving the woman in me
is a gift': 1922–1925 138

PART IV: Paris

8 Fame and poverty: 1925–1927 173
9 'No one needs me here': 1927–1934 190
10 The question of return: 1934–1937 213
11 'It was all unstoppable, unchangeable, fatal':
1937–1939 234

PART V: The Return to Russia

12 Moscow and Yelabuga: 1939–1941 247

vi   *Contents*

Notes   272

Selected bibliography   279

Index   282

Acknowledgements

I should like to thank all those who collaborated with me in making literal word for word annotated versions for my translations of *Selected Poems of Marina Tsvetayeva*; in the first instance, more than twenty years ago, Angela Livingstone of the University of Essex and Valentina Coe; and for the second edition, Simon Franklin, Vera Traill, Jana Howlett, and Bernard Comrie.

For this biography, I am particularly grateful for the help of Richard Davies, of the Russian Archive at the University of Leeds for his translation of Ariadna Efron's *Stranitsy Vospominanii* and *Pisma K Anne Teskavoi*; to Simon Franklin, University Lecturer in Russian at the University of Cambridge, for his translation of all the letters quoted from *Neizdannye pisma*, and passages from Anastasia Tsvetayeva, *Vospominanni*; I should like to thank Vera Traill, not only for her translation of passages from Mark Slonim 'O Marine Tsvetayevoi'; 'A tale of Sonyechka'; but also for her helping me to put questions to both Salomea Halpern and Konstantin Rodzevitch by letter. I am also grateful for the numerous anecdotes of Tsvetayeva in Paris she shared with me. I should like to thank Jana Howlett, University Lecturer in Russian at the University of Cambridge, for her translations of letters to Alexander Bakhrakh; Roman Gul; and Georgy Ivask. I am grateful to the University of Basel for a xerox of the unpublished MS of Part II of 'A Tale of Sonyechka', and to Dr Andrew Kelus, who kindly arranged its transfer to England. I am deeply grateful to Simon Karlinsky's detailed critical books; full references to all these sources will be found in the Bibliography. I am extremely grateful to Natasha Franklin who helped me deal with problems of annotation.

I am particularly grateful to Masha Enzensberger, Margarita Aliger and Yevgeny Yevtushenko for their help in meeting people in Moscow who had once known Tsvetayeva or were working on her poetry, notably Viktoria Schweitzer, now at Ann Arbor; and to Konstantin Rodzevitch, for allowing me to interview him in his Paris apartment, and afterwards replying to the questions I put to him in correspondence through Vera Traill.

Like anyone working on Tsvetayeva, I am deeply indebted to the research contained in all Professor Simon Karlinsky's pioneering books. I should also like to thank Dr Andrew Kelus, who arranged for Tsvetayeva Mss to be shown to me by the University of Basel; Catherine Carver, who took immense trouble with an earlier version of this manuscript; and Olwyn Hughes, who read this last draft with painstaking attention.

ELAINE FEINSTEIN

For Arnold

Introduction

Marina Tsvetayeva is one of the greatest European poets of this century. In her own generation, Boris Pasternak praised her genius as 'golden, incomparable', and Anna Akhmatova numbered her among a grand fellowship of equals that also included Mandelstam. Since her death, poets as disparate as Yevgeny Yevtushenko and Josef Brodsky have paid homage to her. And yet she has only gradually begun to take her rightful place in the consciousness of the West. The years of neglect spring as much from the paradoxes of her personality as from the accidents of exile and isolation.

Poets have traditionally attracted devoted servants to protect their unworldliness. Far from finding any such fortune, Tsvetayeva willingly put herself in harness, for most of her life, to support her family. For all her passionate nature, the deepest bond of her life was closer to a tie of blood. And yet she never failed her own stern muse. Her impracticality often looked like self-indulgence to fellow *émigrés*, whose self-respect depended on retaining some organization in what was left of their worldly effects. They did not grasp the enormity of her struggle.

She was not a ruthless woman, though her daughter wrote of her: 'She was able to subordinate any concerns to those of her work. I insist, *any*.'[1] For most of her married life, she had to work while coping with conditions of unremitting poverty, for which her comfortable childhood had provided little preparation. When in a letter, Tsvetayeva rebuked Boris Pasternak for travelling through Germany without visiting his mother, she added incredulously: 'Among you superhumans I was *merely* a human . . . I have only ever been myself (my soul) in my notebooks and on solitary roads (which have been rare), for all my life I have been leading a child by the hand.'[2] Among those children, she might well have included her own husband.

As a woman, for all her vitality, she came to accept without bitterness the role of worshipper rather than beloved; perhaps she chose it. It was an understanding of love that seized her when she first heard Pushkin's *Eugene Onegin* read aloud when she was a child, and she longed for a love equally devouring and intense. It was an intensity that, as Mark Slonim observed, made her friendship like meeting 'a single naked soul',[3] and unsurprisingly it frightened many away. At the same time, once Tsvetayeva had given her loyalty, it held for life. It was this commitment that held her through all the vicissitudes of a long marriage.

Although she was always to be sustained by correspondence with great spirits, she could rarely number them among her daily acquaintance. There is little to support the conclusion that this distance was in any way preferable to her. She always needed the company of friends and fellow poets, even if there was something inevitable about the antagonism she aroused. Not all of this was connected to her eccentricity.

Even while opposing the Communist regime she always remained loyal to the greatness of poets in the Soviet Union. For Tsvetayeva, the true poet could have no interest in ideologies. She saw the condition of creation as a visitation analogous to dreaming, when suddenly 'obeying an unknown necessity, you set fire to the house or push your friend down the mountain top'.[4] But in the political context of the Thirties, that lofty apprehension was misunderstood; without any other circumstance, she would have come to be distrusted by the emigration.

She came to feel it was only in Prague that a whole city had been suffused with intense, if painful, excitement. Even in 1926, she was already writing to Anna Teskova from Paris of how much she wanted to return there, to live like a human being: 'I have lived inhumanly and I'm tired of living like that. I'm tired in advance.'[5] She wrote of wanting to find some place in the centre of the city where it would be possible to attend concerts and visit galleries, without being altogether bounded by the responsibility of her children.

As it proved, her whole life was an inexorable movement

into the isolation at the peripheries – from Moscow into exile, then from city to outer suburbs, where the drudgery of everyday life became all the more difficult to bear for being so far from the centre of things. It was a sense of the danger of such situations to her psychological survival that made her so desperate not to be isolated in a village outside Moscow when she returned to the Soviet Union. And it makes even more poignant her ultimate loneliness, in the small town in Yelabuga in 1941, the place appointed for her last ordeal.

It is twenty years since I first began to work on translations of her poems (eventually published as *Selected Poems of Marina Tsvetayeva* by Oxford University Press in 1971) and in that time I have come to understand what it was that so attracted me to her. There is nothing like Tsvetayeva in English. It is not only the violence of her emotions, or the ferocity of her expression, but the extraordinary courage of her humanity and honesty. As I learned more of her life, I was astonished by the stamina that must have sustained that achievement.

It was in 1975 that I first undertook a commission to write the life of Marina Tsvetayeva. Before I set off for Moscow, in the autumn of that year, two pieces of good fortune ensured that several important doors would be open to me.

While dining at Churchill College, Yevgeny Yevtushenko learned that a translator of Tsvetayeva lived in Cambridge. He visited me later that evening. We talked for a whole night about Tsvetayeva and her last weeks in Yelabuga, and when I arrived in Moscow, he did everything he could to help me. In addition, Masha Enzensberger, at that time a Fellow of King's College, Cambridge, had arranged a visit to her mother, the poet Margarita Aliger, in Moscow to coincide with my time there. Through Aliger, I was able to meet and talk to some of the people (notably Viktoria Schweitzer) who had helped to prepare Tsvetayeva's work for publication in the Soviet Union; and also those who, like Pavel Antokolsky, had known Tsvetayeva at the time of the Revolution and on her return to Russia in 1939.

In Aliger's comfortably furnished apartment, I recognized a formidably definite woman in Viktoria Schweitzer, and I questioned her eagerly, most particularly about the character of Tsvetayeva's husband, Sergei Efron. (Unhappily, Tsvetayeva's daughter Ariadna had died only a few weeks before my arrival.) Pavel Antokolsky was less direct. He had obviously once been a very handsome man, and still took some trouble grooming his hair and moustache, but his eyelids were maroon, and he had wine-stained pouches under his eyes. His memory was clearer than he claimed, however, and he spoke vividly of Tsvetayeva's changed demeanour after her return to Moscow.

Most usefully, Aliger was able to give me the Paris address of Konstantin Rodzevitch, the hero of Tsvetayeva's 'Poem of the End'. In the spring of 1976, I visited him in his Paris flat, and found him very willing to talk about his relationship with Tsvetayeva in Prague and in Paris. He replied to all my questions with great charm and courtesy, and showed much distress when looking at a photograph of Tsvetayeva's son, Georgy (who was better known by his pet-name 'Moor') who had died in his teens during the Second World War. Later, when I had met many old friends of Tsvetayeva who spoke harshly of the boy and wrote of him with some bitterness, I was to wonder at Rodzevitch's tears.

On my second visit to Moscow, in 1978, Aliger lent me her own chauffeur-driven car and this enabled me to see the place where the house of Marina's childhood in the Street of the Three Ponds had once stood, and to look at the flat in Boris and Gleb Street where Marina had lived, first as a young married woman and then through the famine and civil war.

Two other accidents gave me some contact with people who had known Tsvetayeva personally. Anna Kallin, who had been a schoolfriend of Tsvetayeva's, wrote and invited me to tea after hearing a broadcast of mine on the Third Programme. She was living at the time with Salomea Halpern (formerly the Princess Andronnikova, and the 'Solominka' of Mandelstam's poetry). The two women made an extraordinary impression, and I doubt if I should have dared to press upon them the impertinent questions I needed to ask. However, soon after, I made the acquaintance of another Russian exile, Vera Traill (formerly Suvchinsky). She had been brought to Addenbrooke's Hospital, Cambridge after sustaining serious burns, and over the following years, I saw much of her. A witty, precise woman with a wide-ranging memory, Vera provided a fascinating\link with a whole network of Russians in Paris during the Twenties and Thirties, including Salomea Halpern, Rodzevitch, the critic D. S. Mirsky (Prince Svyatapolk-Mirsky) as well as Tsvetayeva and her family. In addition to a fund of anecdotes, Vera provided invaluable help in correspondence with Salomea Halpern and others, to whom, on my behalf, she put a number of indelicate questions about Tsvetayeva's behaviour.

I have been most fortunate of all in the calibre of the assistance I received from Russianists, whom I should like to thank for the enormity of the tasks they undertook with such generosity. Particularly my early debt to Angela Livingstone, Simon Franklin, Lecturer in Russian, University of Cambridge; Richard Davies, Librarian of Leeds University Russian Archive; Jana Howlett, Lecturer in Russian, University of Cambridge; Patrick Miles, Fellow of Gonville and Caius College, Cambridge, Bernard Comrie and Natasha Franklin. Their particular contributions are listed among the acknowledgements.

Lastly, I should explain that this book is not intended to provide a critical analysis of Tsvetayeva's poetry except in so far as it arises directly out of her own life. In the Select Bibliography, I recommend several books and articles which deal with her linguistic richness, and set her in the context of Russian poetry in her time.

I am also well aware of the distrust felt among the Russian *émigré* community in the United States for Soviet-published memoirs of Tsvetayeva, which needed to suppress those facets of her behaviour that would offend Soviet ideology: I hope I have guarded against any such whitewashing. Discrepancies between the account of Marina's childhood given by her sister Anastasia and Marina herself offered fewer decisions. There, I have chosen to follow Tsvetayeva's account of events whenever there is a clash, not because she is more accurate, but because my own involvement has led me to see her life as personally as possible through her eyes.

Part I

Russia

I

'Childhood is the history of my truths'

1892–1907

The dominant presence in Marina Tsvetayeva's childhood was that of her mother, Maria Alexandrovna, who devoted most of the energy of her short life to the education of her eldest daughter. There was something tyrannical in the intensity of her attention; and that intensity she bequeathed to her daughter: 'After a mother like that, I had only one alternative: to become a poet.'[6]

To look at the gentle face of Maria Alexandrovna at twenty-one, it was possible to miss the intensity, and Professor Ivan Vladimirovich Tsvetayev certainly made that mistake. Maria Alexandrovna herself cannot have married with many illusions. Tsvetayev was forty-five, a greying, slightly stooped figure in gold-rimmed spectacles, with an absent-minded manner. His former wife and mother of his two children had been dead less than a year. It was not a romantic choice, but since the man Maria Alexandrovna still loved was estranged from a wife who refused to divorce him, she had already abandoned hope of passion, and in marrying Tsvetayev, she looked only for some understanding and affection.

She, too, miscalculated badly. Tsvetayev had loved his first wife Varvara Dmitrievna deeply, and there were signs of that love everywhere. Varvara Dmitrievna had been a woman of exceptional beauty, who had once studied singing in Naples. No doubt love of music must have seemed a resemblance

23

between the two women, but Varvara Dmitrievna had only had a light, bird-like gift for singing, whereas Maria Alexandrovna was an outstanding pianist, who had been taught by a pupil of Nikolai Rubinstein. Her talent was far more than a domestic accomplishment; she brought passion and discipline to it. It cannot have helped her marriage to discover that Tsvetayev had no ear for music.

I. V. Tsvetayev was a professor, first of Roman literature and then of fine arts, at Moscow University, and a director of the Rumyantsev Museum. Such positions ensured a comfortable life for all his family, even though his own father had been a priest in the village of Talitsy, and both he and his brothers had grown up in extreme poverty.

For all his dedication to the fine arts, Professor Tsvetayev's face in middle age has a stolid toughness. A man who disliked extravagance, he nevertheless commissioned an artist to paint a portrait of his dead wife, without any thought for the pain it might give his new one. Maria Alexandrovna sadly reproached herself in her diary for jealousy: 'Jealous of whom? Of the poor bones in the cemetery?' Yet jealous she was, and quite soon deeply unhappy. When the portrait was completed, it was hung high on the white-and-gold-papered wall of the drawing room, where it filled the room with the presence of dead beauty. But then, the house itself had been part of Varvara Dmitrievna's dowry: a one-storey, wooden house at No. 8, The Street of the Three Ponds, in Moscow, with seven tall windows and a silvery poplar leaning over the gateway. Inside, there was a fine ballroom, where the piano stood on a polished parquet floor. In Marina's earliest poems, it was 'a marvellous house, a miraculous house'.[7]

Maria Alexandrovna herself had been well provided for by her own father, but she found her husband's temperament oppressive. She also found it difficult to cope with the resentment of her stepdaughter Valeria, who at nine was only twelve years younger than she was. (The son of the first marriage, Andrei, adjusted more easily.) And when Maria Alexandrovna became pregnant in 1892, all her need for love focused upon the child she was carrying, whom she determined must be a son.

Marina Ivanovna was born on 26 September (o.s.) 1892.*

She was not the longed-for son, but she did show early signs of high intelligence. Maria Alexandrovna's loneliness soon led her to treat this first child as an adult friend. The wide-eyed little girl accepted all she was taught as altogether natural. Half-understood hints stayed with Marina for life – the conviction that everyday life was opposed to all that was sacred, for instance, and the necessity of accepting that talent, like a good ear for music, came from God.

Some lessons were stranger. As a child of four, Marina was shown a picture that hung in her mother's bedroom and recorded the duel in which Pushkin was killed by d'Anthès. The small, black, stick-like trees remained in her memory, alongside the two figures helping to lead the poet towards a sleigh. Her mother never explained to her that the cause of the duel had been Pushkin's wife, the famous beauty Goncharova; the child transposed the duel into a myth with only two figures, the poet and his murderer.

Maria Alexandrovna found the story exciting, and expected Marina to imagine the great poet, dying of his wound among the snowdrifts and yet insisting on his own right to shoot: 'He aimed, he struck home, and what's more, he said "Bravo" to himself.'[8] The lesson had more to do with pride and passion than Christianity and Marina remembered it all her life. It was as if the black and white picture flowed out into her mother's bedroom, which held not a hint of colour in Marina's recollection. There was only a black and white window and the trees outside, her mother, and the terrifying snowy picture on the wall.

All the pictures that Marina remembered from the House on the street of Three Ponds (two murders and one apparition) were in some way threatening. They were to be, as Marina herself put it forty years later, 'an excellent preparation for the terrible century'[9] that awaited her.

Marina also understood, in almost the same way that she knew anything, that she was different from other children, and would be judged by different standards. For a Russian

* Or, according to the Gregorian Calendar now in use, 9 October 1892. Tsvetayeva preferred the Julian Calendar all her life.

child of a comfortable family, the need for a female child to acquire ordinary household skills would not have been stressed. Somewhere in the mixture of privilege and exceptional pressure lay the seeds of Marina's deep unworldliness.

It was not Maria Alexandrovna's intention to turn her daughter into a poet. On the contrary, she was determined to turn her into the concert pianist she had failed to become herself. The pressure was tinged with a cruelty, which her next child, Anastasia (Asya), born two years later, escaped. This was because Maria Alexandrovna saw there was no gain in pushing her younger daughter's limited talent: 'So she's like Ivan Vladimirovich,' she would say with sad resignation as she listened to Anastasia trying to sing in tune. She was not punished for lacking gifts Marina possessed in abundance. On the contrary, she was treated much more indulgently.[10] This Marina resented. Only she needed to excel, it seemed; Anastasia was given love without any such requirement. It was an injustice that complicated the relationship between the sisters. Anastasia admired her sister and followed her lead in everything, but Marina was always impatient with her and sometimes malicious. She envied the response given to Anastasia's milder temperament but she could not imitate it. And in any case she could not escape her powerful mother.

Her mother's ruthless training at the piano remained one of Marina's most bitter memories of childhood. (In later years, she recalled the sheer release of no longer hearing a metronome.) Yet she loved the yellowing keys of the Becker piano, and the music she heard when her mother played. She particularly liked sitting with her sister underneath the piano, as if underwater: underwater not only because the music poured over them, but because pots of palms and philodendrons were reflected in the polished wood of the piano as if in a black lake, and the parquet floor became a watery bottom, with green light on faces and fingers and real roots the children could touch with their hands, where Mother's feet and the pedals moved soundlessly.

Although Marina practised every day for two hours, without complaining, her mother saw easily enough that she lacked her own enthusiasm. The knowledge disappointed but did not deter her. She blamed Marina for it: 'Now when I was four, they couldn't drag me away from the piano! *Noch ein Wenig*! If you asked that of me, just once.'[11] Marina never did. In spite of her precocious understanding of the terms on which she could be loved, Marina would not pretend to a pleasure she did not feel. What she absorbed alongside the strength of her mother's love for the piano was the connection between art and worship. She learned to see the piano as a sacred object, on which nothing should be placed – certainly not newspapers. Maria Alexandrovna made that clear with the undefined, lofty persistence of a martyr, every morning, without saying a word, when Marina's father invariably and innocently put them there. Marina remembered her mother's gesture and, when she was much older, recalled the piano's mirror-like, ultimate cleanness and blackness and contrasted it with the disorderly rustling of her father's newspaper. From this she concluded, with great clarity and for the rest of her life, that newspapers were unclean, and belonged to a world that would be ready to let her die under a fence.

Marina had most of her early tuition from her mother, but she was also instructed by governesses. (Her half brother Andrei was, as a young man, given tutors with grander educational qualifications.) Unsurprisingly, neither they nor the nannies who looked after her in other ways figured sharply in her recollections. All were displaced by the central importance Marina attached to her mother. She even acquired her lifelong interest in folklore mostly through her reading rather than through the traditional story-telling of the jolly peasant nannies who looked after her. In fact, more often than not, Marina herself was the hypnotizing story-teller. She enjoyed her ability to win rapt attention and impress them as she never managed to impress her mother.

At six, when Marina was sent to the Moscow music school of Madame Zograf-Plaksina, she had a firm, rounded face, though it was already possible to detect an obstinacy about the set of her mouth that was missing from her sister Anastasia's expression. (Of the two sisters, it was Anastasia who had inherited the narrow face and sharp features of their mother.) Marina was also a tough child physically, able to take on Andrei, even though he was two years older than she was.

Once her mother read a story to the children about two

boys who ran away from home to look for a princess in the
greenery. Neither boy found her, but a strange feeling of well-
being came over the boy who stayed closest to home. When
her mother had finished, she asked, 'Now children, who *was*
that Tsarevna in the greenery?' Andrei answered indifferently,
'How should I know?' while Anastasia hesitated. Marina was
only too eager to give an answer. 'I think it was *Nature*.' And
although it is not clear whether the answer was strictly correct,
for once she was rewarded for being a bright girl. This praise
was unusual, because Marina's early and instinctive love for
literature was discouraged by her mother. She was piqued to
discover how much sharper Marina was than the other children. 'And why is it always *you* who knows, when I am
reading to *all of you*?'[12] Very early on, Maria Alexandrovna
sensed a rival passion would distract Marina from music, so
when she found Marina was reading adult books, she took
them away and, with inexcusable cruelty, ridiculed the first
poems Marina brought to show her. Her antipathy to any such
interest approached the pathological, and led her to destroy the
notebook in which Marina had written her verses.

Fortunately, Valeria, Marina's half-sister who was twelve
years older, enjoyed Russian literature and in this way Marina
had access to Gogol's *Dead Souls*, which her mother had
declared unsuitable, and eagerly devoured Pushkin's *The
Gipsies*. In Valeria's room was the whole tree of knowledge;
a book cabinet of forbidden fruits, all the sweeter for being
under prohibition. A world, too, of female sexuality lay under
Valeria's green Venetian mirror: cosmetics and silver pills
against menstrual pain suggested bewitching secrets. An illicit
compact grew up between Marina and Valeria, as much from
the older girl's feud with her stepmother as affection between
the half-sisters. An erotic version of a childhood devil,
ambiguously sexed, and suggesting all the powerful forces
of the instinctual world denied by Marina's mother always
appeared in Marina's imagination in her half-sister Valeria's
bedroom. It was one more strand in the network of tensions
that made up Marina's childhood.

Others arose from the personality of D. I. Ilovaisky, Valeria
and Andrei's grandfather, a dour and alarming man of
extremely reactionary beliefs, for whom hatred of the Jews

was a particular passion. Remembering his house near Old St Pimens church on Little Dmitry Street many years later, Marina wrote of a place where 'Everything died out except death. Except old age. Everything: beauty, youth, wonder, life.'[13] Ironically, it was from this side of her extended family that she was to receive her first encouragement to go on writing, from Sergei Ilovaisky, the historian's young son.

Ilovaisky was a harsh man in more than his political beliefs. The tuberculosis that infected, and finally killed, all of his children, did not touch him; he kept a cold house, with open windows, and refused to take a horse and carriage anywhere, even as he aged. There was something monstrous in his longevity.

When he arrived at the Tsvetayev household, he brought gold coins for Andrei only. He had no interest either in girls or in the children of Tsvetayev's second wife, never even bothering to distinguish their faces sufficiently to name them correctly. Maria Alexandrovna took the coins gravely away and gave them to her stepson. But as she took them, she insisted that his hands should be scrubbed because 'all money is dirt'.

The entertainment at the Ilovaisky household, usually cards, was overseen by the formidable old man. It was of no interest to Maria Alexandrovna, who went round to Little Dmitry Street as infrequently as possible. Sometimes her husband insisted, saying, 'You haven't been over there for a whole month now. . . Make an effort, my dear.'[14] Although she never discussed the Ilovaisky way of life with her children, the inhuman coldness of it appalled her. She disliked the old man's bigoted hatred of all minorities. She was conscious of her own German roots (her family were Baltic German through her father), loved Heinrich Heine, and admired Rubinstein. To her intelligent understanding, there were 'neither Greeks nor Jews'. This understanding Marina drew from her mother, along with a love for the richness of the German language. It was a part of her mother's life that she was allowed to share.

In contrast to so much family bitterness, Marina's grandfather, Alexander Danilovich Mein, was a jolly, bustling man who brought presents whenever he visited the Tsvetayev household. His background, that of a wealthy Baltic German, played a significant part in Marina's own development. She learned to read and write in the German language only a little later than Russian and, almost as much as Mandelstam (a St Petersburg Jew), could have written of being 'in seriousness and honour in the West from an alien family'.*

Although Maria Alexandrovna often treated Marina with impatient resentment, they did share one pleasure – a passion for playing with language – which was not shared by the rest of the family. Whatever her mother questioned her about, Marina, in answering, looked for rhymes, as if there were a mystical significance in the way one word rhymed with another; and her mother responded gravely, querying the precision of the rhyme, but understanding the premise. The child worked on word associations rather than etymology; when asked for the meaning of 'red carbuncle', she hit on 'red bottle', because of the resemblance to *Karaffe*, and *funkeln*, and was rewarded by an understanding admission that she was at least close to the meaning. Why, then, was there such a strain of malice, even of triumph, when Marina's mother could show that her daughter failed to understand the grown-up world? She mocked the six-year-old's passionate response to a recital from Pushkin's *Eugene Onegin*. 'You didn't understand anything in that. Well, what could you understand in it?'[15] Marina sensed that the antagonism was more than a question of the disappointment of her mother because of her sex.

A year after her first child was born, Maria Alexandrovna met the man she had once loved, quite by chance, at a lecture by Professor Tsvetayev. When he asked politely after her health, she replied: 'My daughter is a year old. She is very big and intelligent. I am completely happy.' It was a brave lie for a young woman who had married a middle-aged widower still in love with his dead wife. Tsvetayeva, writing of the incident four decades later, commented: 'Oh God, how that minute she must have hated me, however big and intelligent, because I was not *his* daughter!'[16]

It was her mother's own suffocating unhappiness that made her feel antagonism to her daughter, but there was more to it

* From Mandelstam's poem 'To the German Tongue' (1932).

than that. An old Ukrainian folk-tale Marina loved tells of a girl going into a church at night and finding a congregation of unnatural quietness. Suddenly she feels someone grasp her shoulder. It is her dead godmother, and her strange advice is to run away, before her real mother (who is also dead) sees her and tears her to pieces. The terrified girl takes to her heels, with her own mother in hot pursuit. But why had the mother been sharpening her teeth and waiting for a chance to eat her daughter ever since the day she died?

Later in life, Marina understood that it was envy. Of course, every daughter is a rival, but Maria Alexandrovna's ambitions and desires had been so thwarted that her jealousy was as bitter as a dead woman's jealousy of one still alive, with all the ferocious awareness that the chance to live would not now be hers.

Professor Tsvetayev was often away and the house in the Street of Three Ponds was very much a house of women. With Valeria sometimes playing a protective role and her mother alternating between encouragement and impatience, it is not surprising that Marina, in later life, turned most successfully to women to build close friendships. Not surprising, either, that she should find an almost erotic excitement in the idea of being kidnapped by Old Believer nuns from a convent near the family's country home in Tarusa.

The Tsvetayev family spent summers at Tarusa, a small town on the Oka river, not far from Moscow, in the province of Kaluga. It was a quiet town, surrounded by forests and far from the railway, with broad fields on both sides of the river. During Marina's childhood, most of the houses were single-storey wooden *dachas* with painted fences, and gardens behind them with closely planted apple and cherry trees. In streets and courtyards, roosters, hens, geese and baby chickens scurried everywhere. It was altogether remote from town life and yet it was a modest countryside, without the majesty of the Caucasus or the richness of Georgia.

The Tsvetayev house in Tarusa had a large garden, or rather several gardens. In the old orchard were apple trees that had been allowed to run wild; these apples the Tsvetayev family gave away. However, there were also other gardens full of fruit that ripened all at once in summer: strawberries, cherries,

currants and elderberries. Marina recalled the redness and illicit
sweetness of those berries in a story about the 'Kirillovnas',
group of Old Believer nuns who lived in the village and were
particularly fond of her. Their fondness took the form of
feeding victoria plums to her and her sister as soon as their
mother's back was turned. They very well understood that
such greed would never be countenanced – Maria Alexandrovna's eyes had made that as clear to them as to the children
– yet they went on pouring berries from their colanders into
the children's daring, hungry mouths.

Marina remembered with longing the nuns' teasing threat
that they were going to take her away to live with them:

> 'Marina, dear, my beauty, stay with us, you'll be our
> daughter and live with us in our garden and sing our
> songs . . .'
>   'Mama won't let me.'
>   'But wouldn't you stay otherwise?' Silence.
>   'Well, of course you wouldn't stay . . . you'd miss your
> mama. She probably loves you a great deal, doesn't she?'
> Silence. 'Probably she wouldn't give you away for money
> either, would she?'
>   'But we won't even ask her mama – we'll just take her
> ourselves!' said one of the younger ones. 'We'll take her
> away and lock her up in our garden, and we won't let
> anyone in. Then she'll live with us behind the hedge.' (A
> wild, burning, unfulfillable hope began to glow inside
> me: would it be soon?)[17]

Although Marina may have wanted to be whisked away
from her family, she loved the family *dacha* at Tarusa and the
way of life there. She remembered her father in his tussore-
silk jacket, her mother in her red handkerchiefs, the yellow
bonfire and the river Oka, and indeed the story of the Kirillovna nuns contains a notably genial portrait of Professor
Tsvetayev himself, resisting his wife's objections to Marina
being allowed to go with the family to watch the hay-making.
Maria Alexandrovna couldn't stand any kind of family outing,
and feared that the ride behind the horses was likely to make

Marina sick. Marina clearly found her father gentler than her mother although he only challenged his wife's opinion meekly.

'I don't get sick to my stomach when I walk,' I inserted in a timid outburst, having acquired courage from Father's presence.

'She can sit facing the horses. We can take some mints with us,' said Father convincingly, 'and another dress, too, for changing . . .'

'Only I don't want to sit next to her! Not next to nor in front of her!' burst out Andryusha [Andrei] whose face had long since turned sullen. 'Every time I have to sit next to her, like the time in the train, you remember, Mama, when . . .'

'We'll take some eau-de-Cologne,' continued Father, 'and I will sit next to her.' ('Only be sure and tell us, please,' he said confidentially to me, 'when you feel dizzy – just say so, and we'll stop the horses, and you can get down and rest a bit.')[18]

Aside from holidays in Tarusa, Marina inherited a Moscow such as Boris Pasternak was to recall – of cloisters, towers and churches with gold-crowned cupolas. The ambience of the Pasternak household was, however, wholly different from that of the Tsvetayevs. Leonid Pasternak was also a member of the teaching staff of Moscow University's School of Painting, Sculpture and Architecture; his wife Rosalya, like Marina's mother, was a talented pianist who had given public concerts before she had abandoned her career to look after her husband and family. Leonid and Rosalya, however, were warmly attached to one another, and their Odessa Jewish descent made for a southern ebullience Marina's family notably lacked. Pasternak's earliest memory was of listening to a trio performed by his mother and two professors from the Moscow Conservatory, but Marina's family seem to have rarely entertained in any such spirit. This is hardly surprising in someone of Tsvetayev's temperament. He was not only absent-minded but inturned, and a little stingy. The bare-footed poverty of his childhood as a priest's son in Talitsy is only part of the story: he genuinely disliked spending money.

For him, even the purchase of new clothing produced misery and apprehension. Awkward, sheepish and eccentric Tsvetayev may have appeared but he was despotically opposed to extravagance, and that asceticism may well have put down roots in Marina's own spirit.

The inwardly turned, almost reclusive character of her family background stunted and narrowed Marina in many ways; she never acquired, for instance, the easy rapport with others that blessed Boris Pasternak for most of his life, and made his tentative stammer a tic that friends remembered with affection. At the same time, Marina's isolation was a source of later strength. She learned unnaturally early to rely on the habit of self-appraisal that was to sustain her through a loneliness few writers have had to endure.

Pasternak was more fortunate. It may have been his father's talent that led Tolstoy to choose him as his illustrator for *Resurrection*, but it was the ease of the elder Pasternak's hospitality that brought Tchaikovsky, Gorky, Rilke and Einstein through their drawing room on the way to the artist's studio. In marked contrast, Marina's memories of her childhood focus almost exclusively on close members of her family. And even there, her relationship with her sister, Asya, was made uneasy both by, first, the inequity of their mother's demands on them, and then by Asya's adoring imitation of everything Marina did or said. For this, Marina showed a proud contempt.

She was far closer to, and more than half in love with, Seryozha (Sergei) and Nadya, children of her Ilovaisky relations, who often joined the Tsvetayev family on holidays in Tarusa. At four years old, Marina stood for hours in complete silence, immersed in watching Seryozha work away at the slope running from the river Oka to the Tsvetayev *dacha*, digging a stairway into the steep side of the hill. Marina's nanny was puzzled by the fascination; Marina herself could only explain it by sighing, 'I'm looking at his blue trousers.'[19]

By the time he was seventeen (and Marina only seven), Seryozha knew her well enough to encourage her to copy out her secretly written poems. It was a request that made her shy. In his presence, her saucy, bold manner deserted her completely, and when the poems were copied, she could only offer them to him nervously, feeling awkward, short-haired and plain. His attention was worth far more to her than he knew, even if it arose mainly from kindness, a kindness (and a deep innocence) that sprang from the knowledge that his own death was approaching. Both Seryozha and Nadya had already contracted tuberculosis. At first, Ilovaisky took them to Spasskoe, where they were fed on a diet of oatmeal and made to sleep with the windows open in a singularly damp climate, but in 1902 he more sensibly took them to Nervi on the Bay of Genoa in Italy.

If Seryozha was Marina's first love, it was to Nadya she attached her deepest passion; the girl's faint smile, dark eyes and flushed beauty (all so unlike her own solidly healthy face) were features that attracted Marina's most romantic feelings. But both loves were doomed. Seryozha died first; a month later, Nadya too was borne off in a coffin through the February snow. It was a crueller death than Seryozha's, for to the end, Nadya had continued to hope and pray for life.

With the loss of these two, Marina experienced the extent of her isolation. It was an isolation that made for precocity, as well as a preternatural voracity for books. (She had read Racine, Corneille, Victor Hugo and most of the Russian classics before she was twelve.) It also gave her the wary self-sufficiency of a natural outsider.

At the age of nine, Marina entered the first year of the Gymnasium No. 4 on the Sadovaya, near Kudrinskaya Square. A heavy, yellow building, it formed part of a network of state schools that taught Greek and Latin as well as scientific subjects. Pasternak attended a similar one. For all her prodigious talents in Russian, French and German (both languages learnt from her mother) Marina hated the change. She never found it easy to adapt from home to school, from school to school or even from grade to grade.

Maria Alexandrovna played the piano more and more to herself in an empty drawing room, dreaming perhaps of an audience that was capable of appreciating what she played. She made no social calls, though sometimes she went to the theatre or to concerts with friends. By the spring of 1902, her health was beginning to fail, and in November of the same year she learned from her doctor that she, too, had tuberculosis. So it was that the family's travels abroad began. Andrei was left in

Moscow with his grandfather, but the rest of the family jour-
neyed to Nervi, which Professor Tsvetayev used as a base
for sculpture-spotting trips around the country. Marina was
hugely excited at the prospect of seeing the sea. She was only
ten, but she already loved Pushkin's magnificent praise of its
elemental force. However, her romantic hopes were shattered
by her first sight of the real thing. 'Is that the sea?' she whim-
pered. 'That's not the sea at all, not at all like the sea.'[20]

As the family arrived at Nervi, Maria Alexandrovna suffered
a serious tubercular attack, and there was no further chance
that day for the children to examine the sea any closer. In
the morning, ill though she was, Maria Alexandrovna forced
herself out of bed and took her seat at the piano. A few minutes
later, there was a knock on the door.

> 'Allow me to introduce myself, Doctor Mangini. And
> you, if I am not mistaken, are Signora thus-and-such, my
> future patient?' (He was speaking in halting French.) 'I
> was passing by and heard your playing. And I must warn
> you that if you continue like that, you will not only burn
> yourself out, you will set the entire Pension Russe on
> fire.' (And with an ineffable pleasure, now in Italian:)
> 'Geniale . . . Geniale . . .'[21]

Of course, he put a long-term prohibition on her playing.

In Nervi, the children's circle of acquaintances broadened a
little. The son of the hotel owner, a boy called Volodya,
offered to show them the town. His appearance did not suggest
reliability, and although the children were eager to go, Maria
Alexandrovna hesitated. It was Valeria who persuaded her
to let them venture out on their first independent explo-
ration.

Marina must have hoped to see the Nervi that she had
imagined from the postcards sent back by her sad, much-loved
Nadya Ilovaiskya – cards on which the sea appeared a deep,
dark blue, with black pines against it, and a brightly lit moon
stood out against blue-black clouds. That blue darkness was
never to be matched in the Nervi that Marina and Anastasia
explored with Volodya. And Marina soon discovered that,
however much her name might suggest an affinity to the sea,

she was much happier walking upright on mountains than she could ever learn to be in the presence of the slippery, pale monster that lived in the Bay of Genoa.

Volodya took a certain pleasure in her clumsiness. While he and Asya climbed happily about the flat slate and rocks on the seashore, Marina almost at once fell in, and had to be hauled out by Volodya, grinning. As she sat disconsolately, emptying water out of her boots, and trying to dry out her dress so that her mother would not be angry, Marina caught a glimpse of the longed-for blueness in the distance. So she came to write on the slate the deepest truth she had learned from the experience, which was the truth from which she had begun: Pushkin's 'Farewell, free element!'

Among those staying at the same pension were a group of anarchists, who taught Marina and Asya revolutionary songs. They had been *émigrés* as a result of their opposition to the Tsar, and some openly discussed the penal servitude they had suffered for their opposition to the regime. One of the servants who had accompanied the family was among the latter.

In 1903 Maria Alexandrovna's health began to deteriorate, and since it was essential for her to go to a sanatorium, Marina and Anastasia were sent away to boarding school in Lausanne – the Pensionnat de Mademoiselle Lacaze.

Marina was not yet eleven, but luckily, her command of French was excellent. She was always academically confident, even though she found it difficult to make friends with children her own age, who found her precocity worrying. With older girls, however, she became something of a pet. Monsieur l'Abbé was less pleased with her opposition to the Catholic church, and set himself the task of winning over her lost soul. The children were taken twice to church on Sundays: once to morning Mass, and again at four in the afternoon. This was unlikely to win Marina's complaisance, and she frequently stopped the hand of her less militant sister as it hovered over the collection plate. By the time the girls had been at the school for a few months, however, both were touched enough by the new faith to write letters that Maria Alexandrovna found alarming. She wrote to Tsvetayev:

It is uncanny how these Catholics bring up children! My

children are no longer little girls. They are turning into nuns. [22]

Evidently Professor Tsvetayev was less alarmed, for they were not immediately removed from Mademoiselle Lacaze's.

It was mainly to bring the children closer to their mother that, in February 1905, they were moved to another school, this time in Freiburg in the Black Forest: the Brinck boarding school. Their mother took a room in a small hotel next door, perhaps to ward off undesirable influence as far as possible. Conditions in the Brinck school were spartan, however, and the severity was in terrifying contrast to the tolerant atmosphere at Mademoiselle Lacaze's. 'Bad marks' were given for sheets not tucked in tightly enough, a single hair left in a comb or an incautious turning of the head towards the window during class. In many subjects, Marina had to be placed in a class three years above her own age group, and this contributed to her isolation.

Although for many years afterwards the landscape of Freiburg and the Black Forest represented German magnificence to Marina, the days at the Brinck boarding school were doleful. The children looked forward desperately to the start of the summer holidays, when Professor Tsvetayev was to come and collect them, as if to a day of liberation. Under the harsh regime of the school, Marina learned a new virulence and anger. She played pranks on her teacher Fräulein Enni – for instance, she knitted a small figure with a tail and horns into a dress she had made in a handicraft lesson. This was felt to be not only brazen, but even wicked, and Marina was summoned for punishment. She was characteristically unrepentant and proud, and when her father received a letter from the headmistress requesting him to come and collect the children before the end of the summer term, she would have been happy to have him agree. Unfortunately he could not leave Russia immediately, and their mother was too ill to be disturbed.

However, there was, out of all this misery, one pleasurable occasion that Marina was to recall most sharply from her stay at the establishment of the Fräuleins Brinck. This was a visit they organized for her to meet a princess – the Fürstin von

Thurn und Taxus. In later years, Marina discovered that the magical figure who listened so kindly to her spirited account of *Heidi* and to her patriotic convictions concerning the Russo-Japanese war was a close friend of the poet Rainer Maria Rilke.

In the winter of 1904/5, Maria Alexandrovna's illness worsened considerably. Tsvetayev was forced to stay closer to her and she had to be transferred from Freiburg to a sanatorium at St Blasien in Switzerland. By this time, Maria Alexandrovna was confined indoors and the girls had little to do, so they went on walks with their father.

Tsvetayev was not a sociable walker. He preferred to stride ahead, lost in thought, neither taking any pleasure in the countryside around him nor talking. He could not even share the grief he felt at the illness of his second wife. Marina tried hard to bridge the gap between herself and her father, but there were often heavy silences. Whatever memories may have stood between him and the expression of his love, in practical matters Maria Alexandrovna's assistance had become essential. It was not only because she wrote letters in French and German for him; she was also the only member of the family who felt, as he did, the fate of the museum as an integral part of her own life. Ill though she was, she had shown a horror equal to his own when she heard of a major fire at the Rumyantsev Museum, and she insisted on his temporary return to Moscow.

Quite soon, Maria Alexandrovna too decided to return to Russia. The children had by now adjusted to a nomadic life and were ready to help with all the suitcases, packages and baskets, but Maria Alexandrovna insisted on doing most of the packing. By now she was very ill, coughing all the time, but still smiling and evidently strong enough to help write some letters on behalf of the museum, which Tsvetayev dictated in Russian and she translated into French. Evidently her spirit was not yet worn out, and the children might be forgiven for being grateful that they were on the road to Russia again.

The family had decided to stay first in the *dacha* of a certain Dr Weber in Yalta, where among their neighbours was Ekaterina Peskova, the wife of Maxim Gorky. They did not live there very long. Professor Tsvetayev disapproved of an attachment that rapidly developed between Marina and Vera, the

eldest of the Weber daughters. Vera was a pale, dark-eyed girl
with plaits, who was stubborn and self-willed, and who at
once became Marina's idol. There were rumours that she was
a revolutionary, and Professor Tsvetayev decided to transfer
to living quarters on the other side of Yalta, so that Marina
might be removed from her dangerous influence. There was
no way, however, of removing the family from knowledge
of the growing swell of revolt, for these were days when
revolution, whether welcomed or feared, was no dream but
an everyday threat, bringing repression, arrests and searches
in its train, even in Yalta. It was the year of a massacre of
workers, bearing icons, outside the Tsar's Winter Palace in St
Petersburg; and the revolutionary Lieutenant Piotr Schmidt's
execution; it was also the year of the mutiny aboard the Black
Sea battleship *Potemkim*.

Professor Tsvetayev and Maria Alexandrovna supported
constitutional democracy by way of moderate and bloodless
reform. That did not suit Marina's temperament, she preferred
individual heroic revolutionaries. But although it was a winter
of strikes and shootings, her heart was racked by a misery
closer to home.

This was the winter when the fatality of her mother's illness
had to be accepted. At the end of March 1906, Maria Alexandrovna had a serious lung haemorrhage, which was the start
of her final steep decline. She had to spend most of her time
in bed swallowing ice, and for the first time she accepted
without any pretence that she was going to die.

The family determined to return to Moscow, but never
completed the journey. Maria Alexandrovna stopped being
able to sleep. She needed more air, and had difficulty in
breathing.

The last mortal thing, June 1906. We didn't get as far as
Moscow, we stopped at the Tarusa station. They had
carried Mother from place to place the whole way from
Yalta to Tarusa. 'I boarded a passenger train and I'll arrive
in a freight,' she joked. Arms lifted and placed her in the
tarantass. But she would not allow herself to be carried
into the house. She stood up and, refusing support, took
those few steps by herself, past where we stood breathless

and immobile, from the porch to the piano, unrecognis-
able and huge after several horizontal months, in a beige
travelling duster which she had ordered made up as a
cloak so as not to measure the sleeves. 'Well, let's see
what I'm still able to do,' she said smiling and it was clear
she was saying it to herself. She sat down. Everyone
stood. And there from hands already out of practice, but
I don't want to name the things yet, that's still the secret
I have with her . . .

That was her last playing. Her last words in that newly
added porch of fresh pine boards, shaded by that same
jasmine were: 'I only regret music and the sun.'[23]

After his second wife's death, the household of Professor
Tsvetayev split up. Valeria left home, Andrei became the ward
of Professor Ilovaisky and the two daughters of Maria Alexandrovna entered the Gymnasium.

The form of Maria Alexandrovna's last will and testament
bears out strongly her fears for the maturity of her daughters.
She left all her money to them, with the proviso that they
could not touch it until the age of forty. Marina herself, in
later years, thought that this provision arose from anxieties
that her adolescent revolutionary fervour might have led her
to give all the money away to a foolish cause. Ironically, the
money was lost altogether when the Communists took over.

A year after Maria Alexandrovna's death there was a service
at the Vagankov cemetery to mark the anniversary, and all the
family returned briefly to the house in the Street of the Three
Ponds. The shutters were half-closed and the house smelt of
camphor balls, but the samovar was gurgling and eggs were
being steamed on its open lid. Marina walked to the piano and
touched the keys, the sounds filling the silence of the room,
but then she firmly closed the lid and walked softly away.
Now Maria Alexandrovna's hopes for Marina's musical career
were finally over. Marina stopped practising, and although
teachers continued to visit her, she no longer cared to perfect
her technique.

While her mother was alive, Marina had made an effort to
give her happiness, knowing that a lack of application would
have been a torment to her. Although at first astonished, the

teachers soon accepted that the importance of music in
Marina's life had now diminished.

> Thus, the sea, receding, leaves pits behind, at first deep,
> then getting shallower, then barely damp. Those musical
> pits, the traces of Mother's seas, stayed in me for good.[24]

Had her mother lived longer, Marina would certainly have
entered the Conservatory and graduated a fair pianist. Luckily,
since she lacked that wondrous quality of slowly developing
genius that took Pasternak through music and philosophy until
he reached his destiny as a poet, Marina was free to emerge
early as her true self as she disentangled herself from the love
she had felt for her mother.

And that farewell of parting was not so different from the
lesson she had learned at that childhood performance of *Eugene
Onegin*, when her enthusiasm had so incensed her mother: the
lesson that love was most sharply felt in parting. It was a
lesson she learned from her mother too, and perhaps other
generations had passed it down.

> A lesson of courage. A lesson of pride.
> A lesson of fidelity. A lesson of fate.
> A lesson of loneliness.[25]

2

'The sweetest of ailments . . .'

1907–1912

Eighteen months after her mother's death a sense of loss still filled Marina's life. She read with pain and sympathy the nine thick volumes of the diary Maria Alexandrovna had kept since she was seventeen. In the description of 'S. E.' (the artillery officer her mother had loved), she found a bitterness that reminded her of Andrei Bolkonsky's in *War and Peace*. Her own romantic imagination was stirred. And as the diary ended: 'I am thirty years old. I have a husband and children, but . . .'[26], followed by a thick wad of stumps, all that was left of the pages that had been carefully cut out, Marina's heart was thrilled with the recognition of intense and unrequited love.

As a child, Marina had always hated her own unromantically healthy appearance. By the time she was fourteen, she was solidly built, tall for her age, often with a short, thick plait arranged around her head. Her huge green eyes were seriously myopic, though she rarely wore glasses. To remove the offensive signs of health from her cheeks, she cut down on food and drank vinegar. She lacked the physical beauty of Anna Akhmatova, but what she did have was vitality, and this she determined her new Russian boarding school should not curb. Unsurprisingly, her wilfulness soon ensured her expulsion.

She was allowed new financial independence, and in 1908

43

she was able to afford to go abroad to study French literature at a summer course at the Sorbonne. Marina was not timid, as her decision to go to Paris on her own demonstrates. If her mother had been alive, she would hardly have allowed it, but Professor Tsvetayev's acquiescence was easy to win. His mind was preoccupied with his own concerns, and he seemed remarkably lacking in paternal anxiety for his self-willed daughter.

In the summer of 1909, she returned again to Paris and was able to see Sarah Bernhardt on the stage. After her performance in Edmond Rostand's *L'Aiglon*, Marina waited outside for an autograph from the great actress – she had found a new heroine. She had also begun to write remarkable poetry, discovering that it was possible to withdraw into a world of fantasy and be sustained by it.

In the same spirit, Marina began to translate *L'Aiglon*, at the end of that summer in the family house at Tarusa; she spent all the winter of her seventeenth year on it. What attracted her to the play, apart from her admiration of Rostand, was her love for the character of Napoleon II. She filled her room with pictures of both the Emperor and his sad son and, in her work, cut herself off from the daytime of people and chores, preferring to live with her books, among the people in the portraits on her walls. She loved to quote Napoleon's words from the play: '*L'imagination gouverne le monde!*', which became one of the epigraphs for her first book of poems, *Evening Album*. Marina's absorption with the life of Napoleon was so profound that she spent half of each day in her own narrow room, as if she had transferred herself altogether into another age and another person's life. She knew Victor Hugo's 'Odes to Napoleon' by heart, and collected engravings of her hero to hang upon her wall.

Her translation has since been lost. After she had finished it, she discovered that it had already been translated by Schepkin-Kuperrik. The rival work was ludicrously prosaic, but Marina, understandably disappointed, threw all her work to one side when she heard of its existence, a gesture reminiscent of a spoiled, imperious child. Yet there was more to it than that: a refusal to compete with the shoddy on any terms.

Soon she was to discover another world, a world of poets

and literary criticism in Moscow itself – and her first romance. At fifteen, Vladimir Nilender entered Marina's life, through Lev Kobylinsky (better known under the pseudonym of 'Ellis'), with whom he shared lodgings. A graduate student in history at Moscow University, and an enthusiastic admirer of Baudelaire, Ellis gained enormous prestige in Marina's eyes as a friend of Andrei Bely. Unknown to her, Bely was titillated in his turn by Ellis's knowledge of the Tsvetayeva sisters, but their meeting would not have suited Ellis. Nevertheless, Ellis was the first reliable critic of Marina's work, and while praising her translation of *L'Aiglon*, he put her in touch with contemporary Russian poetry. Marina (accompanied by her sister) had conversations with both Ellis and Nilender, and recorded them in a dark blue, leather-bound album with gold trimmings, which Marina and Asya called 'Our Evening Album'. Later they wrote out Marina's new poems in the same album, and Marina used the title *Evening Album* for her first published book of poems.

Ellis had the quality of an enchanter, a magician opening up a new world for Marina, and it was in this way that she wrote of him in the 'Evening Album', but it was to Nilender that she was attracted. Probably both sisters enjoyed the discovery of their own attractions. However, both Nilender and Ellis were in love with Marina; indeed, Nilender proposed marriage on the very night that Ellis had dispatched him with a letter to Marina containing a similar proposal. When at last Nilender brought himself to hand over the letter, Marina received it with astonishment. It was Anastasia who was the first to understand that Nilender was as much in love as Ellis, and once she was sure of this, she got up, put on her coat and left, although Marina tried to persuade her to stay. Anastasia knew Marina had no desire for marriage, but was wrong in thinking that Marina did not want to be loved.

That evening, Marina and Nilender walked the streets of Moscow together. After she returned, shivering with cold, she was silent for the rest of the night. Evidently she was perplexed and could not decide what to tell her sister. Several days passed before Marina decided to break the silence, and then she said with despair in her voice, 'It's over. That evening, when we went out for a walk together, we said goodbye and now we shall never see each other again.'[27]

Marina was deeply disturbed by her feelings for Nilender and found that parting painful. One night walking with Anastasia along the Arbat, she was suddenly overwhelmed to recognize Nilender walking towards them. There was only time to acknowledge his sad smile, the wave of his hand and the raising of his hat before he had passed beyond her, but Marina went pale, and said nothing for the rest of the walk. She recorded her feelings in a lyric written in March 1910 called 'Meeting'. She had cared more than she knew, although her affection for Nilender was far less ferocious than later attachments were to prove.

In spite of love poems written to Nilender, Marina's deepest emotions at this time were generated by women. Whoever entered her heart, she began, in a sense, to invent, to endow them with qualities they did not really possess. Yet in the case of Asya Turgeneva, Marina's adoration was shared by many admirers.

In Moscow in 1910, there were many legends surrounding the three Turgenev sisters. The poet Solovev was in love with Natasha, the eldest; Andrei Bely was in love with Asya; and even the youngest (then aged only twelve) was soon to have all Moscow at her feet. Meanwhile, Asya Turgeneva held court, her small head held tilting delicately forward, looking as fine as an etching. Marina observed that her tapered fingers perpetually held a cigarette, and that her lovely head seemed always wreathed in a grey cloud of smoke. On one occasion, Nilender himself was present when Marina visited the sisters. Marina guessed that he too was a little in love with Asya: 'It was impossible not to be in love with her.'[28]

Very little was said on these visits. Asya seems to have been silent in her effortless superiority, and Marina was silenced by the effect of Asya's incomparable elegance. Once Asya wore a leopard skin across her shoulders, and Marina won her attention by exclaiming that she herself was just such an animal. In return, she received a prolonged and serious gaze, and a comment on her own remarkable green eyes.

What Marina liked in Asya, aside from her girlish beauty, was her business-like manner, almost that of a courtly young man, which she recognized as like her own. What lay between them was decidedly more than friendship: a love, rather than an infatuation, as Marina put it herself, because, to her, love was felt for 'what is akin' and infatuation only for what is alien. The two girls had a common wildness and, once conversation had opened, enjoyed their own daring. But it was not a love intended to last, and Marina lost Asya soon after, when the latter married Andrei Bely.

Marina was now seventeen, with bobbed hair and high heels, and she had taken up smoking. At first, she concealed this to spare her father's feelings. (He was indeed rather alarmed at the way she was developing.) However, when he packed her off to Germany in the summer of 1910, he had more on his mind than the thought of her general discipline.

Nilender's connection with Ellis had contributed to Professor Tsvetayev's negative attitude towards Marina's further acquaintance with her young suitor. And it is as well that Marina had no romantic feelings about Ellis, who was soon at the centre of a scandal that involved her father and came close to ruining him. The facts are not entirely clear. In January 1909, a theft of prints from Tsvetayev's museum was discovered when a grand duke found some of them in a Moscow shop and saw that the museum stamps had not been fully rubbed out. The trail led to Koznov, a friend of the museum curator, Shurov. At this stage, Tsvetayev managed to retrieve three-quarters of the stolen prints. Nevertheless, the Minister of Education, Alexander Nikolayevich Schwartz, decided to appoint a special commission of investigation. There was an element of personal enmity in this, a relic of the days when Tsvetayev and Schwartz had been at school together. A check on the museum stocks was made, and several accusations were levelled at Tsvetayev. These criticisms reached the press and Tsvetayev prepared a long written reply. His plans were cut short when he received a letter from Schwartz ordering him to resign within three days. Tsvetayev refused.

In December of the same year (1909), a Senate report followed, declaring that there were no grounds for Tsvetayev's dismissal as Director of the Rumyantsev Museum. Hearing this, Tsvetayev wrote happily to the architect of the new museum, R. I. Klein:

Dear Ivanovich,
Yesterday evening I received from Petersburg dispatches concerning the Senate's conclusions and my moral victory. The Assembly of the Senate unanimously declared the accusations to be groundless . . . this makes me very happy despite the *numbness* that has come over me after such malicious and protracted persecution by the administration and by newspaper reporters.

Somehow, totally unexpectedly, I must have become the object of malice and slander. . . . You never doubted my innocence. . . .[29]

The story should have ended there. Early in 1910, however, Shurov, the museum curator, ordered a new stock-taking at the museum as a result of statements made by two informers on the museum staff. In March, the Senate repeated its rejection of all charges against Tsvetayev, but Shurov sent an aggressive report to the Senate, and by May, the newspapers were once again commenting on the scandal. Why precisely Ellis chose *this* moment to cut some pages out of several books belonging to the museum is by no means clear. It may have been a gesture in support of anarchism, a belief he shared with Bely, who could see no malice in this act towards the Tsvetayev family. Bely's own absent-mindedness led him to believe that Ellis simply forgot which books were his own and which were the museum's. None of the books was particularly rare or valuable. Tsvetayev himself could not conceive that Ellis had acted with criminal intent. However, the matter had by now become a *cause célèbre* in the press, and although the charges against Ellis were subsequently dropped because of insufficient evidence, Professor Tsvetayev was relieved of his duties at the museum. He never recovered from the blow, though he bore it with great courage, and continued to work dutifully on the setting up of a new musuem he planned. But he was a broken man.

The events around her father's dismissal were doubly bitter to Marina since they involved someone whom she had once thought of as an important friend. She had already broken off all contact with Nilender: now a trip to Dresden with her father helped to enforce that break. But she went on thinking of him, and her first book of poems included a number of verse epistles addressed to him, as if they were alternatives to the true letters she had been forbidden to write.

Tsvetayeva's precocity as a poet is clear from *Evening Album*, a volume of poems published at her own expense in 1910, which contained many poems written when she was only fifteen. Many of these are preoccupied with death:

> To be dead for ever. Can it be for this
> that Fate gave me understanding of so much?

but most are filled with the longing for some volcanic passion whose pain she was eager to endure as 'the sweetest of ailments'.

Once printed, she took the volumes to a bookshop and set them down there as if carelessly: however she also sent inscribed copies to the poets Bryusov and Voloshin, whom she had not yet met. Among the poets to notice her at this early age was Gumilyov, the leader of the Acmeist movement in Russian poetry who wrote of her:

Marina Tsvetayeva is inherently talented and inherently original. It does not matter that her book is dedicated to the radiant memory of Maria Bashkirtseva, that the epigraph is taken from Rostand, and that the word 'Mama' is almost never absent from the pages. All this only suggests the young age of the poetess which is soon confirmed by her own lines of confession. There is much in this book that is new: the audacious, at times excessive, intimacy of tone; the new themes such as childhood infatuations; the spontaneous unthinking delight in the trivial details of everyday life. As one would have thought, all the principle laws of poetry have been instinctively guessed, so that this book is not only a charming

book of a young girl's confessions but also a book of
excellent verse.[31]

Marina must have known that, from this moment on, whatever else was to be denied to her, she could walk boldly among
poets in the future.

Marina's adolescence continued its wild course unchecked,
threatened only briefly by the prospect of her father marrying
again. Tsvetayev mistakenly thought the children needed a
mother to look after them, but he backed down from the
arrangement after pressure from Ilovaisky, and no new figure
came into the household.

Marina's literary acquaintance began to grow. Max Voloshin, one of the most enthusiastic critics of her first book,
soon became her friend. He instigated the relationship himself
by calling upon Marina at home: he was wearing a top hat,
and his large face was framed by a short curling beard. Marina
had not yet read the article he had written about *Evening
Album*, and he had brought it round for her to look at. Marina
received the unstinting praise with apparent calm. Voloshin
was amazed to find that she was wearing school uniform, and
Marina explained that she was indeed still supposed to be
attending school, though all she did was write poetry. She
showed no shyness. Voloshin observed she was wearing a cap
to cover her then bald head, and asked for permission to take
it off so that he could feel the shape of the bumps of her skull.
Marina agreed at once, without demur. Voloshin examined
her carefully and declared that she resembled a Roman semi-
narist. The baldness had arisen by accident. That summer, she
had stayed behind in Moscow for a few days while the family
went to Tarusa. She had rubbed a liquid into her hair to make
it grow thicker, but the preparation had contained hydrogen
peroxide and shortly after she arrived in Tarusa, it turned
Marina's hair a bright yellow. To remove this humiliation,
she had resorted to extreme measures.

She and Voloshin then went up to the old nursery, a room
the size of a ship's cabin, which was papered with gold stars
on a red field. Voloshin squeezed his huge bulk into the room,
and looked over all Marina's icons, particularly the pictures of
Napoleon. He scrutinized the narrow couch hemmed in by a

writing table. Then, almost as equals, the two of them began to talk about writing, and how to write; what books she still had to read, and which books she most admired. Voloshin was astonished at the gaps in her knowledge, but when, the next day, he sent her a package of books, Marina received it indignantly, because it contained a book by Henri de Regnier that she found pornographic. Voloshin was not particularly penitent. It was he who introduced Marina to the *Memoirs of Casanova*, and this at least she found altogether fascinating. She read it in French and was soon carried away by the fiery diversity of Casanova's character.

Voloshin knew exactly how to treat the young girl. He had a particular talent for drawing out women favoured with the gift of poetry. He was, moreover, particularly kind to those who were 'unbeautiful favourites of the gods'. Much later in life, Tsvetayeva was to recall that no one had treated her mature poems with the worshipful care given by the thirty-six-year-old Voloshin to her early verses.

Soon Marina was invited to literary evenings where she met Adamovich and Khodasevich, among others. Her talent was already becoming celebrated among poets and writers, and through Voloshin she was introduced to Musaget (a literary café and publishing house) and soon she was invited to give readings. Marina and her sister Anastasia had grown closer with their awakening interest in the opposite sex. Marina not only confided in Asya, she also drew support from her, and because of this, she asked Asya to appear with her at the reading. The two of them went on stage in their Gymnasium uniforms and read together, standing side by side, every rise and fall in intonation fused as one voice, Marina with her as yet uncut hair modestly pulled back to relieve her forehead, and Anastasia with her thicker and shorter hair falling to her shoulders. They did not so much recite as use the natural rhythm of the voice, avoiding all theatrical rhetoric. When they reached the end, there was a moment's silence and then the whole hall burst into applause, even though applause was actually forbidden. The two girls stood there, confused and bowing awkwardly. It was an occasion that, decades later, Anastasia was to recollect with pride as a high point in determining the course of her own developing talent.

★

In the autumn of the same year Marina moved out of her mezzanine room with the golden stars on its dark red sky, into what had once been the maids' room downstairs. (Later, it became a storeroom.) She now slept close by the little table on which, in their childhood, a paraffin stove had warmed milk for them in a white-and-blue-streaked saucepan. Her new room was square, with a low ceiling. She began to keep indoor plants (especially luxurious ones, such as begonias) and a favourite cat. She also acquired a gramophone, and from that ancient mouth flowed Schubert's Serenades, the music of Glinka and all the melodies that recalled her mother and her childhood.

Marina was eager for adventure, and when Voloshin talked enthusiastically of his *dacha* at Koktebel in the Crimea, where he kept open house with his mother Pra, she determined to take advantage of his hospitality. She was still only eighteen years old but she was able to talk her father into letting her travel to the Crimea before the end of the school term, and was also able to get his agreement for a visit to Koktebel. Meanwhile, Anastasia's life was also exciting: at a skating rink, she had met the man whom she was to marry, Boris Trukhachev. Marina's travel plans became increasingly elaborate – for instance, she wanted to visit Pushkin's Gurzuf – as if she wanted to take in the whole of her Russian heritage in one gulp.

Marina wrote to her family from Gurzuf: about the charm of being alone, of moonlit walks and the joy of being by the sea. She also mentioned a Tartar boy who was so attached to her that he followed her everywhere, but it is clear that her own heart was whole.

After a month of solitude among the ruins of a fortress there, Marina arrived at Koktebel on 5 May 1911. Voloshin's mother, a remarkable woman who wore her grey hair swept back to reveal the profile of an eagle, greeted Marina in her long white kaftan sewn with silver and blue. Her nickname 'Pra' came from 'Pramater', meaning 'the mother of these regions'. Pra, indeed, ran a matriarchal society in Koktebel. The house was isolated, being the only house on that part of the Black Sea shore, and was surrounded by a Kimmerian landscape, traditionally supposed to be the home of the

Amazons. Max himself delighted in myths and created many of his own about the landscape, the grottos and the coastline around his home. He also kept dogs, some of them of the Crimean sheepdog breed, which closely resembled huge wolves. But Koktebel was chiefly notable for the informal friendliness and hospitality Max delighted to extend, particularly to young writers, and it was there, at Voloshin's *dacha* at Koktebel, that Marina met the man who was to become her husband.

Marina was eighteen, and Sergei Yakovlevich Efron seventeen, when they first met on a deserted shore near Koktebel, with the noise of the sea in their ears. The shore was strewn with small pebbles; Marina had been collecting them when Sergei began to help her. He was a particularly slender boy, not so much handsome as sadly and meekly beautiful, with astonishingly huge eyes. Marina at once sensed in him the enormity of his need to be loved. With an instant reckless decision (often recalled), Marina predicted: 'If this boy finds and gives me a cornelian, I shall marry him.'[32] He found the cornelian immediately.

Sergei was the sixth child of nine from an extraordinary family. His mother, Elizaveta Petrovna Durnovo (1855–1910), came of an ancient aristocratic lineage of which Marina was proud in later years. Elizaveta was the only daughter of an army officer who had been adjutant to Tsar Nicholas I. On the other hand, her husband Yakov Constantinovich Efron came from a large and literary Moscow family of Jewish origin, some of whom had been rabbis. Sergei's father had been a student at the Moscow Technical College, and only politics had brought him and Sergei's mother together. They were both members of a revolutionary party (which they had joined in 1879) that had as its aim a juster re-allocation of land. Sergei's mother was then a beautiful, black-haired girl who appeared at revolutionary meetings dressed in a ball gown and velvet cape, but however aristocratic her appearance, Elizaveta's political views had been formed under the influence of Kropotkin and she was a member of the First International. She was also extremely courageous. In the early stages of their friendship, Yakov and Elizaveta carried out several acts of terrorism. For example, on 26 February 1879, it was Yakov who, with two others, assassinated the police agent Reinstein who had succeeded in penetrating their Moscow organization before being exposed as an *agent provocateur*. At first it was not discovered who was responsible for Reinstein's murder, but in July 1880 Elizaveta was arrested for carrying seditious litera- ture and materials for building an underground printing press from Moscow to St Petersburg. As a result, she was imprisoned in the notorious Peter and Paul fortress.

She was luckier than she might have been. Although her father was appalled to discover that she had anarchist sympa- thies (he was himself an unshakeable monarchist), he had wide- spread contacts and was able to arrange for her to flee abroad, and Yakov was able to follow her. There they were married and spent seven years in exile. Their first three children were born in exile.

The Efron family returned to Russia to find most of their friends in prison or deported. Yakov himself knew he was under constant watch by the police. In any case, he only had the right to work as an insurance agent, employment with no joy or prospect, and his small salary hardly allowed him enough money to feed and clothe his large and ever-increasing family. Elizaveta's parents were wealthy and could easily have helped, but they disapproved strongly of their daughter's life. Knowing this, she was too proud to ask for help. At any rate, they provided nothing.

The daily troubles of the Efron family were increased by the loss of three of the youngest children through illness: meningitis and hereditary heart disease. Nevertheless, it was a harmonious and loving family and continued to be a remark- ably idealistic one. In the late 1890s, Elizaveta joined some of her old comrades and began once again to help in printing declarations, manufacturing explosives and even hiding arms.

Some of the older children joined, too. In photographs from that period, Elizaveta's face looks grey and tired. Although she had not been broken by the hardships of life she had to face, her high narrow forehead had become wrinkled early and there were lines round the corners of her mouth. Her modest clothes had begun to look too loose for her body, and the grandeur of the days of ball dresses and capes had changed into a worn toughness. There is one photograph of husband

and wife together, in which Yakov's face has some of the characteristics that were to mark Sergei. His face is simple, open and defenceless, with very bright clear eyes. He and his wife are seen surrounded by their children, many of whom were to continue with revolutionary activities against the Tsar in later years.

Elizaveta's political activities, however, reached their peak in the Revolution of 1905. In that year, police repression came down upon the family and shattered it. Elizaveta was sent briefly to the Butyrki prison, but Yakov was able to secure her release (she was threatened with hard labour) by paying a ruinous amount of money as security, money that had been raised with the help of his friends. As a result, he was able to take his wife abroad; but she was sick and exhausted and was never to return to Russia. Both of them died in exile. Elizaveta survived her husband's death, but when a short while later, the youngest of the sons who had followed them into exile fell ill and died, she lost heart altogether. She died the next day, at her own hand.

In 1905 Sergei was only twelve. He took no direct part in the Revolution, and perhaps resented the way his loving family had been fragmented in its name. When his mother and father had to leave Russia, his entire existence lost its centre. There was no longer a family home. While still an adolescent, he fell ill for the first time with the tuberculosis that was to recur throughout his life. His illness, and his longing for the mother he felt had deserted him, brought him such bitterness and grief that his family thought it wiser to conceal the fact that Elizaveta was dead – an error of judgement, although an understandable one. When Sergei finally discovered the truth, it was too late to mourn in any traditional way.

Such was Sergei's tragic background. He, too, thought of himself as a writer, and he had many friends among writers and poets, both in Moscow and in St Petersburg. In spite of his continuing sadness, he was very much part of the group of young people who went regularly to Koktebel. However, it was only in Marina that he found someone who was able to release him from the lonely misery that had filled him since his early years . . . and she enjoyed her role as rescuer.

Through the autumn of 1911, the two of them continued

to lead a strange, childish, playful life, even though Marina
soon regarded herself as engaged to Sergei. When Anastasia
travelled to the Crimea to join her sister at Voloshin's *dacha*,
Marina took part, with Sergei, in an extraordinarily elaborate
practical joke that involved all Voloshin's guests.

Marina had become not only part of the group, but a dominant member of it, and she had also changed her general style
of dress and behaviour from her Moscow self. She now looked
like a boy. Her hair was tightly curled, and touched with gold
by the sun; the skin of her face, neck and legs (which were
bare below the knee) was almost black. Marina had once loved
high heels in Moscow, but in the Crimea, she wore sandals,
and *sharovary* – wide boyish trousers of Turkish style. She
looked younger and altogether freer than Anastasia, who
arrived from Moscow carefully dressed in a proper travelling
coat and a wide-brimmed straw hat. Perhaps it was this
contrast in manners that tempted Marina, but the practical
joke that followed was unkind and silly. It depended upon
inventing elaborate new identities for the other guests, one of
whom had to pretend to be mentally defective, and another
deaf and dumb. In particular, Marina pretended to find Sergei
ridiculous. Afterwards, Anastasia was greatly upset that she
had let herself join in poking fun at the unknown young man;
and when next morning she found Marina and Sergei sitting
close together over breakfast, so engrossed that they hardly
noticed her arrival, she was exceedingly embarrassed. Pride
prevented her from showing her shock, and yet she felt it cruel
that they had all played such a joke on her. Later on, she felt
the one thing that could not be corrected was being led to
describe Sergei's face as handsome but stupid.

That evening, Marina confessed to her sister that she was
deeply in love with that same Sergei, who was all the dearer
to her because of the tragedy in his life. His close escape from
death after hearing of the suicide of his mother had made
Marina want to love and protect him for ever. She particularly
loved his physical frailty. However, despite Marina's intense
happiness at this time, she remained perverse and teasing, as
she invited her sister to compare the love she felt for Boris
with her own for Sergei. Anastasia was stiff and cold in reply,

because she was worried: Boris had promised to come to the Crimea, but had not yet arrived.

Like everyone else, Anastasia felt Sergei Efron's charm. All Russians love affectionate names, but few people shortened Marina's after her childhood. However, everyone knew Sergei as Seryozha, a diminutive that followed him throughout his life. It was part of his eternal boyishness.

Seryozha and Boris met for the first time at the Koktebel railway station when Anastasia and Boris came to see off Marina and Seryozha who were to journey back to Moscow ahead of them. The four young people stood on the platform, looked at the clouds over the town, waiting for the train. The two boys were about the same age. The sisters talked about their father, who was ill at the time, and had been ordered by his doctors to Bad–Neuheim. He had been very reluctant to go, because the new museum was not yet ready to open. At last, the two young couples shook hands rather than kissed, and Marina and Seryozha set off for the House on the Street of the Three Ponds.

By July, Marina and Seryozha were travelling to the Urals together; and when they returned to the House on Three Ponds Street, Marina's father was away, and they moved into her family home together. Later, they moved in with Seryozha's sisters.

Marina's marriage to Seryozha in January 1912 can hardly have pleased her father. She was only nineteen, and there was much to find alarming in Seryozha's background. Quite apart from the anti-Semitism of the Ilovaisky family, there would have been a gaol sentence and a suicide to conceal, on the Durnovo side of Seryozha's family, if Professor Tsvetayev had chosen to have a large wedding. Accordingly, the wedding was celebrated quietly. Afterwards the newlyweds travelled to Sicily, and also paid a brief visit to Paris before returning to Moscow to set up their new home.

3
'I could not love anyone else . . .'
1912–1916

The two years between their first meeting and the start of the First World War turned out to be the only period of shared happiness in Seryozha and Marina's lives. Thanks to the second wife of Marina's Grandfather Mein, they could afford to buy a house in the old merchant quarter. Two years later, they decided to move, in order to be more centrally located. They chose a three-bedroom flat at No. 6 Boris and Gleb Street in Old Moscow, which belonged to a priest who served in the church opposite. It was a modest apartment, but prettily painted, and they lived in it irresponsibly and without questioning their privileged gaiety.

Marina knew that her happiness with Seryozha depended on the child-like quality that held them as if they were part of the same dream. In a poem written to him at this time, she declared her intention of staying a small girl, and bewitching him into remaining young for ever. Childhood for her was the golden time of Huck Finn and Tom Sawyer, the Prince and the Pauper. These were the years when she and Seryozha were closest and most equal.

Seryozha had his own literary ambitions (he put together a manuscript of short stories), but his talent was to lie more in recognizing the greatness of others than in any other use of his gifts. He loved to be surrounded by lively and talented practitioners of all the arts, and it had been no accident that

he and Marina had met at Voloshin's *dacha*. He was not envious
of Marina's genius because her attention and devotion to him
were so unmistakable, and in the readiness with which he was
accepted by others, she saw the confirmation of her own high
opinion of him.

In many ways, his easy charm made him more attractive on
first meeting than Marina, and this was particularly true
among actors and actresses. Marina was not exactly shy with
them, but their extrovert, non-intellectual company disturbed
her and she was piqued by her inability to impress them. She
had always hated to feel that her own special qualities were
going unrecognized; when she knew as much, she became
sullen. Seryozha's easy gaiety made up for that awkwardness
in her, and ensured their entry into the friendly world of the
players.

Marina and Seryozha thus bolstered one another. His weakness and his good nature both sprang from the same source:
the desire to please. There was no one he desired to please
more than Marina, and so they clung to one another happily.

Seryozha continued at drama school, and Marina's second
book, *Magic Lantern*, was published in 1912. However, for the
first time in her life, she no longer put writing before everything else, and she no longer even wrote every day. Their
first child, Ariadna, was born on 5 September 1912. At her
christening, her godfather was Professor Tsvetayev and her
godmother was Maximilian Voloshin's mother, Pra, and the
child was named Ariadna, though she was usually called Alya.
Suddenly, there were many new interests, and many distrac-
tions, and in all of them Seryozha was also concerned.

Even after her marriage, Marina dealt with all her father's
correspondence as her mother had once done. She was
delighted to hear that not only was the Tsar to be present at
the opening of her father's cherished new Museum of Fine
Arts, but also that Professor Tsvetayev was going to be
awarded the Order of the Guardian of Honour. Both daughters
now felt considerable affection for the old man, and together
they bought him a splendid silver tray. He accepted this gift
with surprise, only grumbling mildly that, as married women
(Asya and Boris had married soon after Marina and Seryozha),
they needed the money more than he did. It was a generous

grumble, though Marina (in a memoir written in the 1930s) made gentle fun at his continuing parsimony, which led him to insist on shopping for his daughters' clothes himself, to make sure that the fabric was sufficiently durable.

In old age, and after obstinately continuing to work on through all his adversities, there was a charm in his unworldliness. On the day of the museum's opening, he was dressed in an old greenish-grey dressing gown when an old friend called on him to present him with a laurel wreath. This he declined out of modesty, though he did stand for a moment with the wreath on his head, without any sense of looking comic.

When the Tsvetayev family entered the museum, it was packed with the grand and the distinguished, many wearing medals. Among them, Marina (then pregant with Alya) and Seryozha seemed preternaturally young. For Marina, one of the high points of the day was watching the Tsar talking to her father; indeed, she was so excited by the Imperial presence, that she insisted afterwards that the Tsar had looked directly at her. Her father phlegmatically agreed that he might well have done, since 'a person does have to look at something'.[33] She had no qualms about the magnificence of the occasion, being far too stirred by the visual ceremony and by her pleasure in her father receiving a deserved honour to consider the politics of the time. Besides, she was not among those who saw in the Tsar and the opulence of Court festivities an intolerable indifference to the squalor and misery of the Russian masses. Seryozha, too, for all his Jewish and revolutionary inheritance, remained remote from the reforming ferment among the intelligentsia.

Marina's father died unexpectedly on 30 August 1913, fifteen months after the opening of the museum. He had lived economically all his life, and Marina was well provided for. She had never been as passionately attached to her father as she had been to her mother, yet as he had come to need more help from her, she began to feel greater warmth for him. She had always respected his wish to serve the visual arts and the courage with which he had met his critics. Now his death left her an orphan, and made her even more eager to draw the bonds between herself and Seryozha closer than before, for reassurance. Not everyone understood how deeply Marina loved Seryozha. Indeed, on 7 March 1914 she wrote to a friend: 'I could never love anyone else . . . no one, not a single one of my friends, understands my choice.'[34]

However, for a year following her father's death, there was no other change in the pattern of her life or in the pleasures that she sought and continued to share with her young husband. One of these was her passion for the theatre. It had been important to her since her first efforts at the verse translation of *L'Aiglon*, and Sarah Bernhardt had, of course, been among her early heroines. Both Seryozha and his two sisters were pupils at a drama school, and took part in studio performances; the oldest brother, Pyotr, had been a professional actor. Seryozha had some dramatic talent, though nothing outstanding, and he enjoyed his performances on the boards, while Marina was at first happy enough simply to be a part of the group. These young people could not have anticipated how short a lease their life of gaiety had left to run, and in any case, they were temperamentally disinclined to do so. If they looked into the future at all, it was by fortune-telling, enjoying a *frisson* at the thought of the unknown world ahead.

New Year 1914 opened with just such an occasion at Koktebel. By now, Marina was looking her most voluptuous: her face full without podginess, her dresses long and rich-fabricked, with many chains and amulets on her plump bosom. She wore stiff silks, deeply cut bodices and long voluminous skirts. She and Seryozha arrived with Asya and Boris, through a snowstorm so alarming that their drivers had been reluctant to risk the journey. They were received into Voloshin's welcoming bear hug. The exhilaration of arriving through such weather gave the evening a special enchantment and they began telling fortunes using Voloshin's Bible, too absorbed in the game to realize that the tower in which they were sitting was on fire until they could actually smell smoke and see it rising through cracks in the floor boards. In later years, Marina recorded a vision of Voloshin lifting his hand towards the flame and uttering words of magical power, while the others rushed more practically to bring buckets of sea water to the flames. In her memory of the incident, the fire died out at

Voloshin's command. It was not an image that suggested she had much grasp of the events to come.

When the war began, Seryozha was a student in his first year at Moscow University and he was eager to take part in the fighting. His motives were not, as we shall see, only those of intense patriotism, and in any case, he was sent to the front as a male nurse with an ambulance train. He tried, at first unsuccessfully, to persuade several medical boards that he was fit enough for active service, and his intense determination finally won him admission to an officers' training school for which he was not particularly suited. A fatal ingredient in his desire to see action was a need to impress Marina. His duty in the ambulance corps had already separated him from her for the first time since they had been married; now, after long periods apart, he sensed an unwelcome shift in her attention. She had begun to write again, and her writing was growing in confidence. He could not mistake her enormous energy, and he already knew that she had ceased to direct her passion towards her family alone.

Marina's life at this time was frenetic and wilful but retained a firm domestic structure. This was partly a question of money. She could afford a nanny to look after Alya, and was well able to run a complicated household in her own peremptory fashion. In her memoir, Alya reported a succession of nannies but it is quite clear that the ruling spirit was always Marina's. One nanny was sacked for taking the small child to the wrong church, and another for having dirty hands. Marina decided everything, including the time when toys had to be put away and when Alya was to go to bed. Walks with Marina were delightful adventures, however, even though she always insisted on Alya being dressed with formal correctness: 'boots, hoods, gaiters, straps, hooks, buttons, *endless* buttons'.[35] Marina's will decided every move the family made. To Alya, it seemed as if Marina had magical powers, since she could transform winter into summer by suddenly deciding to go south, leaving their familiar Moscow world behind for the *dacha* at Koktebel.

Alya was brought up to speak clearly and coherently at all times, and Marina treated her like an adult almost as soon as

she could speak at all. In many ways Marina's behaviour
recalled that of her own mother, even to instances of occasional
cruelty. When Alya drew her first little man, with arms and
legs like sticks and a head like a cabbage, and called her mother
to see it, she must have been expecting praise. Instead, Marina
pretended to find difficulty in making out any figure at all.
Then she counted the fingers on the monster's hands, and
made Alya count her own to see the absurdity of her mistake,
before turning to make fun of the matchstick legs, the teeth
that resembled a fence, and all the other features of the drawing
that were out of proportion.

Alya always felt that Marina's mockery then was more
merciless than the occasion seemed to merit. More must have
been under threat than a child's first artistic experiments.
Marina could hardly have forgotten her own childhood misery
when her mother mocked her first attempts at poetry. Now,
as if in mimicry, she herself began to insist that Alya must
love poetry before any other art.

Marina was determined that no opportunity to form Alya's
growing intelligence should be wasted and took responsibility
for every facet of her daughter's development. She taught Alya
to read and write herself, as soon as she saw that the child was
capable of forming letters. Even a visit to the circus could not
be undertaken casually. Marina would never let her child gaze
about vaguely, watching the stagehands about their electrical
business high above the ring. She seized Alya's head to make
her concentrate on the animals in the ring instead. Sadly, the
one thing the child enjoyed was the uproarious slapstick of the
clowns, and for that Marina rebuked her. Marina was far from
humorless, but she wanted Alya to know it was wrong to
laugh at people who were ugly or unfortunate enough to put
their feet in the wrong place. As a result of this intense personal
teaching, Alya continued to hear the voice of her mother inside
her head like the voice of conscience for years afterwards.

However, in spite of so much that was imperious and arbitrary, Marina was often an enchanting mother, particularly
when she took her daughter backstage at the theatre, or to
watch a parade of colourfully dressed soldiers on horseback
behind a golden drum. Rewards for good behaviour were
usually gifts of Marina's presence: she would read to Alya

from a favourite book or take her for a walk. A visit to her mother's room was a very special privilege, since Marina maintained the privacy of that room totally. To run into it without permission was quite forbidden. Alya recalls Marina's room as a place of enchanted clutter,

> a many-cornered, multi-faceted room, with a magical blue chandelier from the reign of the Empress Elizaveta hanging from the ceiling, and a wolf's skin (rather frightening but fascinating at the same time) by the low divan. . . . I remember my mother's quick bending down towards me, her face next to mine, the smell of Corsican jasmine, the silken rustle of her dress and the way she would quickly settle down with me on the floor.[36]

At the centre of Marina's privacy, of course, was her writing desk, upon which she had portraits of Sarah Bernhardt and Maria Bashkirtseva (whose candid diary Marina much admired); a varnished pencil-case with a portrait of the young hero of 1812, General Tuchkov; and a clay bird coated with silver that represented Sirim, in traditional Russian folklore a bird with a woman's face and breasts. One of her most prized possessions was a book of the tales of Perrault with illustrations by Gustave Doré, which she allowed her daughter to look at only if her hands were first carefully washed and only if she treated it with respect. Marina was punctilious about books; indifference to *things* was not yet part of her style.

There were many objects in Marina's private room that recalled her own childhood, and made it a magical place for a child to enter. For instance, there was her grandmother's musical box, which played a minuet, and there was also a gramophone on which Marina liked to play gypsy songs that she had first heard sung at a concert. At this time, Marina's interest in gypsies was part of her love of everything exotic. She liked to believe in the Romany gift for telling the future, and she enjoyed their confidence-trickster patter. Some premonitory intuition of her own led her to praise their 'imperial fecklessness' to her young daughter.

Marina's faults as a mother were those of an attentive severity rather than neglect. It is hard not to flinch, however, when reading this account of her mother from six-year-old Alya's journal:

MY MOTHER

My mother is very strange.

My mother is not at all like a mother. Mothers always admire their child and children generally, but Marina does not like little children. She has light brown hair; it curls up at the sides. She has green eyes, a hooked nose and pink lips. She has a slender build and arms which I like. She is sad, quick and loves Poems and Music. She writes poems. She is patient and tolerant to the extreme. Even though she gets angry she is loving. She is always hurrying somewhere. She has a big heart. A gentle voice. A fast walk. Marina's hands are full of rings. Marina reads at night. Her eyes are nearly always full of fun. She does not like being pestered with silly questions, then she gets very angry.

Sometimes she walks about like someone lost, but then she suddenly seems to wake up, starts to talk and again seems to go off somewhere.[37]

The clarity of this vision shows an unrelenting honesty that is truly remarkable in a child and recalls the astonishing precocity of Marina herself, who had begun to write poetry at the same age.

Marina's life was once again centred around the love and admiration she felt for the poets she had begun to meet. Few of them were her equals. One was Tikhon Churilin, a minor surrealist poet, to whom she addressed this poem, written in 1916.

> Today or tomorrow the snow will melt.
> You lie alone beneath an enormous fur.
> Shall I pity you? Your lips
> have gone dry for ever.
>
> Your drinking is difficult, your steps heavy.
> Every passerby hurries away from you.

Was it with fingers like yours that Rogozhin
clutched the garden knife?

And the eyes, the eyes in your face!
Two circles of charcoal, year-old circles!
Surely when you were still young, your girl
lured you into a joyless house.

Far away – in the night – over asphalt – a cane.
Doors – swing open into – night under beating wind.
Come in! Appear! Undesired guest! Into
my chamber which is – most bright![38]

Their relationship was intense, but not necessarily sexual. In an
autobiographical poem published in *Julistan* in 1916, Churilin
dedicated a section called 'Love' to Marina Tsvetayeva. On
Marina's side, an infatuation provided excitement without
necessarily involving disloyalty to Seryozha.

However, Marina's most passionate erotic involvement in
the years between 1914 and 1916 was with a woman; Sophia
Parnok, best known at the time as a translator of poetry
(though she was later to write some remarkable poems of her
own) and an unashamed lesbian all through her life. She came
from an affluent Jewish family in southern Russia, and the
descriptions of her in Marina's poetry suggest an arrogant
bearing and handsome, even heavy features – 'Beethoven's
face', with eyebrows like a heavy ridge.

The relationship between the two women began immediately after their introduction in October 1914, and continued
until February 1916. Marina was very much the intoxicated
lover throughout, and for once, sensuality rather than infatuation was the key to the relationship: Sophia understood how
to give Marina a deeper sexual pleasure than she had yet
experienced.

Marina made no attempt to hide her love affair, and began
travelling around Russia with Sophia, staying occasionally at
places of historic interest and making love wherever they slept.
Unsurprisingly, Seryozha found not only the affair but also
the attendant gossip bitterly humiliating, perhaps all the more
so since Marina's emotional attachment was far from equally

reciprocated, Sophia Parnok never feeling the slightest compunction in taking up with other women. Part of his determination to join in the war undoubtedly came from his wish to escape from the pain of the situation.

For six months in 1915, after Seryozha joined the ambulance train in March, Marina and Sophia lived together openly as a couple, even though Marina continued to feel as if she still belonged to her husband in some other, more enduring way. She wrote to him every other day and, though she felt his suffering like a burden upon her heart, insisted that she 'loved Sergei for life'.

It is, however, the love for Sophia Parnok that occasioned the following strange and beautiful poem:

> We shall not escape Hell, my passionate
> sisters, we shall drink black resins –
> we who sang our praises to the Lord
> with every one of our sinews, even the finest,
>
> we did not lean over cradles or
> spinning wheels at night, and now we are
> carried off by an unsteady boat
> under the skirts of a sleeveless cloak,
>
> we dressed every morning in
> fine Chinese silk, and we would
> sing our paradisal songs at
> the fire of the robbers' camp,
>
> slovenly needlewomen (all
> our sewing came apart), dancers,
> players upon pipes: we have been
> the queens   of the whole world
>
> first scarcely covered by rags,
> then with constellations in our hair, in
> gaol and at feast we have bartered away heaven
>
> in starry nights, in the apple
> orchards of Paradise.

– Gentle girls, my beloved sisters,
we shall certainly find ourselves in Hell.[39]

For all this almost gleeful declaration of sinfulness, love
between women was not thought of as especially horrendous
in the society in which Marina usually moved. Her guilt came
from the pain she knew she was causing Seryozha and, increasingly, from her own jealousy as her relationship with Sophia
became more and more stormy. In January 1916, she rushed
over to Sophia's house one evening and discovered another
woman seated on Sophia's bed. Even if Marina had been
willing to accept that blow to her pride, Sophia made it
impossible for her by declaring that their love affair was at an
end. Months of unforgiving hatred followed in Marina's heart,
and years later, she described her rejection by Parnok as the
first catastrophe of her life.

Most of Marina's poetry written between 1915 and the
Revolution was published in a literary journal, *Northern Notes*,
edited in St Petersburg by a wealthy Jewish couple, Sophia
Chatskina and her husband Jacov Saker, and the magazine also
serialized her translation of the Countess de Noailles's novel
La Nouvelle Espérance. Marina refused to take any money from
them as fees, but accepted gifts instead; the perfume 'Jasmine
de Corse', which Alya remembered, was probably such a
present.

At soirées given by literary and theatrical personalities of
the time, Marina appeared elegant and self-assured; and when
she was given the opportunity to give a reading in St Petersburg in January 1916, she was greatly excited, even though it
meant parting from her daughter for the first time.

Her great wish was that Anna Akhmatova would be in her
audience that evening. She was not, but Tsvetayeva still read
as though she were. As she was to put it two decades later:

I wasn't reciting against Akhmatova, but for her, *to* her. I
read as if Akhmatova were the only person in the room.
I read for the absent Akhmatova. I needed this success as
a direct line to Akhmatova. And if in that moment, I
wanted to present *Moscow* in my own person, I couldn't
do better – not with the aim of conquering Petersburg,

but giving Moscow to Petersburg as a gift, to give
Akhmatova Moscow in myself, in my love, to present it
to her and to pay homage.[40]

In the audience, Kuzmin* lay back smoking, listening and
waiting for his turn to read; Mandelstam, Tsvetayeva
observed, had eyes 'like a camel's'. Tsvetayeva's poems were
applauded, even though she read a poem against the war and
in praise of Germany, in which she swore that she would love
Germany to the grave. She also read a poem, written the
previous year:

> I know the truth – give up all other truths!
> No need for people anywhere on earth to struggle.
> Look – it is evening, look, it is nearly night:
> *What* do you speak of, poets, lovers, generals?
>
> The wind is level now, the earth is wet with dew,
> the storm of stars in the sky will turn to quiet.
> And soon all of us will sleep under the earth, we
> who never let each other sleep above it.[41]

Altogether Tsvetayeva was intoxicated by her reception,
and she had a joyous sense that, contained in the *Northern
Notes* offices, with their walls lined with books and dark blue
wallpaper and with white bearskins on the floor, was a miraculous new world; one in which, when the telephone rang at
two in the morning and a voice inquired, 'Is it too late to
come over?' the reply came in the very spirit of Tsvetayeva's
own desires: 'Of course not, we're reading poetry.' This
exalted state, more than any particular events, helped to heal
the wound of rejection by Sophia Parnok and encouraged
Marina to open a relationship with Osip Mandelstam, whom
she had first met at Voloshin's *dacha* at Koktebel. Shortly after
the recital at St Petersburg, Mandelstam began to visit her in
Moscow. He also spent part of the early summer of 1916 with

---

* Mikhail Alexeevitch Kuzmin (1875–1936) a poet, playwright and
composer, who had earnt some notoriety by writing of love between
men.

her in Alexandrov in Vladimir province where she was taking
a brief holiday to visit her sister Asya.

It was probably the only love affair with a man of the many
Marina embarked upon with such intensity during this period,
that was physically consummated. In the nature of things, it
is hard to be sure even about that. Salomea Halpern,* in
correspondence with Vera Traill (formerly Suvchinsky) in
1979, remarked, 'I had always assumed Osip and Marina were
lovers,' though a few lines later she adds, 'Osip and I never
discussed these things.'

Nadezhda Mandelstam (Osip's wife), writing (in *Hope
Abandoned*) of their friendship, acknowledged that Marina's
love stemmed from the finest impulse of her noble woman's
soul. At the same time, Marina's enjoyment in being with
someone so young and finely gifted had a kind of narcissism
about it – understandable because both poets clearly felt that
being together transcended the ordinary world. It was as if,
by looking into one another's eyes, they could recognize and
confirm their own uniqueness.

Both poets write of walking about Moscow, smoking and
talking together as a sleepless, even sexless, intoxication. It is
one of Marina's few relationships with a poet of her own
stature that was not to depend largely on correspondence.
What Madame Mandelstam recognizes as her 'generosity' lay
in her lack of possessiveness. She treated Mandelstam as a wild
creature. At this period of her life, Marina clearly felt herself
so powerful that she could keep, or release at will, anyone
who came into her orbit. She did not even resent the fact that
it was Mandelstam who became restless first.

In 1916 Tsvetayeva wrote lyrics for Mandelstam in which
she offered him Moscow; she also wrote of their night-time
walks. It is not often that poems by two different poets that
clearly record the same occasion can be put side by side.
Marina wrote:

> You throw back your head, because
> you are proud. And a braggart.

* Then the Princess Andronnikova, addressed as 'Solominka' in
Mandelstam's poetry.

This February has
brought me a gay companion!

Clattering with gold pieces, and
slowly puffing out smoke, we
walk like solemn foreigners
throughout my native city.

And whose attentive hands have
touched your eyelashes, beautiful boy, and
when or how many times your
lips have been kissed

I do not ask. That dream my thirsty
spirit has conquered. Now
I can honour in you the
divine boy, ten years old!

Let us wait by the river that
rinses the coloured beads of street-lights:
I shall take you as far as the square
that has witnessed adolescent tsars.

Whistle out your boyish
pain, your heart squeezed in your hand.
My indifferent and crazy creature –
now set free – goodbye!⁴³

In the same year, Mandelstam wrote this poem, later published
in *Tristia* (1922):

With no confidence in miracles of resurrection,
We wandered through the cemetery.
Here on earth, you know, ubiquitously
.. ..
.. ..
.. .. ★

★ These lines are lost from the surviving Russian version.

Where Russia stops abruptly
Above the black and god-forsaken sea.

An ample field escapes
Down these monastic slopes
I did not want to leave the spacious Vladimir
To travel south,
But to stay with that lacklustre nun,
In the dark [the wooden]
Village of god's fools,
Would have been to court disaster.

I kiss your sunburned elbow
and a wax-like patch of forehead –
Still white, I know,
Under a strand of dark-complexioned gold,
I kiss your hand whose bracelet
leaves a strip of white:
Touris's ardent summers
Work such wonders.

How quickly you became a dark one
and came to the Redeemer's meagre icon
And couldn't be torn away from kissing –
You who in Moscow had been the proud one.
Music remains,
A miraculous sound,
Here, take this sand:
I am pouring it from hand to hand.[44]

The shared darkness and the shared tenderness of the following
poem bring out Marina's sense of Mandelstam's youth and
physical beauty:

Where does this tenderness come from?
These are not – the first curls I
have stroked slowly – and lips I
have known darker than yours

as stars rise often and go out again

(where does this tenderness come from?)
so many eyes have risen and died out
in front of these eyes of mine.

and yet no such song have
I heard in the darkness of night before
(where does this tenderness come from?):
here, on the ribs of the singer.

Where does this tenderness come from?
And what shall I do with it, young
sly singer, just passing by?
Your lashes are – longer than anyone's.[45]

For all Tsvetayeva's sensual pleasure in the younger man's
beauty, the sexual element was not as strong in Mandelstam's
attachment. As Marina often complained bitterly, men loved
something other than the woman in her. Madame Mandelstam
stresses Mandelstam's realization that to stay with such a 'mist-
wreathed nun' would have destroyed him, and points out how
many of his poems written at the time have premonitions of
a terrible death. Even allowing for Madame Mandelstam's
reasons for jealousy, it was certainly Osip who became restless:
bored, perhaps with the calm landscape of Vladimir province
and longing for the Crimea. And it was Marina who continued
to insist on their relationship, even across the miles that separated them. Moreover, she continued to feel proprietorial long
after their parting. Many years later, Nadezhda found herself,
as a wife, necessarily excluded from their glorious acceptance
of one another by Marina's manner, and she says justly,
'Though I met Tsvetayeva several times, we never really
became friends . . . she was totally intolerant of the wives of
her friends.'[46]

How did Marina's infidelity affect her husband? He found
it painful, if only as a sign of her failing attention. And the
physical betrayal was only a part of it. There is one key lyric
in the 'Insomnia' sequence in which Marina's excitement in
moving alone around streets at night rises to a sense of magical
liberation.

In my enormous city – it is night,
as from my sleeping house I go – out,
and people think perhaps I'm a daughter or wife
but in my mind is one thought only – night.

The July wind now sweeps a way for me.
From somewhere, some window, music though faint.
The wind can blow until the dawn today.
In through the fine walls of the breast rib-cave.

Black poplars, windows, filled with light.
Music from high buildings, in my hand, a flower.
Look at my steps following nobody.
Look at my shadow, nothing's here of me.

The lights are like threads of golden beads,
in my mouth is the taste of the night leaf.
Liberate me from the bonds of day,
my friends, understand: I'm nothing but your dream.

The beauty of the poem cannot disguise the fact that what was
being celebrated was a year of independent adventure, in which
no one's feelings but her own mattered. The first ecstatic
happiness of her love for Efron has been replaced by something
closer to brotherly camaraderie. This did not prevent her from
being deeply dependent upon her husband for emotional
support. On 27 April 1916, she wrote a poem for him in
which she penitently pleads for help and understanding and
declares him her 'lawful tsar'.

Seryozha was away enough to be aware of Marina's behaviour only through gossip, or when she confided in him. He
feared to probe too closely. He was young, married only four
and a half years, and by no means as indifferent to ordinary
human jealousy as Marina wished to imagine. Sexual liberty,
assumed as natural among the Russian upper classes of the
time, was taken up by the intelligentsia before the Revolution,
but Seryozha had always been unusually psychologically
dependent on his wife's love, which had to replace that of a
much-loved mother. Salomea Halpern married (according to
Vera Traill) with her husband's agreement to allow her to

sleep with whomever she chose, but Marina and Seryozha had no such understanding. Certainly there was nothing *hidden* about Marina's passions. She often turned to Seryozha with her problems, and from all accounts, he was both supportive and uncritical. And yet it must have been agonizing for his vulnerable, self-distrustful nature.

Part II

Civil War

4
'Loyalty held us, firm as an anchor'
1917–1920

At the time of the February Revolution of 1917, Marina was in Moscow expecting her second child, and the sudden and total collapse of the regime in March left her alarmed at the rioting and none too clear about what was happening. She was not alone in her confusion, though it says little for her political astuteness that she could mistake Kerensky, even briefly, for Bonaparte. In poems written in April 1917, which deal with the abdication of the Tsar, the note of reproach is directed towards the Tsar himself, who is asked to remember his duty to his descendants. Tsvetayeva began to observe something treacherous and Byzantine in the eyes she had once been so flattered to meet. However, the desperation of people who supported the Bolsheviks did not move her because she could distinguish no single heroic figure among the rebels (unlike Stenka Razin, the legendary bandit whom she had always admired) – only a mob, 'the colour of ashes and sand'. She was by no means the only writer to find herself untouched by the revolutionary cause – Mandelstam, for instance, did not feel the need to leave his friend's *dacha* in the Crimea, and continued to meditate on the myths of his much-loved Mediterranean throughout the years of upheaval. In July 1917, he had as intense a dislike of the Bolsheviks as Tsvetayeva, and in October published a poem calling Lenin an upstart. Tsvetayeva, who had given birth to a second

79

daughter, Irina, in April 1917, had every reason to hope for civil order, and felt no impulse to welcome, as Mandelstam began to do by 1918, the 'great, clumsy creaking turn of helm'.[48] What was decisive in Tsvetayeva's case was Seryozha's involvement with the White cause. It was a commitment that, as so often, was made with the wish to impress Tsvetayeva in mind. Whatever other radical opinions Tsvetayeva may have held, she still saw God and the State united in the Tsar's person. Later on, her hatred of 'all organized violence, no matter in whose name it may be perpetrated or by what name it may be called', gave a moral stature to some lyrics of *Swan's Encampment*,★ which otherwise found nobility in a very questionable group of opponents to Bolshevism. One lyric, at least, shows an unerring humanism:

> On either side, mouths lie
> open and bleeding, and from
> each wound rises a cry:
> —Mother!
>
> One word is all I hear, as
> I stand dazed. From someone
> else's womb into my own:
> —Mother!
>
> They all lie in a row,
> no line between them,
> I recognize that each one was a soldier.
> But which is mine? Which one is another's?
>
> This man was White now he's become Red.
> Blood had reddened him.
> This one was Red now he's become White.
> Death has whitened him.[49]

But she was surely right to assert of the journals she kept during the civil war: 'There are no politics in them.'[50]

★ This has been translated as *The Demesne of Swans* in Robin Kemball's translation of the complete cycle of these poems.

The chaos of the days following the outbreak of the civil war threw all plans into confusion; and Marina's own plans involved her crossing Russia four times. In October 1917 she was at Koktebel with Max and Pra, and she eventually included diary notes of those days in her memoir of Voloshin. She heard the news of the Bolshevik victory in Moscow at Max's *dacha*, from two officers who had been involved in the last hours of fighting.

On 2 November, on her long journey back towards Moscow, Marina crouched in the corridor of a crowded train, uncertain of what news to believe. News-sheets on pink-coloured paper, handed down the train, told of the destruction of Tverskaya Street, the Arbat* and the Metropole hotel; the streets were said to be piled high with corpses. Worse, she did not know whether her own house was standing, or if Seryozha were safe. At this moment, all her thoughts were for her husband. In the diary that she scribbled on that three-day journey back, she promised: 'If God leaves you among the living, I shall serve you like a dog.' And again: 'I have not once thought of the children. If Seryozha is no more, then nor am I; and nor are they. Alya would not live without me, she wouldn't want to, wouldn't be able to. Like me without Seryozha.' No one should dismiss these feelings as false in the light of Marina's other entanglements. Her emotional commitment to her husband was to prove decisive and disastrous at every turning point in her life.

A pass was necessary to enter Moscow, and Marina arrived there just before dawn. The city was black and guns were still rumbling but it was possible to take a cab through the almost uninhabited streets even at 5.30 in the morning. In her imagination, Seryozha was involved, at that very moment, with the last White resistance, and she feared to arrive and hear the news of his death.

At the Church of Boris and Gleb, and the entrance to the side street where she lived, she was stopped by a group of houseguards who would not allow her to enter her own house. Only the intervention of the peasant woman Dunya (who

* A famous boulevard in Central Moscow.

worked for Marina) sufficed to convince them that she should
be allowed in to see her children.

When at last she burst in, she found that her fears for
Seryozha were exaggerated – he was, in fact, safely in bed –
but she still put the urgency of his departure from Moscow
before every other consideration. They set off for the Crimea
the very same day, leaving the children in Moscow with
Seryozha's family, to be collected later. Seryozha's intention
was to join the White Army regrouping in the south, and in
this Marina vigorously encouraged him.

In Tsvetayeva's notes of the time, she recorded:

Moscow, 4 November 1917. In the evening of that same
day we leave: S., his friend Goltsev and I for the Crimea.
Goltsev manages to collect his officer's pay in the Kremlin
(200 roubles). That gesture of the Bolsheviks ought not
to be forgotten

   ..   ..

Arrival in a frenzied snow storm in Koktebel. The grey
sea. The huge, almost physically searing joy of Max V.
at the sight of Seryozha alive. Huge white loaves.

   ..   ..

The vision of Max on the bottom steps of the tower, with
Thiers on his knees, frying onions. And, while the onions
fry, Seryozha and I listen to this recital aloud of Russia's
tomorrow, and the day after tomorrow. 'And now,
Seryozha, such-and-such will happen . . .' Stealthily,
almost rejoicing, like a good sorcerer to children, he gave
us in picture after picture, the whole Russian revolution
for five years to come: the terror; the civil war; the
executions; the barriers; the Vendée; men turned to beasts,
the loss of decency, the unleashed spirits of the elements,
blood, blood, blood. . . .[51]

Into the true chaos that had begun to engulf Russia Marina
bravely set out again to collect her children. Marina and
Seryozha had wildly misjudged the situation in leaving them
behind. She was lucky enough even to enter Moscow, for the

city was now sealed off by the Red Army; leaving again was out of the question. And so it was that Marina and Seryozha were separated and forced to live apart for the next five years.

They were to be years of great terror and hardship, but at first Marina met them with high-spirited gaiety. Seryozha was the single person she continued to care most about in the world. It was a familiar, domestic loyalty, which did not inhibit amorous adventures, although these were usually more a matter of nervous excitement than physical expression.

The closest relationships Marina formed with men during this period existed mainly to sustain her imagination. Marina needed to be in love in order to feel alive. It was not necessary that those she loved should share her emotion; all that mattered was that Marina could feel strongly.

Pavel Antokolsky (or 'Pavlik' as Marina called him) was a young poet whose verse Marina heard first in 1917, recited by a cadet on the train as she travelled back to Moscow alone. She was so struck by the quality that she sought out the poet himself and invited him to visit her at her flat. There in her kitchen, surrounded by pots and pans, they became friends. They were both young. Marina, then twenty-five, thought of Pavel as seventeen, the age Seryozha had been when she had first met him; in fact, Pavel was twenty-one, but on that first occasion at least, he seemed a schoolboy. He even wore his school uniform, with the correct buttons, and dressed in it he resembled a little Pushkin with black eyes, the Pushkin of Marina's legend. It was a meeting that Marina described as being 'like an earthquake. Because I understood who he was, just as he understood who I was.'[52] Whether or not Antokolsky was her lover as well as her friend, 'he stayed days, he stayed mornings, he stayed nights . . .'[53] the encounter was important because he introduced her into the very centre of the group of young people attached to the celebrated Vakhtangov Studio, which was an experimental part of the Moscow Art Theatre – a group to which Marina had been only peripheral part before.

Marina loved them all; not only for their beauty and gaiety, but also for the sense they had of being part of a joint endeavour: the play. The idea of 'play' as an adult joy was in

itself intoxicating to her. The theatre seemed like a licensed
fairy tale, and in the same spirit, she fell in love with one
participant after another in turn. Many of them were equally
in love with one another, and Antokolsky himself was part of
a particularly intense homosexual attachment.

In the winter of 1918/19, Marina met a young actor from
the Vakhtangov Studio whom (in her memoirs) she called
Volodya. Theirs was an unusually formal relationship – for
instance, Volodya never spoke to Marina without using her
patronymic. Nor was the bond between them, as was usual
in Marina's relationships, poetry: she never read poetry to him
nor even spoke to him about it. Yet she rapidly came to feel
that he was indispensable to her. This dependence was not
surprising, for despite all the bustle of the crowd attached to
the Vakhtangov Studio, Tsvetayeva was often bitterly lonely.
Politics played some part in this: she could not help despising
those who supported the White cause and yet had not gone
off to fight for it, and she refused to make close friends with
Red supporters. Seryozha was risking his life to stem their
conquest, and she felt there 'could be no friendship between
victors and vanquished'.[54]

Meanwhile, Volodya's first words set the tone of their
relationship: 'You remind me of Georges Sand. She too had children, and she wrote, and she had a hard life in Majorca.'[55]
Touched by the image he had of her, Tsvetayeva invited him
to her flat the following morning; there they ate some bread
together, and then wandered about with it in the street. After
that, Volodya began visiting her perhaps twice a week after
the performance at the theatre (that is, after midnight), but the
relationship remained a chaste one: they always sat at opposite
ends of a divan and talked. This may not have been altogether
Tsvetayeva's decision. There is something erotic in her
description of the pleasure she took in his appearance: '. . .
like a triangle upside down. The shoulders have all, the waist
– nothing.' She liked his dark eyes and straight nose, 'the
whole face in a straight line, as straight as his figure'.[56]

Volodya's friendship helped to dispel the fear that nobody
cared any longer what happened to her (even her sister was
far away in the Crimea). Late on Holy Saturday 1919, Marina
and her daughter Alya felt so alone in their flat that Marina

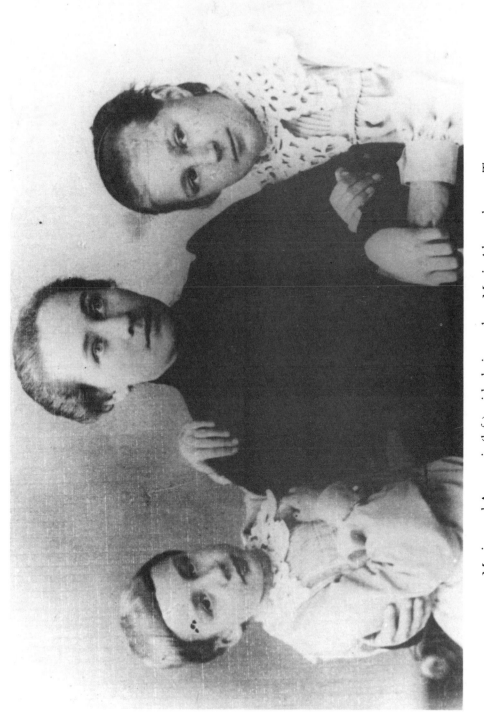

Marina and Anastasia (left) with their mother, Maria Alexandrovna Tsvetayeva

Marina and Anastasia (left) as young girls, with a friend

Tsvetayeva with her son Georgi (Moor) in Paris, late 1930s

Two portraits of Tsvetayeva
by Konstantin Rodzevich,
Prague, *c.* 1923

said, 'Alya, when one is forsaken by people as you and I are, there is no use crawling to God, like beggars. We aren't beggars. Let's go to bed like dogs.'[57] So they both got into the kitchen bed, which had once been the maid's. Alya fell fast asleep just as she was, in her dress. Marina too was still dressed but she found it harder to sleep. She was burning with the misery of spending Easter night alone for the first time in her life and without hearing the miraculous words: 'Christ is risen!' It was Volodya's light, sharp knock that reached into her loneliness. He had come to take them both to midnight Mass. Alya thought that his surprising arrival amounted to a miracle. 'Perhaps,' she said, 'God couldn't come Himself, or perhaps He was afraid He would frighten us, so He sent Volodya.'[58]

It was on that night that Volodya decided to go and join the White Army. Later, when he came to say goodbye, he took a signet ring off his finger and gave it to Marina, who was particularly moved by the gift because she was usually the one to give presents. To receive one now from Volodya set a seal of difference upon their friendship.

In other ways, their relationship followed a pattern that was to be repeated many times. Volodya himself perceived that she found qualities in him that she had invented. When he came to say farewell that afternoon, Marina was astonished to see him, as if for the first time, in daylight and to observe that his hair was not (as she had imagined) black, but auburn. Volodya was amused at her mistake, saying, 'Marina Ivanovna, I am afraid . . . you always saw all the rest of me in your own way, too. All of me, not just this.' And he waved contemptuously at his hair. 'So, did I see anything bad?' she queried. 'No, Marina Ivanovna. Good, even too good. That's why I've always dreaded being in daylight with you. Today you see me blond. Tomorrow you might see me boring. Mightn't it be just as well I'm leaving?'[59]

As they parted Volodya kissed her forehead and her lips almost ritually, and Marina made the sign of the cross over him three times. He left her with a book about Joan of Arc on which he had written as a dedication: 'You and I love the same things.'

★

Despite her devotion to Volodya, Marina's most intense attachment during the civil war years was again to a woman. It was a passion much less sensuous than she had felt for Sophia Parnok, and closer to the loves of her childhood, notably Asya Turgeneva. In those, there had always been a wistful quality; she would so clearly have preferred to be loved as a beauty herself than to celebrate the beauty of others. Yet in her relationship with Sonya Holliday, her feelings were clearly returned.

Lonely as Marina often was, friends from the theatre continued to make their way up to the ancient one-and-a-half-floor flat, with its odd internal staircase. In the winter, Alya and Marina and the baby had to live downstairs in the warmest and darkest of rooms. In the summer, they lived in a long, narrow, attic-like closet with a single window. This room was Marina's favourite, because Seryozha had at one time chosen it for himself. Now it was filled by new voices: argument, conversation, rehearsals and declamations.

Pavlik Antokolsky continued to be a constant visitor, and one evening, in 1919, he brought a friend who was the lover of a girl called Sonya Holliday, and so it was that Sonyechka came into Marina's life. In one of Marina's letters to Anna Teskovà, who was to become a friend in later days in Prague, she wrote that Sonyechka was 'the woman I loved more than anybody else in the world. Simply – she was Love in a woman's form.' She had black plaits, enormous black eyes, and burning cheeks. Marina described her as

A living fire. All of her burns! Cheeks burning, lips burning, eyes burning, white teeth and two black plaits – as though curling in flames – one round her back, the other on her chest. And out of these flames comes a look of such delight, and at the same time such despair! It was as if at the same time she's saying, 'I am frightened! I love!'[60]

On that first occasion, Sonyechka and Marina parted with nothing more than a glance – a questioning, doubting, hesitant glance – but very soon after Sonyechka telephoned to ask whether she could come and see Marina sometime – without

Pavlik. Marina agreed and asked only 'When?' Evidently Sonyechka arrived that very day.

It was the reading of Marina's verse play *Snowstorm* to a studio audience that confirmed Sonyechka's own response to Marina. There, alone on the stage, Marina read her play as if it were one of her poems. There was a bright stage, and a black hall and, afterwards, wild enthusiasm from the beautiful girl who came up to tell her how moved she had been. Nearly twenty years later, Tsvetayeva could still recall the exact words of Sonyechka's delirious enthusiasm: 'Marina, I was so frightened! And afterwards I wept so much! As soon as I saw you, and heard you – immediately I loved you madly. I understood – it's impossible not to love you madly . . .'[61] A love can be passionate without being expressed sensually, and there is something innocent even in the extravagance of Sonyechka's words.

Such an affirmation of love was something Marina looked for from the men she loved throughout her life. For all her beauty and talent, Marina offered men a passion that was more intense than they could bear, more devouring than they could endure. Only from Sonyechka was a love of the same ecstatic absoluteness offered freely. It was a miracle for Marina. That Sonyechka had such a love for *Snowstorm* was only part of the intensity of the love she felt for Marina. As Sonyechka said: 'Marina, will you love me always? Marina, you must love me *always* because I am going to die soon, I know, and that is why I love so madly and so hopelessly.'[62]

There is something childish in her style of expression, as there was in her whole personality. Marina herself said that Sonyechka could not play any of her adult heroines: 'I had to write of little girls.'[63] Both Rosa Fortuna, a little girl in *An Adventure*, and Francesca in *Casanova's End* were roles that Marina wrote for Sonyechka.

Childish or not, Marina found much of what Sonyechka said memorable – for instance, when she explained once how something had affected her: 'My tears were so enormous – they were bigger than my eyes!' Marina was so struck by the poetry of the phrase that she threatened to steal it. Sonyechka eagerly agreed, willing to offer anything: 'Do take it, Marina!

Take everything you need for your poetry. Take the whole of me!'[64]

This offer must be interpreted only in emotional terms for (like Marina herself) Sonyechka loved men too, and (unlike Marina) was slightly guilty about the numbers who had received her kisses. One touching conversation is recorded:

'Marina, do you think God will forgive me for having been kissed so much?'
'Do you think God counted?'
'I didn't count either. . . .'[65]

There was no thought of fidelity between them. But this did not prevent Sonyechka being petulant, and a little jealous, if she visited Marina and found her with anyone else. Marina ironically questioned whether Sonyechka spent the rest of her time alone. Sonyechka replied 'I? I'm a lost soul. I am so afraid of death that when there is nobody around – there are such dreadful hours sometimes – I feel like climbing on the roof to find the cat, just so as not to be alone. And not to die alone. . . .'[66]

Sonyechka was particularly jealous of Volodya, and before he left for the White Army they made a strange threesome at Marina's flat. Sonyechka and Volodya preferred to come separately and at different times, although there was a close relationship between them too. When the three of them were in Marina's flat together, they sat, with Volodya on the left and Marina on the right, rather as though Sonyechka were the child and Marina and Volodya were the grown-ups protecting her.

Marina lost track of Sonyechka in the year she found her. There was no goodbye. It was from someone else that she learned of Sonya's departure the day before, and the person who brought the news was astonished that she had not come to say farewell to Marina. No one knew exactly where she had gone.

For Marina, her room grew suddenly old at the news; the walls and floor faded in colour; everything became dull and grey at once. She felt neither insult nor betrayal in Sonyechka's surprise departure. She understood that Volodya had come because he couldn't leave without saying goodbye. Sonyechka didn't come because she *couldn't* say goodbye.

Many years later, reflecting on what she had lost, Marina said: 'She was my sugar. I needed her like *sugar*. We all know – sugar is not necessary and one can live without it as we all did in the four years of the Revolution, replacing it with treacle or scraped beetroot or saccharin or nothing – drinking plain unsweetened tea. One doesn't die of that. But one doesn't live, either.'[67]

Throughout 1918 and 1919, the conditions in which Tsvetayeva lived with her two children grew daily more difficult. By September 1918, Marina needed to make forays into the countryside to barter for food – that is, pig fat and millet – and to get official permission to travel she had to pretend to be going to the Institute for Dames of the Order of St Catherine (by then turned into the Department of Fine Arts) 'to study hand embroidery'.

Marina made notes on the dangerous journey to and from Usman station in Tambov province with a certain wild glee. The first train she settled in was requisitioned by the Red Army before it left the sidings, and she knew she was not safe even when the second train arrived at Usman station near midnight. There, people made themselves comfortable wherever they could, in the only house with accommodation to let. A woman who had a son in the Red Army made what use she could of that connection; her reward was the landlady's pillows and featherbed. Marina made do with the clothes she had brought with her.

In the middle of the night, she was woken by a heavy knock, the sound of feet, laughter and swearing. By matchlight, it was difficult to make out what was happening, but it turned out to be yet another official 'requisition' squad. Tsvetayeva jotted her impressions of the savagery of the search in her notebook:

Cries, tears, the tinkling of gold coins, bare-headed old women, featherbeds ripped open, bayonets . . . they rummage everywhere.

'Doing pretty well with your icons, aren't you! All this
for the saints, too! Gods like gold too, I suppose.'

'But we haven't got anything . . . Listen to us. Young
man! You'll be a father, too, one day!'

'Shut up, you old crone!'

A candle flame flickers and dances. Huge shadows of
Red Army soldiers on the walls.[68]

Tsvetayeva was not a shrewd businesswoman. Told to ask
for 3 poods (108 lb) of fat for a reel of cotton, she was too
timid to ask for more than half a pood, and her bargaining
got off to a bad start. In any case, the peasants resented
everyone who came from Moscow, convinced that no
Muscovite could know anything about hard work. Tsvetayeva
records how she ended up buying a wooden doll and a necklace
of dark amber and giving away three boxes of matches. At
the time, she was angered by the peasants, but afterwards she
came to feel that she had more in common with them than
with some of her boorish fellow travellers, who looked her
over and either despised her for her cheap stockings, or recognized in her short hair and style of speech something of the
hated bourgeoisie.

For all her mother's liberal opposition to anti-Semitism,
Tsvetayeva had never grasped the complexity of the Jewish
situation in Russia and, even though Seryozha was half-Jewish,
shared many Russian prejudices about those she met on this
journey. She identified a Communist (with a gold ingot round
his neck) and his wife as Jews, and treated their memories of
their old tailor shop in Petrograd (formerly St Petersburg) as
absurdly self-important. But the dialogue she records is also
touched with pathos:

We had such a nice little apartment, a dear, sweet place!
Three rooms and a kitchen, with a small pantry for the
servant. I never allowed the maid to sleep in the kitchen,
that's slovenly, hair could fall into a pan. One room was
the bedroom, another the dining room, and the other,
sky-blue, was the drawing room. I had very important
people giving me their orders, you know, and all the best
people in Petrograd wore my jackets. Ah, yes, we made

a lot of money, every Sunday we received guests, wine, the best food in the shops, flowers . . . Iosya had a whole smoking set, a small filigree desk, Caucasian, with all sorts of pipes and little odds and ends, ashtrays, matchboxes. . . . We bought it by chance from some factory-owner. . . . And people used to play cards at our house, too, and, I assure you, not for any measly insignificant amounts, either.[69]

Aside from countryside forays, Marina decided to improve their situation by letting out rooms. She found a young man called Zaks, a decent if humourless Communist, who felt sorry for her. He first suggested she might get a job as a file clerk at the People's Commissariat for Nationalities, which was located in the same building as the Cheka, the secret police. Iks had to reassure her that she would not be involved in working for the Cheka itself (they would have been unlikely to take her anyway), but what finally convinced her was the building itself: it was the Sologub family mansion, which had been Tolstoy's model for the Rostovs' house in *War and Peace*. The job had no particular advantage, such as special rations, and Iks then wondered if she might not be better off working in a bank. In spite of her desperate situation, Tsvetayeva asserted grumpily, 'I can't add up.'

On 13 November 1918, therefore, she found herself in the Information Department of the Commissariat for Nationalities. It was hardly a job requiring complex attention, and Tsvetayeva found it grindingly monotonous. (The burden of looking after Irina fell largely on Alya.) Marina's account of that time in journal jottings gives a sharper picture of it than her later essay in *My Jobs*, which is clearly based on the same material.

November 15, my third day at work. I am compiling an archive of newspaper cuttings. That is to say, I put down in my own words what Steklov and Kerzhentsev say, reports on prisoners-of-war, the advance of the Red Army and so forth. I set down one and then another (I transfer them from the 'journal of newspaper cuttings' on to 'cards'), and then glue these cuttings on to huge sheets of paper. The newspapers are thin and the type is hardly readable, but to write headings in a lilac-coloured pencil and then more glue is totally useless, and it will vanish into dust even before it is burned hereafter.

To my left there are two dirty, down-at-heel Jewish★ women, like herrings, and ageless. Further on is a blonde, dressed in red, also frightful looking, like a person who has become mere sausage meat. She is a Latvian: 'I knew him, such a nice man. He took part in a conthpiwathy, and now they've sentenced him to be thot. Click-click!' And she titters excitedly. She is dressed in a red shawl. Her neck is a bright pink and fat protuberance.[70]

Monotonous, distasteful or not, Marina needed the money urgently, and she hung on to her job for five and a half months. She was fair enough to note, when she resigned, that 'under the old regime they would have kicked me out as soon as they took one look at my work'.

Soon afterward, she found herself a job in the Institute of Noblemen, a government department in which she was expected to deal with index cards in a room resembling a coffin. The supervisor was forty years old and seemed to Tsvetayeva to be a 'frightful old woman, like a gaol keeper'. Certainly this woman was ironically amazed at how slowly Marina toiled. She could tell that she was not familiar with the work and commented acidly: 'Our normal quota is 200 cards a day.' Even the knowledge that her children depended on her for food did not prevent Marina from walking out after a single morning.

It was not the noble gesture she made of it in *My Jobs*, in which Tsvetayeva explained her behaviour: 'My feet took me out without my being conscious of it. This is what is called instinct.'[71] However, it was certainly not a conscious decision. She had forgotten to register for dinner and the first reason she gave for needing to leave the office was to go home for food. She was given half an hour to do so, since she lived quite close, but her morning's work had made her weep so much that an old woman seeing her pass in the street thought

★ See p.90 for Tsvetayeva's ambivalent attitudes.

she must have been robbed. Marina said as much, and as she thought of what she had said, her words in some way restored to her a sense of her own freedom.

This was one of the last of Marina's actions to be characterized by a kind of spoiled child's refusal to accept responsibility, which took no account of her two children, dependent for their lives on her support. It is probably the only example of Marina's behaviour throughout her life that I find personally antipathetic, however understandable it might have been.

On 14 July 1919, she was offered a reading at the Palace of the Arts at which she chose, with some insolence, to read to fellow writers a group of poems that condemned the threefold lie of 'freedom, equality and brotherhood'. The reading lasted at least forty-five minutes and she was to be paid sixty roubles for it, but she refused the money. It was only paper of course, virtually worthless, and would have bought little, but the gesture had an arrogance in keeping with her refusal to perform menial work while her resources were dwindling.

The Moscow famine of 1919 could not be endured only through the possession of printed paper, but money did help. Marina's attempt to realize some by selling an antique clock worth 10 000 roubles resulted only in the loss of the clock to the man who had promised to find her a buyer. She noted the disaster with resignation, since the money would only have bought a pound and a half of flour. Friends helped her: some gave her the occasional luncheon voucher; an actress brought some potatoes and some beams ready sawed for fuel; a literary friend brought matches and some bread. However, the squalor and poverty of the family situation were unremitting and would have been so for even the most careful housewife. This Marina was not.

In her journal, Marina noted:

I live with Alya and Irina (Alya is six, Irina two years seven months) in our same flat on the lane of Boris and Gleb, opposite two trees, in the attic room which used to be Seryozha's. We have no flour and no bread. Under my writing desk, there are about twelve pounds of potatoes which is all that is left from the food 'lent' by my neighbours. These are the only provisions we have.[72]

This laconic catalogue of resources is very far removed from
the usual voice of Tsvetayeva's daily record of her life, which
reflected the inner world of emotions. There is no ecstasy, no
joy in the use of language here, simply a sober note, as if to
a future reader after Marina's death, recording the details of
her desperation and the ages of her children.

She did what she could. She returned bottles to the kinder-
garten to get the money back on them; went with coupons
from a bootmaker to the 'Prague' eating house; and walked
all over Moscow looking for bread for sale. Whatever she
managed to beg or buy, she usually carried back without help.
If Alya came with her, Irina had to be left alone, tied into her
chair for safety. But Marina could not handle the situation, as
her journal makes clear:

> I feed Irina, then put her to bed. She sleeps on the blue
> armchair. There is a bed, but it won't go through the
> door. I boil up some coffee, drink it, and have a smoke.
> I write. Alya writes or reads. There is silence for two
> hours. Then Irina wakes up. We heat up what remains of
> the mashed goo. With Alya's help, I fish out the potatoes
> which remain, or rather have become clogged in the
> bottom of the samovar. Either Alya or myself puts Irina
> back to bed. Then Alya goes to bed. At 10 P.M. the day
> is over.[73]

These were the years when the bond between Marina and
her daughter Alya was drawn most tightly. They often slept
in the same bed for warmth, sometimes fully clothed. Marina
used her daughter's intelligence to make her into a precocious
confidante. The child responded gravely, imitating her mother
in many ways, sharing ideas drawn from books such as *Don
Quixote*, which Alya had already read by the age of six, or
imagining how Marina could have brought her up in the
eighteenth century. Marina depended on her child, not only
for help in grappling with slop buckets and wood chopping,
but also for spiritual assurance. In some ways, the relationship
recalled the few moments when Marina had been closest to
her own mother.

Marina remained unworldly, but luckily not all the peasantry were eager to cheat her, and she found it easy to make friends with the milk-woman, Dunya, who continued to come with pails of milk right up to the winter of 1920. Her willingness to accept paper money for the priceless milk touched Marina deeply. It was a bond between mothers: Dunya had three sons and two daughters of her own. Marina frequently gave Dunya something from her chaotic household, while Dunya sometimes brought crushed potato-rye cakes or a precious hard-boiled egg from hers.

All of them were hungry, all of the time. Irina once tried to stuff a raw cabbage into her mouth. And she looked sickly. In June 1919, her former nanny, a peasant from Vladimir province, begged Marina to let her take the child back to her village: 'Our milk is still milk, white under the Tsar, white without the Tsar, and our potatoes are alive, not frozen to death, and the bread has no whitewash in it. And your Irina will come back – ho! ho! – you wait and see.'[74] Marina did let the peasant woman take Irina away for a time, and her charity staved off the child's hunger for several weeks.

Alya fell seriously ill and Marina kept her alive only with a tremendous struggle – there was no help from anyone. At last it looked as if Irina could only survive in a state orphanage. The decision was a tragically mistaken one, however: Irina – whom Alya described as a little girl with a straight forehead, fair ringlets and grey eyes, always singing 'Maena [Marina], my Maena' – died of hunger in the winter of 1919/20, at the age of two years ten months in the care of the orphanage that Marina had hoped would save her.

The horror and confusion of the period come through in a letter that Marina wrote to her sister Anastasia in December 1920:

> Forgive me if I keep writing the same things – I'm afraid of letters not getting through.
>
> In February of this year Irina died – of hunger – in an orphanage outside Moscow. Alya was badly ill, but I kept her alive. Lilya and Vera [Seryozha's sisters] behaved worse than animals – in fact just about everybody turned their backs. Irina was almost three. She could hardly speak

yet. It used to be distressing to see her. She would spend
all the time rocking and singing. Her ear and her voice
were astonishing – if you should find any trace of S.,
write [him] that it was from pneumonia.[75]

5

'I think of him day and night'

1920–1922

Marina was always to remember the shock of standing in the Street of the Three Ponds and finding that the much-loved house of her childhood had been destroyed; a house made of pine timber, it had been demolished for firewood. For years afterwards, Tsvetayeva had only to shut her eyes to recall at once the ruins of the house she loved. Meanwhile, she and Alya now lived in the dining room of the flat on Boris and Gleb Street, and to heat that one room they had to burn the furniture from the others.

Marina was in pain whenever she remembered Irina, or allowed herself to be chilled by the thought of Seryozha's possible death. Yet she and Alya were not altogether isolated; in famine-stricken Moscow, others battled against the same conditions. In 1919, when Marina met Boris Pasternak in the street, he was on his way to sell valuable books from his family library to buy bread. They were not close friends, but they felt themselves to be part of the same community of poets.

Their politics were widely different at that time. The February Revolution had filled Boris with exhilaration, as if 'the lid had been snatched off the whole of Russia'.[76] Although the fine poems of his book *My Sister, Life* make little reference to particular events of the year of revolution, he himself 'saw on earth a summer that seemed to recognize itself – natural, prehistoric, as in a revelation'.[76] Marina, reading the collection some years later in exile, recognized how deeply he had conveyed that mood 'without hiding from the Revolution in any of the available cellars'.

Although, in a conversation with Marina some time during the spring of 1918, Boris mentioned his plans to write fiction as well as poetry, he was not intimate enough with her to talk about the complex politics of the changing situation. They could hardly have argued peaceably. Pasternak was still writing to Valery Bryusov in August 1922 that the stage of revolution closest to the heart and to poetry is its 'morning, its explosion', and unlike Yuri in Dr Zhivago, he as yet had few qualms. His opinion was unshaken, even though during the whole of the civil war he had remained in a flat in Volkhonka Street and endured Moscow's three worst winters of famine, disease and desperate fuel shortage.

On one point, however, Marina and Boris could have agreed: by the spring of 1920 the situation was beginning to improve, at least in Moscow. Marina was allocated a government ration of food, and this led her to encourage her sister to return from the Crimea to Moscow. From Voloshin's letters, she knew how disastrous the situation was there. Corpses were being eaten, not by dogs but by people. In the last month of her life, before she died from emphysema, Pra ate eagles.

In December, Marina had heard from the novelist Ilya Ehrenburg of her brother-in-law Boris's death, but nevertheless she wrote to Asya of her refusal to believe it. It was so close to her own worst terror. Marina's only comfort, in the absence of news, was her faith in Voloshin's insistent reassurance: 'Don't be anxious about Seryozha. I know that he is alive, and will remain alive.' Her refusal to believe in one death went hand in hand with her own need for hope. And, after all, other friends kept turning up, alive even if ill. So she wrote:

Asya! . . . Come to Moscow. You have a miserable life. Here things are returning to normal, but it will be a long time before that happens where you are. We have a lot of bread; there are frequent distributions for children; and

– since you insist on having a job – I could arrange (my great connections!) a wonderful position for you, complete with large rations and firewood. Apart from that, you would be a member of the Palace of the Arts (formerly Sologub's) and receive three decent meals for almost nothing. Forgive the household themes, but I want to get them over with at the start. You will be all right in Moscow; there are many acquaintances and semi-friends; I have relations; we will manage. *You can be sure of it.*

I hate Moscow, but at the moment I cannot travel, because this is the only place [Seryozha] can find me – if he's alive. I think of him day and night. I love only him and you.

I'm very lonely, even though all Moscow is full of acquaintances of mine. They are not people – believe that literally – or else they are already so worn out that I, with my temperament, feel awkward, and they feel perplexed.

All these years I have always had someone next to me; but still felt utterly desolate in my need for people![77]

It was clear that the old way of life had gone for ever: 'I no longer hold anything dear except for the maintenance of my rib-cage. I am indifferent to books; I sold off all my French ones; whatever I need, I shall write myself!'

In the same letter, she records a visit from her friend Lann (whom she writes about with the hyperbole that suggests a lover) who brought presents and news of Asya's son Andryusha. His visit emphasized the homesickness that the thought of her sister aroused, as she wrote:

Asya! I'm waiting for you. It's *years* that I have been alone (a highly populated wasteland). We *must* be together. You'll be all right here.

How easy dying is. But – it's strange – throughout these years I have been completely unworried about you (the highest form of trust!), just as about myself. *I have known that you were alive.*

Asya! Boris's death has wounded me for life. It is a great and terrible grief. I only believed it when Lann confirmed it. I loved Boris like the brother we never had. I write drily. You will understand!

This letter carries a series of postscripts:

Asya, wait until the trains start and write how much money you need for your departure. I'll send it . . . I shall write to you every day. Forgive me that my letters are telegrammatic.

Alya is not very big; thin, fair – like Psyche. Her letter and poems were in the first letter.

Immediately after the occupation of the Crimea I sent Max a telegram through Lunakharsky. Did it really not arrive! Moscow is without fences (burned), and full of sacks and boots.

If I knew [Seryozha] was alive, I would be completely happy. I need nothing apart from you and him.

Each morsel that I eat sticks in my throat, and I despair that I cannot send it to you. I shall find out about transferring money, and I shall send it off straight away. Do not abandon the thought of moving to Moscow.

Tender kisses for you and Andryusha. I am touched by his little letter.[77]

Marina's letter to her sister suggests that she had little time for the literary life around her, and she speaks contemptuously of opportunities the new regime offered to hold meetings and put on plays. Marina found the audiences as motley as a circus crowd and complained that she was rarely allowed to appear, and had not printed a single line, because the poet Bryusov controlled the publication of all literature.

Bryusov had been one of the four poets to review *Evening Album*, Tsvetayeva's first book of verse, and he had taken exception to many of the qualities that had so attracted Gumilyov, particularly a spontaneity of expression that he found slovenly. He would hardly have become so bitter an enemy, however, if the eighteen-year-old girl had not, in return, written an angry letter to him about his attitude to Rostand and, later, directed a mocking poem at him, accusing him of following fashion blindly. In spite of this undisguised antagonism, Marina was not completely excluded from taking part in the life of the Palace of the Arts. The luxurious cuisine that characterized the restaurant in later years as the Writers' Union grew richer was not yet an important attraction, but the portions of the three, nearly free meals a day were plentiful, and the restaurant was already a place where it was possible to meet and exchange gossip with writers of every political persuasion. There, in 1920, she was allowed to read her poem *Tsar Maiden*. This poem is a folk-tale in verse, in which can be found elements of two of Alexander Afansiev's tales and also the theme of Phaedra's incestuous love for her stepson Hyppolytus. The heroine, a warrior woman in love with a delicate man, finds he is wooed at the same time by the black arts of his stepmother. The theme of such incestuous love runs through much of Tsvetayeva's writing of the Twenties.

In the winter of 1921 Marina was invited to take part in a reading by 'women poets' organized by Bryusov, a grouping that, in itself, Marina found an insult; she did, however, agree to take part. As Bryusov introduced them all with arch references to the feminine skill in writing of love and passion, her fury was confirmed. In contrast to the frilly dresses of the other women, Marina chose to dress in a belted leather cassock and grey felt shoes. When her turn came, she mounted the platform and read poems from *Swan's Encampment* praising the White Army. This was more than a wilful risk, as Marina knew, and she later wrote of it as 'obvious insanity'. As she put it:

I was guided by two, no, three, four aims: (1) seven poems by a woman without the word 'love' and without the pronoun 'I'; (2) proof that poetry makes no sense to an audience; (3) a dialogue with anyone, a single person, who *understood* (perhaps a student); (4) and the principal one: fulfilling, there in Moscow of 1921, an obligation of

honour. And beyond any aims, aimlessly, stronger than
aims, a simple and extreme feeling of: *what if I do?*[78]

Among the most important readings she attended were
those of Alexander Blok. Marina had always admired him
with fervour, and had begun writing a cycle of poems for him
in 1916. She felt a reverence for his genius, which, for her,
surpassed that of all living poets.

> Your name is a – bird in my hand
> a piece of – ice on the tongue
> one single movement of the lips.
> Your name is: five signs,
> a ball caught in flight, a
> silver bell in the mouth
>
> a stone, cast in a quiet pool,
> makes the splash of your name, and
> the sound is in the clatter of
> night hooves, loud as a thunderclap,
> or it speaks straight into my forehead,
> shrill as the click of a cocked gun.
>
> Your name – how impossible, it
> is a kiss in the eyes on
> motionless eyelashes, chill and sweet.
> Your name is a kiss of snow,
> a gulp of icy spring water, blue
> as a dove. About your name is: sleep.[79]

It was an enthusiasm she had shared with Antokolsky during
their weeks of intimate friendship in 1917, when he brought
a book of Blok's poems into her house and read them aloud
to her, but she did not hear Blok himself read until 1920, when
she had the opportunity to hear him twice in the course of a
few days: once at the Palace of the Arts, a second time in the
Polytechnic Museum. She did not know him personally, and
she did not take the risk of introducing herself to him, though
she was far from shy. Instead, at the Palace of the Arts reading,
she sent Alya to him with an envelope containing some of her

poems and a letter. Later, she was to regret having missed the opportunity.

All the pink velvet seats seemed to have been taken by the time Marina and Alya arrived at the Palace of the Arts, and it was only through Antokolsky that chairs were found for them before Blok arrived. Even as they sat down, an excited whisper went round the crowd: Blok was about to appear.

He did not share the excitement of the audience. His eyes were lowered; his face was a dull brown and his mouth looked dry. There was a completely dead expression in his eyes and on his lips, and his whole face looked as if it had been stretched over his bones. At first, he read a poem called 'Reverence' about Byron and the youngest daughter of an ancient English noble family who was enchanted by him. The audience clamoured to hear 'The Twelve', but Blok refused: this was Blok's controversial poem in which Christ suddenly appears at the head of a group of ruffians and drunks who bear the standard of the Revolution. He could not read it, he said simply. And the audience understood this as a failure of health and energy.

Marina's experience of the reading at the Polytechnic found its way into a lyric that appears towards the end of her cycle 'Poems for Blok':

A weak shaft of light through the blackness of hell is
your voice under the rumble of exploding shells

in that thunder like a seraph he is announcing
in a toneless voice, from somewhere else, some

ancient misty morning he inhabits, how he
loved us, who are blind and nameless who

share the blue cloak of sinful treachery
and more tenderly than anyone loved the woman who

sank more daringly than any into the night of evil,
and of his love for you, Russia, which he cannot end.

And he draws an absent-minded finger along
his temple all the time he tells us of

the days that wait for us, how God will deceive us.
We shall call for the sun and it will not rise.

He spoke like a solitary prisoner
(or perhaps a child speaking to himself)

so that over the whole square the sacred
heart of Alexander Blok appeared to us.[80]

The 'tender spectre', the unkillable spirit of Marina's lyrics,
had become a sick man whose hold on life was failing. He
died in August 1921.

Among the poets Tsvetayeva came to know well was
Konstantin Balmont. They had been friends for some time:
he had been one of the earliest critics to appreciate her work,
and in the first year of the Revolution, they had appeared at
the same literary soirées. Now he was grateful for her (for
once) calm friendship. She was too sorry for him to develop
more febrile emotions. His fame was fading. Before the Revolution, he had been a legendary figure, but in 1920, when the
new government organized a jubilee for him at the Palace of
the Arts, there was not much applause. Balmont was already
yellow in the face and wrinkled, with misty eyes, a bumpy
nose and a strange, lost-looking smile. He no longer made
jokes, and he spoke with a slight pause between every word.
Even his serenity suggested loss: the fire was gone, the tran-
quillity was grey. All this was enough to make Marina, always
a friend to the helpless, gentle. However, her circumspection
arose also from an acknowledgement of how close he was to
his wife. Elena accompanied him everywhere: a small, thin,
vibrant creature with huge violet eyes, always tending him
and seeing to his every need. Marina also helped, waiting with
her in one shopping queue after another, and even harnessing
herself to Alya's sleigh to help Elena carry frozen potatoes,
fuel or some other essential goods home to the Balmont house.
In addition, Marina was generous: when she received her
ration of two ounces of tobacco, she poured out half for
Balmont, and there were occasions when he and Marina would
smoke a single pipe together to economize on tobacco, sharing
puffs like Red Indians.

The Balmonts lived two steps away from the Arbat, near the former home of the composer Scriabin, maintaining as best they could their large room with windows leading on to a front garden. Their flat was heated by a small, sooty stove that Elena tended while Balmont wrote his poetry. When Balmont visited Marina, she would be stoking her own small stove with similar difficulty. By contrast, the Scriabin household was clean, ordered and warm.

When the Balmonts began preparing to go abroad, they were understandably hesitant, and indeed they kept changing their minds altogether. Marina and Alya eventually saw them off twice. On the occasion of their first departure, the Scriabins gave a farewell party where everyone was served potatoes with pepper (a luxury), and real tea in real porcelain cups. The next day, however, some trouble arose over their Estonian visa, and their departure was delayed. The final farewell took place in an indescribable mess. There were clouds of tobacco smoke and samovar steam, as the Balmonts left their house rather as gypsies might strike camp. Nevertheless, many friends came to see them off, and Marina was the most cheerful of all. She told anecdotes, laughed and made others laugh, as if she wanted to prevent any thought of the separation. It was a journey into emigration from which the Balmonts were not to return.

Throughout these years of famine and dislocation, Marina was not ill-treated officially, and in the winter of 1921, she made friends with P. S. Kogan, a convinced Bolshevik, and his wife. Kogan felt that no good writer (even Andrei Bely of whom he disapproved) could be hostile to the Revolution. He was among the most benevolent of the new Soviet officials, and the conversations with him that Marina later recorded show that her relations with the new government were still surprisingly good. She had already been given a ration card, and now her *Tsar Maiden* was accepted for publication. Her sympathies, never hidden, were overlooked on the grounds that writers were a necessary part of new Soviet life.

The previous spring, Marina's sister had come back from the Crimea with tales of people staying alive by boiling moss. Gaunt and ragged though she was, Asya was determined to go out and find a job, and ironically, she found one at the museum that their father had founded, and which continued to function. Asya's contact with Soviet officialdom was less successful than her sister's. By coincidence, the new regime had installed as director a young man, little enough qualified for the post, who had once been a suitor to both the Tsvetayeva daughters. They had been contemptuous of him then; now the reversal of fortune was complete. In Marina's account of the meeting Anatoli, sitting at their father's desk, did not bother to stand up as they entered, and when Asya asked for a job, he told her briskly that there was none available. It was only when she pointedly suggested that some position might be found for her in view of her special connection with the museum that he promised to think it over. A week later, a letter arrived with the offer of a job as a non-staff employee, at a pitiful salary.

News of the deaths of friends came in constantly, and there was still no word from Seryozha. Returning from Koktebel in the autumn of 1920 to find Marina in 'frantic solitude', Ilya Ehrenburg had looked at her cycle of poems *Swan's Encampment*, and tried to explain how very differently her heroes of the White Army had been behaving. Evidence of the looting and murder of innocent villagers was, in fact, overwhelming, and she must have heard of it from many sources other than Ehrenburg. But she was too obstinate to believe any account of brutality in an army that included her tenderly loved Seryozha. That 'difficult character' to which Ehrenburg refers ruefully (in his memoirs *People, Years, Life*) made it impossible to persuade her by argument.

Meanwhile, the civil war was beginning to resolve itself into a Bolshevik victory. But even as the fact of peace was assimilated, a new threat began to show itself. The intelligentsia both in Petrograd and in Moscow (and always suspect in Russia), suddenly found that their political credentials were to be seriously examined, and among many others, Akhmatova's divorced husband the poet Gumilyov was arrested. The uneasy atmosphere of August 1921 was caught by Nina Berberova, as she described how everyone first learned to speak in whispers in the Writers' House, and the House of the Arts in Petrograd.

Everywhere there was silence, waiting and uncertainty.
The 24th August arrived. Early in the morning, when I
was still in bed, Ida Nappelbaum came over. She came
to tell me that on the street corners were posted the
announcements: all had been shot . . . sixty-two persons
in all. . . . That August was not only 'like a yellow
smoke' (Akhmatova); that August was a boundary line.[82]

Like many other exiles-to-be, Berberova had had no respect
for Tsar Nicholas II nor any desire to defend the tyranny or
ineptness of his government, but she felt that August 1921
marked a line dividing 200 years of legitimate political aspira-
tion from the planned destruction of the whole fabric of society
that was to follow.

Akhmatova was a poet whose excellence had excited Marina
to write a cycle of poems for her in 1916, and these were so
much prized by Akhmatova (who was used to praise and too
proud to be flattered by it) that she kept them with her through
all her own later wanderings. However, the two poets could
hardly have been more different. For one thing, Akhmatova
was an acknowledged beauty, whose style and pride had
already been caught in a line drawing by Modigliani, and
many men had fallen in love with her. Yet, for Gumilyov she
continued to feel the bond of a love that had never been equally
requited, and the memory of a generously affectionate spirit
(the lovers she had chosen to succeed him had proved much
more tyrannical). He was, moreover, the father of her only
son. When she heard of his execution, she was struck with
despair, as she recorded:

> Better to lie against the bare boards
> Of a scaffold raised out on the green square
> And to the cries of joy and the groans
> Pour out red blood to the end.
>
> I press the smooth cross to my heart:
> O God bring back peace to my soul.
> The sickly sweet smell of decay
> Is given off by the cold sheet.[83]

She must also have understood her own danger. In Moscow, rumours began to circulate that she had taken her own life.

The passion that went into Marina's letter to Akhmatova of 31 August, offering her loyalty, was characteristically reckless.

31 August (O.S.) 1921
Dear Anna Andreyevna,
Of late, gloomy rumours have been circulating about you, becoming more persistent and unequivocal with every hour that passes. I write to you about this, because you will hear in any case. I want you to be correctly informed, at least. I can tell you that, to my knowledge, your only friend among poets (a friend indeed!) turned out to be Mayakovsky, as he wandered among the billboards of the Poets' Café looking like a slaughtered bull.
Slaughtered with grief – it's true, he really did look like that. But he it was who, via acquaintance, sent a telegram inquiring about you, and it is to *him* that I am indebted for the joy of hearing tidings of you . . . I shall not talk about the other poets – not beause it would be painful for you: who are they, that this could cause you pain? I simply do not want to blunt my pen.
I have, in the hope of finding out about you, spent these last few days in the Poets' Café. What monsters! What squalid creatures! What curs they are! Everything is here: homunculi, automatons, braying stallions and lipsticked sleeping-car attendants from Yalta. . . .[84]

Marina went on to give an account of a contest between poets who wished to be considered as full members of the Writers' Union. She had sat impatiently through this, until at last she had to send up a note to Aksyonov on the platform to beg for true news of Akhmatova's fate. She took his nod to mean that Akhmatova was alive.

Dear Anna Andreyevna,
To understand what yesterday evening was for me, to understand Aksyonov's nod to me, one would have to know how I lived the previous three *unspeakable* days. A horrible dream. I want to wake up, but I cannot. I

confronted everybody, beseeching your life. A little
longer and I would actually have *said* 'Gentlemen! See to
it that Akhmatova be alive!' . . . Alya comforted me:
'Marina! She has a son!'

At the end of yesterday's proceedings, I asked Bobrov's
permission to make an official journey – to Akhmatova.
Laughter all round. 'Gentlemen! I will give readings – ten
evenings in a row for nothing – and I always have a full
house!'

These three days (*without you*) Petersburg ceased to exist
for me – Petersburg! . . . Yesterday evening was a
miracle:
   'You became a cloud in the glory of rays.'
   I shall, in the near future, give a lecture about you –
the first time in my life: I harbour a loathing for lectures,
but I cannot yield this honour to another! In any case, all
that I have to say is: Hosanna!
   I conclude as Alya concludes letters to her father:
                    Kisses and deepest respect, M.Ts.[85]

Perhaps Marina's recklessness sprang from the lifting of her
own uncertainty. Only two months before Ahkmatova lost
Gumilyov, she had had definite news from Ehrenburg that
Seryozha was alive. In the spring of 1921, as one of the first
Soviet citizens to go abroad, Ehrenburg had discovered that
many soldiers from the defeated White Army had made their
way to Prague and been given places at the university,
Seryozha among them.
   As soon as she was sure of this, Marina applied for a passport
to go abroad. Mirkin, at the People's Commissariat for
Foreign Affairs, remarked: 'One day you will be sorry you
are leaving.' Ehrenburg, who recorded the anecdote, does not
record her reply, but afterwards, her daughter was to reflect
that Marina made two decisions because of Seryozha for which
she was to pay bitterly: the first was to follow him into exile;
and the second was to follow him back to the Soviet Union
before the outbreak of the Second World War. However, in
1921, Marina was in no doubt about what action she should

take. The terror she felt in the succeeding weeks resulted from an almost overwhelming superstitious anxiety that the miraculous possibility of seeing and holding Seryozha again would be denied her by malevolent fortune.

Tsvetayeva decided to leave the Soviet Union at the very point when her poetry was beginning to win a qualified acceptance by the new regime. In a letter of 22 January 1922 to Evdoxia Fedorovna Nikitina, she mentions that two of her long poems were to be published, and that a large advance of two million roubles had already been paid for them. There was, however, nothing political in her decision to go abroad, and it is extremely unlikely that she realized the enormity of her decison – or its inexorable results. Ehrenburg said of her: 'In what is known as politics, Tsvetayeva was guileless, obstinate and sincere.' It was on 1 July 1921, at ten o'clock in the evening, that Marina received the first letter from Seryozha. For him the news that Marina was still alive had been transfiguring and had sent him wandering about the town, all day long, out of his mind with joy. Their dependence upon each other was deep, and felt with intensity by both equally: Marina needed, above all else, the certainty of being wanted and irreplaceable; and to Seryozha, she represented the only secure and protective love he had known since his mother had died. Seryozha wrote:

Our meeting was a great miracle, and our future meeting will be an even greater one. When I think of it – my heart stops beating – frightening – for there could be no greater joy than the one that awaits us. But I am superstitious – so I shall not talk about it. . . .

All the years of our separation – every day, every hour – you were with me, in me. But, of course, you must know that already.

It is hard to write about myself. All the years I have spent without you have been like a dream. My life is divided into 'before' and 'after', and 'after' is a terrible dream, I'd like to wake up, but I can't. . . .

What can I say about my life? I live from one day to the next. Every day is struggled for, and each one brings our meeting nearer. This last gives me happiness and strength. Otherwise everything around is very bad and hopeless. But I'll tell you all about that when we meet.[86]

Marina's own journal notes for this period are incoherent. As her husband suggested in his earlier letter, anxiety mounted as the possibility of happiness approached.

Yet even in this state, Tsvetayeva continued to write. From the day she received her husband's letter until the day of her departure in the spring of 1922, she wrote more than a hundred poems, including the long poem *Side Streets* (a poem of magical virtuosity which tells the story of a girl who learns to use witchcraft to seduce and deceive men.) She also began another long poem, *A Peasant*. Alya writes in her memoirs of notebooks filled with conversations and stories picked up on trams, in second-hand shops and in queues. Alya's desire to emphasize Tsvetayeva's awakening interest in working people may well be political, as Karlinsky suggests

Just before her departure, Osip and Nadezhda Mandelstam knocked on her door. Delighted as she was to see Osip again so unexpectedly, Marina could hardly bring herself to offer Nadezhda her hand. Indeed, if Madame Mandelstam reports her correctly in *Hope Abandoned*, she behaved with abominable rudeness, saying to Mandelstam, 'Let's go and see Alya,' and then adding to Nadezhda without so much as a glance: 'You wait here. Alya doesn't like strangers.' Accordingly, the total disorder of Marina's rooms at this time was recorded with wry detachment in Madame Mandelstam's memoir.

'Like all former upper-class apartments, it was now given over to dust, dirt and decay, but here there was also an atmosphere of witchcraft into the bargain. The walls were hung with stuffed animals of all kinds, and the place was cluttered with old-fashioned toys which the Tsvetayeva sisters – all three of them in their turn – had no doubt played with as children. There was also a large bed with a bare mattress, and a wooden rocking horse. I thought of all the giant spiders that might be lurking unseen in the darkness, the mice frisking about, and Lord knows what other vermin beside; all this was supplied by my spiteful imagination.'[87]

By the time Marina and Alya came to leave, they were

living in three rooms: the dining room, the nursery (which may explain the toys and rocking horse) and Marina's own room. Alya describes their last day in Moscow, packing up, with great poignancy. So many things had to be left behind. Some of them were deeply prized, not as *things* but because they were so completely imbued with memories. (Marina's sister was deputed to take away as many of them as she could.) There were favourite books, portraits of Seryozha, the music box that had belonged to Marina's mother, the photographs of Marina and Seryozha in their youth, Marina's childhood notebooks.

All the valuables they did take were listed in one of Marina's notebooks, with a few extra notes appended in Alya's hand:

> Pencil-case with the portrait of Tuchkov IV
> The Chabrov inkwell with the little drummer boy
> The plate with the lion
> Seryozha's glass-holder
> Alya's portrait
> Sewing box
> Amber necklace
> (*In Alya's hand*)
> My felt boots
> Marina's boots
> The red coffee pot
> The new blue bowl
> Primus, needles for the primus
> Velvet lion

The 'plate with the lion' was heavy porcelain with a golden-brown design, which showed 'a king of the beasts with the face of Max Voloshin'; the silver glass-holder with Seryozha's initials had been a wedding present. Marina also chose to take a plush rug that had been her father's last present to her, some hand-made toys and, rather unexpectedly, a Soviet alphabet book with cartoons of Lenin wearing an apron and bow-legged imperialist enemies flying into a ditch. Her listed objects were sacred to her, and except for one piece, she was never to be parted from them through all her wanderings until she brought them back to the Soviet Union in 1939. The rough amber necklace with a coarse waxed thread, however, was exchanged for bread by Alya long afterward during a hungry year near Ryazan.

The actor Podvaetsky-Chabrov, whose inkwell is on the list of treasures, was packing to go into exile at the same time as Marina, and he helped her on the final day of departure. Marina liked Chabrov's sharpness, and his ability to see the funny side of the most extreme disasters. However, the great difference in their lifestyles precluded any more than a gay camaraderie, for as she pointed out rather dolefully in a letter to Ehrenburg, 'He is a nobleman, able to live a pampered life, while I? Who am I? Not even a bohemian.'[88] Nevertheless they could both joke about the business of preparing for exile.

The moment of departure arrived. Marina sat in a cab, with her daughter on her lap and her luggage around her feet, and crossed herself as she went past the familiar white church of Boris and Gleb. She told her daughter to do the same. In that way, she chose to say goodbye to Moscow, ceremoniously recognizing each church as they passed it.

Mixed with the sadness of leaving was a terrifying anxiety, which took the form of worrying continuously that they would be late for the train. They were not. Everything was in order. There were no crowds and not much noise. Alya remembered sharing the compartment with a modestly dressed lady on crutches who had evidently lost her leg in the civil war and was being sent abroad for treatment. Chabrov gave Alya a prettily wrapped parcel for the journey, which turned out to be a box of sweets. Alya recorded that Marina snatched the box from her hands, before she had time to do more than peep at the NEP-style⋆ brunette on the cover, saying: 'How moving! We'll take this to Papa.' Chabrov also passed a message in to them saying that Isadora Duncan was travelling in their carriage. This interesting tit-bit of information turned out to be false, as they discovered when the train set off. They had only Miss Duncan's companion, who was following her mistress out of the Soviet Union and looking after eight weighty trunks of the celebrated dancer's baggage. These

⋆ Lenin's New Economic Policy (NEP) allowed some limited freedom to entrepreneurial activities.

evidently contained mainly the used relics of Russia: dried-out tubs, hornless oven prongs and tattered bast baskets – a collection of junk that was to bewilder the many customs officials who boarded the train on the journey.

Alya remembered the ring of the three bells that were struck before the train began to move: 'So we left Moscow, unnoticed, as if we had suddenly shrunk to nothing.'

In that sad record of leave-taking, nothing is more conspicuous than the absence of Marina's literary friends of the period. It was, after all, not yet an offence to leave the country. Could it already have been felt to be dangerous to come to the station to say farewell? It is true that friends had come to say goodbye at the flat (for instance, one of Voloshin's daughters), but they were mostly casual acquaintances. The last friendly, helpful face Marina was to see in Moscow was that of Chabrov, a courteous aristocrat soon to be in exile himself.

Part III

Emigration:
Berlin and
Prague

6

'You are not a child, my dear, golden, incomparable poet'

1922

The journey to Berlin lasted four days. Tsvetayeva made no attempt to sleep, or even to lie down, on the bed provided. She smoked incessantly. At Riga, they had to change trains, and waited for almost a whole day. At any other time, Tsvetayeva would have enjoyed that ancient city with its jumble of elegant Gothic buildings and the unsophisticated signs (keys, biscuits, bottles, gloves and so forth) that hung above the shops in the crowded streets. But now her inner chill prevented her from taking an interest in anything. She walked around the cobbled streets in a daze, refusing to eat and wanting only coffee. Her tension did not relax until, just as it was growing dark, they were at last able to get on the train for Berlin. Then she let her eyes close, and slept sitting up.

In the morning, she and Alya looked out at the landscape of a Germany that (to Alya's astonished delight) looked like something out of a childhood picture-book. It was an extraordinarily precise and ordered landscape after the confusion they had left behind in Moscow.

They arrived in Berlin – to await Seryozha's arrival from Prague – in bright sunshine on 15 May 1922 and a porter, dressed in green, was at their side immediately to carry their belongings to a cab. At once, Berlin (which even after the war remained a city of considerable chic) opened out before them. Tsvetayeva made for the Pragerplatz, a small, friendly square around which many Russians housed themselves. Ilya Ehrenburg was staying at a pension there and was expecting them. Moreover, to Tsvetayeva's relief, he was there to welcome them, and immediately put a large, dark, book-filled room at their disposal.

Berlin was intoxicating after the poverty of Moscow. The coffee might be poor, but the smell of oranges, chocolate and good tobacco was an overpowering reminder of a lost world. Even if the rate of inflation was already alarming, people still looked well-fed and comfortable.

There were a great many Russians in Berlin. Dozens of Russian restaurants had opened, with balalaikas, gypsies, pancakes and shashliks. Russian could be heard on every side. There were three daily newspapers and five weeklies appearing in Russian, and in one year, seventeen Russian publishing houses were started. At this period, the line between *émigré* and Soviet literature had not yet been harshly drawn, and writers who had aligned themselves with the new regime still met and talked easily with those who had rejected it. And, most important, books from Berlin circulated in Russia itself and were reviewed in the Soviet press.

In those days, there were many who found themselves in exile almost by chance, who had fled in panic and, bewildered, were now earning their living by washing dishes or other menial tasks. Even among those who had made more considered decisions, the sense of a time of transition prevailed.

Many writers and publishers lived at the pension in which Tsvetayeva and Alya now found themselves. Close by was the Pragerdiehle, a particularly popular café. Often joining Ehrenburg and Tsvetayeva there, was the young publisher A. G. Vishniak, who chose to be known by the name of his publishing imprint: Helikon. Marina soon knew all the regular customers of the café well and, as well as Vishniak, made close friends with Ehrenburg's wife, the artist Liuba Kosintseva and Liudmila Chirikova (the daughter of the famous writer).

At ten, Alya made notes on her impressions of Helikon,

which show how much she had absorbed her mother's way of looking at the world.

Helikon is visited by a variety of figures: an old gentleman with his watch on a piece of dog-chain (his gold chain has been sold); thin, dull widows of writers, who come in the hope that Helikon will give them their husbands' allowances. Every useless person comes. Helikon tries not to offend anyone, but everyone curses him for paying so poorly.

Helikon is a man who has two sides to him – his everyday life and his soul. Everyday life is that little weight which holds him down on the earth and without which, he thinks, he could immediately shoot up into the sky, like Andrei Bely. In fact, he would not break loose so easily – he has too little soul, so that he mainly needs peace, rest, sleep, cosiness, which is precisely what the soul does not give.

When Marina looks into his office, she is exactly like an incarnate soul, which troubles and raises someone to its own level, rather than lowering itself to him. In Marina's friendship there is no kind of rocking asleep. She cannot help *pushing* even a child *out of the cradle*. She thinks all the time she is rocking him asleep – but it's a kind of rocking that leaves you not feeling too well. Marina speaks to Helikon like a Titan. She is as incomprehensible to him as the North Pole would be to an inhabitant of the East, and as strangely tempting. I have seen how he reaches towards Marina as if to the sun, like a crushed little stalk. But the sun is far away, because the whole of Marina's being is reserve and pursed lips while he himself is pliable and soft, like a pea shoot.[89]

Not everyone found Tsvetayeva quite so formidable. Although in her adolescence the name of the writer Andrei Bely had been uttered reverently by Ellis throughout their friendship, Tsvetayeva had never been allowed to meet him. Later on, his marriage to Asya Turgeneva had made acquaintance possible though never close. Jealous as she was, because of her own infatuation with Asya, Tsvetayeva still forgave

Asya's choice of Bely because they were of the same kind, those who *wrote* poems, rather than inspiring them. Tsvetayeva met him in the Pragerdiehle, at Ehrenburg's table. Bely recognized her suddenly: 'You? You? . . . Here? How happy I am! Have you been here a long time? Have you come for good? Were they following you on the way?'[90] Bely lived quite nearby, in Zossen, and though he was a difficult person to help, Tsvetayeva knew how to speak with those whose nerves were stretched beyond endurance. At this time, Bely's grief at the break-up of his marriage to Asya Turgeneva had brought him to the verge of madness, but even though her own future was far from settled, Tsvetayeva gave Bely a sense of refuge. In June 1922, he wrote to her:

> My kind, kind, kind, kind Marina Ivanovna . . . during these last particularly difficult, burdensome days you *again* sounded the only true note towards me . . . a tender, tender, remarkable note; of trust. There are miracles after all![91]

Some of the fellowship Bely felt for Tsvetayeva came from the fact that they were both the children of professors. Bely had always declared he would have preferred to have been the son of a coffin-maker, but now, meeting Tsvetayeva, he took great joy in stressing their closeness not only as orphans and poets, but also in the very brand they shared as a result of their fathers' profession. For her own part, Tsvetayeva had never felt her father's position in any way oppressive, but she understood Bely's situation and noted in her memoir of Bely, written after his death in 1934, 'every pseudonym is subconsciously a rejection of being an heir, being a descendant, being a son. A rejection of the father.'[92] Andrei Bely had rejected his father altogether by inventing a new name for himself.

At the time of their meeting Bely had not read Tsvetayeva's book *Separation* (which included her poem 'On a Red Steed' dedicated to Akhmatova, published that year in Berlin, so she gave him a copy. The next day she received a letter of incredulous admiration, and for days afterwards Bely repeated his praise of her work. He himself claimed to have written no poems in three years, and felt he could hardly call himself a

poet any longer. His generous praise for Tsvetayeva's work
led him to place two of her manuscripts, *Tsar Maiden* and
Versts, with a publisher – a remarkable gesture from someone
who was almost incapable of doing anything on his own
behalf.

It was not Tsvetayeva's habit to analyse the natures of those
she loved, and since as Bely could not see the strangeness of
his behaviour, or even take control of his own life, she made
no attempt to force him into anything so uncongenial. She
responded to his innocence, and did not see how often he hurt
other people in alleviating his own pain. His was the kind of
weakness that Tsvetayeva loved to help in the most practical
way possible – by heating up his stove in Zossen, for instance,
or sweeping away his rubbish.

During the weeks she was in Berlin waiting for Seryozha,
Bely frequently came over from Zossen on overnight visits to
see her. Alya (now nine years old) and his publisher's five-
year-old son, who was often in the apartment, found him easy
to tease, and sometimes put rubber animals filled with water
in his bed. This did not particularly distress Bely, who usually
reported his experience to the children in the morning in great
detail. His problems with insomnia went far deeper than the
presence of children's toys in his bed: one of his greatest fears
was to wake up under a staring face. Tsvetayeva was one of
the few people whose presence in a house gave him peace. As
he put it, 'she brings sleep to me. I am going to sleep, sleep,
sleep.'[93] In contrast to his own nervous disorder, Bely recognized her vitality and health.

Bely was unhappy in Berlin. To his brilliantly distorting
eye, it seemed to him that what trees there were cast no
shadows, and that the birds did not sing. He disliked even the
name of the suburb where he lived: *Zossen*. He found it fleshy,
'like noodles for soup'. However, his deepest grief was over
the loss of the woman he loved and the jealousy he felt for
the man who had supplanted him. His distress was pitiful, and
in her attempt to comfort him, Tsvetayeva took less notice of
Alya, though she always took the child with them wherever
they went. Alya was always very quiet on these occasions, as
if recognizing that an encounter between two poets was of
great importance. For Tsvetayeva, who had always seen Alya

as an extension of herself, capable of sharing all her thoughts, the exclusion was unintentional: she simply began to overlook the fact that Alya had needs of her own. As a comic instance of this, Alya recalled that, on one long walk with Bely, she had needed to find a lavatory, but was so afraid of interrupting their conversation, that she had at last to resort to relieving herself in the open air. Not all the changes produced by Tsvetayeva's dedication to Bely were so uncomfortable, however – she showed a new and welcome tolerance towards Alya's behaviour. For example, the young girl was now allowed to drink beer, once strictly forbidden, whenever she wished.

It says something for Tsvetayeva's greatness of spirit that she had the strength to deal gently with Bely in his state of frenzied desperation. For her, it was both a time of great excitement and continuous suspense. She could now, through Ehrenburg's generosity, afford to buy presents for her husband (such as warm underwear, socks, and a cigarette case), but Seryozha had not yet managed to reach Berlin, and until he did so, every such gesture seemed to tempt fate. Her years in Moscow had taken their toll, and Berlin confirmed her sense of a whole world in flux, in which she might lose track of Seryozha even as she hoped to find him.

The exact date of Seryozha's arrival was uncertain. In the event, the telegram with the time of his train was delayed, so that after weeks of waiting, Tsvetayeva found herself rushing helplessly towards the station to meet a train that had already arrived. As if in a nightmare, she found that the passengers had already dispersed, and there seemed to be no one except Alya and herself left in the whole vast cathedral of a station. No one could give them any information; there was no message. Tsvetayeva began to wander about in the deserted white square in front of the station, incredulous and confused, until suddenly she heard Seryozha's voice, and they were able to hold one another close, weeping, after all their fears. They were together again after five years' separation. And for the moment, that seemed to be all that mattered.

In a letter to Maximilian Voloshin of the autumn of 1923 (published in Simon Karlinsky's life of Tsvetayeva), Efron wrote of the way his relationship with his wife had changed over the period of their separation: 'Marina is a creature of passions. To a much greater degree than previously – prior to my departure. To plunge headlong into a self-created hurricane has become a necessity for her, the air of her life.' He added bitterly that he had long felt useless himself for stoking the furnaces of her passions, and referred to a brief and unreciprocated passion Tsvetayeva had felt for Vishniak: 'A few days before my arrival, the furnace had been kindled – but not by me.'

This in no way invalidates the joy that husband and wife felt on greeting one another after the long years apart. Their relationship had changed in character, but there can be an intense love between brother and sister, still more, perhaps, between mother and son, and as early as Seryozha's first letter to Marina of July 1922, he showed that he was aware of this possible turn in their relationship. 'Just go on living', he declared then. 'I will make no demands on you. I need nothing from you except that you stay alive.'

That night, the Ehrenburgs gave a huge party to celebrate the reunion. There was even champagne. Alya's sharp eyes, observing her father, noted:

Seryozha, who was nearly twenty-nine, still looked like a boy who had just recovered from a severe illness: he was so thin and big-eyed and still seemed lonely – even with Marina sitting next to him. She in contrast seemed to have grown up altogether – once and for all! – right up to the threads of her early greyness, which already glittered sharply in her hair.[94]

This insight of Alya's was extraordinarily perspicacious and pointed unerringly to what lay ahead. The loneliness she remarked in Seryozha is easy to understand. He (unlike the others) had made himself irrevocably an exile, and had already tasted the bitterness of it. And in his absence, Marina had matured and changed.

Seryozha's first visit to Berlin was a short one. He had to return to Prague to prepare for the next academic term. He planned to study Byzantine Art under Nikodim Kondakov and he was not finding the work easy. Before then, however, there were many decisions to be taken. The first was to move out of Ehrenburg's large room into a little hotel in Trautenaustrasse where the Efron family could afford to rent two tiny rooms and a balcony. The most important decision was not so easy to make: it concerned the move to Czechoslovakia.

Clearly, there would have been financial problems in staying in Berlin. The small fees Tsvetayeva was earning from Russian publishing houses there could easily dry up whereas there were grants to help students at the university in Prague, provided by Tomáš Masaryk's government. Worse, in the economic crisis hanging over Germany at that time, there was little likelihood of a Russian finding a job. In Czechoslovakia, on the other hand, there was a firm source of money, and the sympathetic government was already giving funds to Russian scientists. Moreover, the country was Slav, and the city of Prague itself, as Seryozha described it, was as beautiful as a fairy tale.

Tsvetayeva put aside her sense of Berlin as a centre of Russian publishing, and their decision was made. Once it was arranged, Seryozha left for Prague. He had been in Berlin only a matter of weeks, arriving in early July and leaving by the end of the month. When he had gone, Tsvetayeva made her first, rather forlorn, attempt to see something of the city with Liudmila Chirikova, and Alya.

Tsvetayeva had been working very hard. During the two and a half months she had lived in Berlin, she had seen very little, but her output of work had been staggering: thirty poems, a story entitled 'Florentine Nights' and an essay on the poetry of Boris Pasternak, called 'A Downpour of Light', which showed how deeply she had been reading and responding to his work.

By a strange coincidence, it was at this time that Pasternak too first picked up Tsvetayeva's volume *Versts* in Moscow and was moved to write to her and explain how much that experience had changed him.

The letter from Pasternak arrived on 27 June 1922, forwarded by Ehrenburg; Pasternak had particularly instructed him to read it, presumably to ensure Ehrenburg's continued protection of Tsvetayeva. It is an extraordinary letter, and initiated the correspondence that was to be one of Tsvetayeva's main emotional supports in the long years of exile.

Dear Marina Ivanovna:
Just now I began reading your 'I know, I shall die at dawn, on one of them' with trembling in my voice to my brother – and I was struck down, as if by a stranger, by a wave of tears which forced its way to my throat and finally broke through. When I transferred my attempts from this poem to 'I shall tell you about the great deception', I was likewise thrown down by you, and when I transferred them to 'Versts and versts and versts and stale bread', the same thing happened.

You are not a child, my dear, golden, incomparable poet; and I hope you understand what that means in our times, when there is an abundance of poets and poetesses, not only of such as are only known to their union, an abundance not only of Imaginists, but an abundance even of unstained talents, like Mayakovsky's and Akhmatova's.

Forgive me, forgive me, forgive me!

How could it happen that treading with you behind the coffin of Tatiana Fedorovna Scriabina* I did not know whom I was walking next to?

It is entirely understandable that Tsvetayeva did not reply at once to such praise – and that she chose an unusual way of doing so. In her letter to Pasternak, a note almost like anger sounds in the opening. She clearly wanted Pasternak to sense the mixed feelings she had felt when she had read his letter for the first time. And her whole letter is tinged, not with reproach precisely, nor with regret, but more with a recognition of loss that she would endure so often, of which her failure to make more than superficial contact with Pasternak in Moscow had been a significant part. And there is something else too: not pride, not shyness exactly, but the same reluctance that had prevented her from going to visit Pasternak before she left Moscow; the same shyness that had prevented her

* Scriabin's wife.

meeting Blok. Tsvetayeva was always capable of the most female, human anxiety: What if I cannot live up to his expectation of me? Here is her reply:*

Berlin, 29 June 1922

Dear Boris Leonidovich,

I write to you in the sober light of day, having overcome the temptations of night and my first impulses.

I have let your letter cool off, become interred under two days' rubble. So what survives?

Well, from underneath the rubble:

Glancing over it, the first thing I felt was an *argument*. Somebody was arguing, somebody was annoyed, somebody was calling me to account: there was somebody I had not settled with. I felt the pangs of hopelessness, of uselessness. That was before I had read even a single word.

I start reading (still not understanding who it is) and the first thing that penetrates through the unfamiliar sweep of the handwriting is: *he is rejected* – I still do not realize who. (And my unbearable response: All right, so somebody is dissatisfied, indignant. But good Lord! How am I guilty for the fact that he read my poems?) – and only towards the end of the second page, at the mention of the name of Tatiana Fedorovna Scriabina, like a blow on the head . . . Pasternak!

Now hear further:

Some time in the spring of 1918, you and I sat next to each other at dinner at the Tsetlins. You said, 'I want to write a major novel; one with love in it, and with a heroine. Like Balzac.' And I thought: how fine; how precise; how above conceit! A Poet.

Then I invited you: 'I would be happy if you could. . . .' But you did not come because novelty in life is unwelcome.

The originals of these and other letters to Pasternak have been lost. svetayeva kept rough drafts of all her letters to him; it is from these quote.

11 April (Old style) 1922, Tatiana Fyodorovna Scriabina's burial. She and I were friends for two years. I was the only woman friend she had all her life. Ours was a stern friendship, a business and conversational friendship, a masculine friendship, devoid of the tenderness of earthly tokens.

And so, I accompanied her large eyes on their way into the earth.

I walked with Kogan, then with somebody else, and suddenly, hand on sleeve like a paw – you. (Later I wrote of this to Ehrenburg.) We talked of [Ehrenburg]. I asked you to write to him. I spoke of his boundless affection for you. You listened perplexedly, even dolefully:

'I completely fail to understand why . . . How difficult . . .' (I felt pity for Ilya Grigorievich and did not include this in my letter.)*

'I read your poem on hunger. . . .'

'Don't remind me. It disgraces me. I wanted something completely different. But you know, it sometimes happens like that; milling masses above your head; then look down, and the paper is still white; the poem has floated past, without touching the table. That poem I wrote at the last moment. People pestering me, telephoning me, but it wouldn't come together. . . .'

Then you talked of Akhmatova. I asked about her most basic personal qualities. You looked hard at me and said:

'Total attentiveness. She reminds me of a sister.' Then you praised me ('although one should not say this to your face') for having, all these years, in spite of everything, gone on writing – oh, and I forgot the main thing!

—'You know who liked your book very much? Mayakovsky.'†

This was a *great* joy: the gift of all that is *alien*: conquered space (time?).

I truly brightened, inwardly.

And the coffin. White. Without wreaths. And, already

* This note must be addressed by Tsvetayeva to herself.
† The poet and dramatist Vladimir Mayakovsky (1893–1930).

close, the comforting arch of the Novodevichii Monastery; blessed repose.

And you. . . .

'I am not with them; this is a mistake; you know, how you give away your poems to various anthologies. . . .'

Now the *most important thing of all:* we stand by the grave. No longer hand on sleeve. I feel with my shoulder (as always in the first second after parting) that you are beside me, a step further off.

I reflect on Tatiana Fyodorovna. Her last moment in the air of this earth. And, with a jolt; a feeling of *dislocation*. It did not occur to me – since I was engrossed with Tatiana Fyodorovna – to watch her through to the end.

And when I look round, you are no longer there. *Disappearance*.

This is my last vision of you. A month later, to the day, I left. I had wanted to call in to please Ehrenburg with an eye-witness account of you, but I felt: a house I don't know, and he probably won't be at home, etc.

Later, I was even ashamed to face Ehrenburg, after such weak ardour for his friendship.

That, dear Boris Leonidovich, is my 'History with you' – also dislocated.

I know little of your poetry. I once heard you at a public reading. You kept forgetting everything. I had not seen your book.

What Ehrenburg said struck me at once; lashed me, rattling, twittering – everything at once. Like life.

Running in a circle; but the circle is the world (the universe!) and you – at the very beginning, and you never shall finish, for you are mortal.

Everything is only outlined – with sharp points – and on, allowing no time for recovery. The poetry of design. Agreed?

I say this going by the five or six poems that I know.

Soon my book *Remeslo* comes out. Poems of the last eighteen months. I shall send it to you with pleasure. In the meantime, I am sending you two diminutive booklets which appeared here without me – simply to pay for my passage: *Poems for Blok* and *Parting*.

I shall be in Berlin a long time. I wanted to travel to Prague, but the conditions of life there are hard.

Here I am close to nobody except the Ehrenburgs, Bely and Helikon, my publisher.

Write how things stand with your departure. Are you really coming (in the concrete world – that of visas and forms and milliards)? It is fine living here. Not the town (one is another), but anonymity, space. One can be completely without people. A little like in the Other World.

I press your hand; I await your book and you.

M. Ts.

My address: Berlin Wilmersdorf
             Trautenaustrasse 9
             'Trautenau-Haus'[95]

Pasternak's parents had already left the Soviet Union for the West and had settled in Berlin. News came through of Pasternak's imminent arrival in Berlin, though it was not known whether or not he intended to move into exile. Tsvetayeva (by then living in Czechoslovakia) could have seized this opportunity to travel to Berlin to see him. She did not go, though she must have been aware of the possibility that this could be her last chance to meet him. Her decision may have been swayed by the fact that he was to be accompanied by his wife, whom he had married the previous spring – Yevgenia Vladimirovna Lurye, an artist of great beauty. (Tsvetayeva was never to mention his marriage during their long correspondence.) The fares, too, presented difficulties: Tsvetayeva never felt entitled to deplete the family budget for entirely selfish reasons. Nevertheless, when Pasternak invited her to come to Berlin, she considered it and decided against the journey, for reasons that were both practical and perversely her own. In an incomparable letter, she explained them:

Mokropsy, 9 March (new style) 1923*

Dear Pasternak,

I shall not come. I have a Soviet passport and no certification of a dying relative in Berlin, and no connections to force it through. A visa would take two weeks, at best. (Immediately after receiving your letter, I made the most precise inquiries.) If you had written sooner, and if I had known that you were to leave so soon. . . . A week ago, a cursory mention in a letter from Lyubov Mikhailovna Ehrenburg: Pasternak is preparing to leave for Russia. . . . And that was it. Everything slipped by, without any mention of the date.

Dear Pasternak, I have nothing, except my *fervour* for you, and that will not help. I kept waiting for your letter, not daring to act without your permission. And I did not know whether you needed me or not. I simply lost heart. (I write in a cheerful fatal fever.) Now I know that it is too late.

On receipt of your *Themes and Variations* – no, earlier, from the news of your arrival – I said: 'I shall see him.' With your lilac-coloured book, this came to life, turned visible (blood), and I started on a large book of prose (correspondence!), counting on finishing by the end of April. I worked every day without a break. What is the connection? It is clear. I have no right (in front of my living persona) so to uproot myself. I (those surrounding me) have a very difficult life. With my departure, all this damned routine falls on them. I began fervently. Now it is too late. A book there will be, but no you. I need you, not the book.

One final word: and this is no wily cunning. You will remember me more if I don't come. *Not* more – that's a lie. No calculation (I shall remember too much if I see you! *Too much* in any case; it could not be more!), and no cowardice (to disappoint, to be disappointed).

Even so, it is monstrous. Your departure, whether from the Berlin platform, or from my Bohemian hill, from which I shall, on the eighteenth, all day (for I do not

* Gregorian Calendar. All subsequent dates are so set out.

know what time!), see you off, so long as I have the strength.

I shall not come, because it is too late, because I am helpless, because Mark Slonim, for example, is getting permission [a visa] at one o'clock, because that is my fate – loss.

Now about Weimar [where Pasternak had suggested that they meet in two years' time]. Pasternak, don't joke. I shall live by this for two years running. And if in those years I should die (I shall not die!), this will be my penultimate thought. Only please don't joke. I know myself. Pasternak, I was just returning along the rough country road (I had gone to check on the visa from those who had just recently travelled). I was feeling my way. Dirt, potholes, dark lamp posts. Pasternak, with what force did I then think of you; no, not of you; of myself without you, of these street lamps and roads without you. Oh Pasternak, my feet will walk milliards of verses before we meet! (Forgive me for such an explosion of truth; I am writing as if about to die.)

Now the prospect of massive insomnia. Springs and summers – I know myself – every tree that my eyes single out will be you. How can one live with this? It is not that you are there, while I am here; the point is that you will be *there*, that I shall never know whether you exist or not. Yearning for you and fear for you, wild fear; I know myself.

Pasternak, this began with *My Sister, Life*; I wrote to you. But then, in the summer, I stopped it, cut it short with my departure for another country, for another life. But now my life is you, and I have nowhere to go.

Now, to put it more sharply: *what* precisely? What is the matter? I am straightforward and clear; I do not, I swear, know the *word* for this. I try them all in turn! (You will see how much I don't know – from my February poems.) A meeting with you would be, for me, a sort of liberation from you, one might predict. Is that clear to you? A breathing out! I would exhale myself into you (from you!) Only don't be angry. These are not superabundant words, but boundless feelings; *feelings*, which already exclude the concept of bounds! And what I say is less than what exists. . . .

Pasternak, two years' growth lie ahead, *before* Weimar. (Suddenly – like a madman! – I begin to believe it!) I want to make you one promise. I make it mutely. I shall send you my poems, and tell you everything that happens to me. I shall speak of you, the poet, to others. I do not repudiate a single word of mine, but if that will be a burden to you, then I shall be silent. But then there will be only one thing left: to write to you directly about myself that which I have most painstakingly, for your own sake, avoided. Pasternak, should things suddenly become difficult for you – no, that's not necessary, I make no requests; but this I demand: break off. Then I shall banish myself to the depths, shall break off – that it may rot under the ground; as then, in February – my poems.

Now it is two in the morning. Pasternak, will you be alive? Two years – what is that? I do not understand time. I understand only Space. I have just been walking down the sharp declines of a hill, and I saw a train in flight. I thought: 'That's it!' Pasternak, there will be no trains for . . . wait a moment – 730 days! So that [gap] . . . Your elegant communication . . . I 'm giving nothing away! I get flustered. 'Since you are good enough to let me think that I address you, I reply to you'. . . . And then, have I forgotten? No, I have not forgotten. If *I* forget, then my thoughts of you will not forget.

And as for that which you refuse to have anything to do with – this is how it should be read: 'Perform a miracle' (I write 'succeed in . . .'), 'be, at last, he who. . . .' That 'at last' is not meant for you. It just fell off the pen.

Do not be afraid. There will be only one letter like this. I have become no stupider, no more beggarly, through choking on you. It is not only my estimate that is burdensome to you, but also my attitude. You still do not understand that you endow with inspiration. I shall observe due moderation. In my poems there is none. But you will forgive that in poetry.

My Pasternak, perhaps I shall, one day, really and truly

become a major poet – thanks to you! I do have to speak without bounds to you, to unfold my heart. In conversation this is done through silence. But I have only a pen!

Two emotions struggle within me, two fears: the fear that you will not believe me, and the fear that, *believing* me, you will recoil. I do not only sin with my external immoderation. Externally, everything is too much for me; both from other people and, particularly, from myself. My grief (*already* grief!) in relation to you is in the fact that, for me, the word is *almost the same* as feeling; the innermost thing. Were you and I to meet, you would not recognize me; there would be immediate relief. I use words to make good my losses, as sometimes I shall, in that just and generous world, make good my losses from the crookedness and meanness of this world. Is that clear to you? In life I am boundlessly wild – not to be brought to heel.

Pasternak, how many questions I have to put to you! We have not talked about anything yet. In Weimar we shall have a long conversation.

Pen out of my hand. . . . Must leave the kingdom of words. . . . Now I shall lie down and think of you. First with eyes open, then with eyes closed. From the kingdom of words, into the kingdom of dreams.

Pasternak, I shall think only good of you, only the real, the important. As if after a hundred years! I shall admit not a single accidental or self-willed thought. Lord, all the days of my life belong to you! As all my poems.

I shall finish writing this tomorrow morning. It is now past three, and you have long been asleep. All night I have been talking to you in your sleep.

M. Ts.

10 March Morning
A whole page is still in front of me, a whole blessed, white page – for everything'! . . .

There is one poem of mine that you do not know: *A*

Peasant. I have lived on it since you (in autumn) and before you (before February). Reading it through, you may be able to clarify a lot. It is a savage work – it was totally unable to part with me. Another of the requests: send me poems. That is just as much a liberation for me as my own. Describe *ordinary life*, where you live and write, Moscow, the air, yourself in space. This is important to me. I can tire (of happiness!) of thinking into 'nowhere'. There are many streets and street lamps. When a person is dear to me, then his *whole* life is dear to me; the most mundane detail is valuable. To put it into a formula: your daily routine is dearer to me than another's existence!

Yesterday evening (I had not yet unsealed your letter, which I held in my hands), my daughter's shriek: 'Marina! Marina! Come here!' (I, mentally: the sky? Or a dog?) I go out. Alya points with an outstretched hand. Half the sky, Pasternak, looking like a wing; a wing in half the sky; unprecedented. There are no words for the colour! Light, becoming colour. And it rushes, wrapping tight half the sky. And I came straight out with 'The wing of your departure!'

I shall live by such signs and *omens*.

I am sending you my poem 'The Emigrant'. I would like you to read it while still in Berlin. The rest (from the first to the last) will be in the letter that I shall send off after it. And my affectionate and insistent request: that you should only read them in the carriage, when the train starts moving.

If in Moscow I should be very much abused for 'White Guardism', do not be distressed. That is my cross. My *voluntary* cross. With you, I transcend it.

Last words: be alive. That is all I need.

Leave your address.

Marina[96]

For all his pleasure in seeing his parents again, Pasternak was very unhappy in Germany. He was disappointed in Bely.

He disliked the throngs of Russian expatriates in Berlin. And when he found, on visiting the University of Marburg, that his old professor, Hermann Cohen, had died, the city had lost all magic for him. He was soon homesick for Russia, and had little hesitation in deciding to return there with his bride.

Tsvetayeva went on waiting for her meeting with Pasternak as an imagined possibility for most of her life in exile. Probably everything she created in the Twenties and early Thirties was in some sense inspired by or directed towards Pasternak alone. His praise, which was to continue warm and unstinting through the years, was to be a rare voice as the excitement of her arrival among the Russians of the emigration declined into disapproval and bewilderment. Tsvetayeva herself later wrote to Pasternak: 'No one's praise and no one's recognition is necessary for me apart from yours.' But by then she was writing out of unhappiness about what was necessary for survival, not for joy.

It is not hard to see why the theme of *A Peasant* was so attractive to Tsvetayeva then and in the years to follow. She felt herself increasingly drained of life by having to care for her sick, tired husband, and the burden of first one child and then, later, another. No wonder a folk-tale about a young girl who falls in love with a vampire struck a chord. However, when the village maiden Marusya (Marina's own childhood name) discovers that her fiancé is a vampire, she does not denounce him, even though her mother, brother and, finally, she herself are to be murdered by him. Tsvetayeva was increasingly aware of the one-sidedness of her relationship to Seryozha, though it was not for years that she made her first truly despairing comment upon it: 'Marriage and love destroy. It's an ordeal. So thought Goethe and Tolstoy. As for an early marriage, like mine – it is a catastrophe. . . .'

She herself gives no hint of any personal connection with the theme of *A Peasant*, but she does describe, in her essay 'A Poet on Criticism', the moment in the folk-tale that most excited her:

I read a folk-tale 'The Vampire' in Afanasiev's folklore collection and I was puzzled. Why is it that Marusya, who

is afraid of the vampire, so persistently refuses to admit
what she has seen, knowing that deliverance lies in
naming it? Why does she say no instead of yes? Fear? But
fear can not only make us bury ourselves in a bed, it can
make us jump out of the window. No, not fear. Granted
fear, but something else as well. Fear and what? When
someone says to me, do this and you will be free, and I
don't do it, that means I am not particularly interested in
freedom; it means that my non-freedom is more precious
to me. And what is the precious non-freedom that exists
between individuals? Love. Marusya loved the vampire.
That is why she never named him, and so lost, one after
another, her mother, her brother, her life. Passion and
crime, passion and sacrifice. . . .

That was my task, when I started working on *A
Peasant*, to uncover the essence of the tale, already implicit
in its skeleton. To release the poem from its spell. And
not at all to invent a 'new form' or a 'folkloric form'. The
work wrote itself, I worked on it, listened to every word
(not weighed – listened). The labour that went into the
poem is confirmed (1) by the fact that the reader is not
aware of it, and (2) by my drafts. But all that is the
poem's development, its realization, and not my initial
conception.

In 1922 Tsvetayeva had no way of knowing how isolated
she was to become as a writer. That year a slim volume of
her lyrics to Blok, which first appeared in her book, was
published in both Moscow and Berlin. Two others also
appeared, one reprinting the poems to Blok, and a second,
part of her forthcoming *Remeslo* ('Craft'). Ilya Ehrenburg was
powerfully promoting her work, and had included it in two
important anthologies, one of them called *The Poetry of Revolutionary Moscow*. She and Akhmatova were spoken of everywhere in the same breath – even by Trotsky who did not
approve of them.

Whatever her letter to Pasternak of June 1922 suggests, she
had no intention of staying long in Berlin. Her heart at this
time was entirely set on living with Seryozha. She imagined
with joy some countryside village preferably close to Prague,

with paraffin lamps and water that had to be brought from a well. So it was that Tsvetayeva and Alya set off to Czechoslovakia.

7

'To have someone loving the woman in me . . .'

1922–1925

Afew weeks after her husband had returned to Prague, Tsvetayeva and Alya followed him and, in August 1922, began their new life in Czechoslovakia. Their first twenty-four hours were spent in a hut as guests of two women students who were friends of Seryozha. The landlady was very strict about everything, down to the times allowed for boiling a kettle, so it was fortunate that the Efron family were soon able to move on to the village of Horni Mokropsy, separated from Prague by the river Berounka.

There they found a room in a three-room house, where seven other people, a dog and a few chickens also made their home. Tsvetayeva was allotted a small stipend by the Czech authorities, in addition to the grant offered towards Seryozha's studies, and all over the village were other Russian students, also supported by the generous Czech government. Nothing could have been less like the table at the sophisticated Pragerdiehle café in Berlin, where Tsvetayeva had so recently taken her place with Bely, Ehrenburg and Helikon.

Nevertheless, Tsvetayeva felt happy. The Efron family were at last reunited, and though it was cramped living in one room, they were surrounded by orchards, pine forests and hills covered with lilac. In comparison with their lives during the civil war, they were all living luxuriously.

Tsvetayeva and Alya soon established a daily routine, which for the latter was particularly arduous. Both got up about 8 A.M. Tsvetayeva cooked breakfast, and Alya made the beds, cleaned the tables and the window sills, and swept the floor with the landlord's broom. She then went to collect the milk, carried out the slops and brought water from the nearby well. After breakfast, she washed the dishes, while Tsvetayeva made the lunch and sat down to write. After lunch, Alya went for a walk and sometimes Tsvetayeva went too. In the evening Alya read and drew and went to bed early.

Seryozha usually stayed four days of the week in the students' hostel in Prague, in the Svobodarna, studying as hard as he could, and editing a university magazine called *One's Own Way*. Otherwise he lived in the village, where he wasn't easy to look after, often angering Tsvetayeva by refusing to eat in the morning although she insisted on giving him cocoa instead of tea and forcing him to put butter on his bread. He was still very thin and tired. After breakfast, he sat on his grey bed, surrounded by books, or walked to and fro trying to learn his notes by heart.

In spite of her new responsibilities, Tsvetayeva continued to write furiously. Indeed, the first entry in her Czech notebook (dated 6 August 1922) was made only a few days after their arrival. The first poem in it begins:

> Sybilla: burned out, Sybilla. A post.
> All the birds have died out. Yet the god arose

and is a meditation upon departing youth, grey hair and the still unchanging prophetic fire of poetry. Tsvetayeva herself was not quite thirty. She was recording the disappointment she felt in her situation, but she was fortunate in Alya's loyalty, and she was not yet cowed.

At the end of September, the Efron family had to make a second move, to a bright yellow house closer to the forest, which could only be approached by a slippery muddy path. This limited access meant that, in order to shift their baggage,

Seryozha had to strap bags and hold-alls over his shoulders, and even ten-year-old Alya had to help.

Despite the discomfort, and the damp, the three of them laughed a good deal, and Tsvetayeva sustained her correspondence with Pasternak.

Mokropsy, 19 November 1922

My dear Pasternak,

My favourite mode of communication is in the world beyond: a dream, to see in a dream.

My second favourite is correspondence. A letter is, as a form of other-worldly communication, less perfect than a dream, but the rules are the same.

Neither can be ordered. We dream and write not as *we* want, but as *they* want. A letter *has to* be written; a dream *has to* be seen. (My letters *always* want to be written!)

Thus, never, right from the start, gnaw at yourself (not even the most peripheral gnawing!) if you do not reply, and do not speak of any gratitude. Any powerful feeling is an end in itself.

I have just received your letter at 6.30 in the morning. And this is the dream you fell into the middle of. I make you a gift of it: I am walking across some sort of a narrow bridge. Constantinople. Behind me, a little girl in a long dress. I know that she will not fall behind, and that it is she who is guiding. But as she is so small, she cannot keep pace, and I take her by the hand. Through my left hand runs a flood of striped silk: the dress.

Steps. We climb them (I, in my dream: 'A good omen'. . .). Striped planks on piles, and below – black water. The girl has crazed eyes, but will do me no harm. She loves me, although not for that was she sent. I, in my dream: 'I shall tame with timidity!'

And then – your letter. My husband brought it over from the Svobodarna (the Russian students' hostel in Prague). Yesterday they celebrated an anniversary – right through the night – and my husband arrived here on the first morning train.

So that was how I received your letter. Chance, and the suspicion of necessity.

★

Now listen *very* attentively. I have known many poets, have met them, sat with them, talked with them and, in parting from them, have more or less known (guessed) the life each of them leads in my absence. So they write; so they walk around; so they go for their rations (in Moscow); so, they go to the café (in Berlin), etc.

But with you, a remarkable thing. I cannot conceive of your day. (And you have lived through so many of them, through *each* one, hour upon hour!) You do not, for me, fit into *life*. Obviously (forgive my boldness) *you do not* live in it. One has to seek you, to follow your traces, elsewhere. And not because you are a poet and 'unreal'. Bely is also a poet, and also 'unreal'. No: is this not an echo of what you write about deltas, about the *intermittent* quality of your being. This is evidently so strong that I transferred it to apply to your *everyday life*. *It is as if, instead of yourself, you send into life your shadow, giving it full authority to act.*

'Words on a dream'. It was summer then, and I had my own balcony in Berlin. Stone, heat, your green book [*My Sister, Life,* 1922] in my lap. (I used to sit on the floor.) I lived by it then for ten days, as if on the high crest of a wave. I surrendered to it and did not choke; I had exactly enough breath for those eight lines which, to my great joy, you liked.

One line still causes my heart to sink.

I do not like meetings in real life. Foreheads knocking together. Two walls. You just cannot penetrate. A meeting should be an arch. Then the meeting is *above*. Foreheads tilted back!

But now people are parting for too long, so I want to know, soberly and clearly, for how long you have come out, and when you are moving on. I shall not conceal the fact that I would be happy to sit with you in some shabby, God-forsaken café in the rain. Elbow and forehead. I would also be happy to see Mayakovsky. He is obviously behaving himself appallingly – and I would be in a most difficult position in Berlin. And perhaps I shall be.

How was your meeting with Ehrenburg? He and I have fallen out, but I love him dearly, and mindful of his great love for you, I would wish that your meeting went off well.

My best memory of life in Berlin (two months) is your book and Bely. I have known Bely almost since childhood, but only this summer did I really become friends with him. He lived on air, eating oatmeal given to him by his landlady, and going out into the fields for walks. There, one evening at sunset, he talked marvellously about Blok. That has remained with me. He lived, incidentally, in an *undertakers' village* and, unaware of this, he used to be naïvely surprised at why all the men wore top hats and all the women wore wreaths on their stomachs, and black gloves.

I live in Czechia (near Prague), at Mokropsy, in a village hut. The last house in the village. There is a stream under the hill, and I carry water from it. A third of the day goes on stoking the huge tiled stove. Life, as far as its *everyday routines* are concerned, differs little from that in Moscow. Possibly it's even poorer! But there is a bonus to my poetry; the family, and nature. *For months on end* I see nobody at all. I write and walk all morning. There are wonderful hills here.

Take from Helikon (Vishniak) the poems sent to *The Epopeia*. They are my life.

In conclusion, I would like to copy out for you my favourite poem – also recent, written in Czechia [the poem *Grey Hair*].

I would be happy if you would send me your new poems. Everything is new for me. I know only *My Sister, Life*.

As for what you write about certain coincidences, correspondence, guesses – that really is not, the Lord knows, foreheads knocking together! When I wrote of you, my forehead was tilted back. It was natural that I should see you.

M. Ts.[100]

Pasternak, I have a request. Give me a Bible for Christmas. A German one, and be sure that it is in Gothic type. Not a big one, but not pocket-size either. And inscribe it. I have already been asking Helikon for one for four months – in vain.

I shall carry it with me all my life!

The reasons for the break between Ehrenburg and Tsvetayeva were partly political: Tsvetayeva remained totally opposed to the Soviet regime, even though she had remained in Russia long enough to see its first attempts to put its precepts into practice; but by 1922 Ehrenburg was prepared to justify most of what he had denounced in poems written just after the October Revolution.* However, the main reason was personal anger at his attitude towards her. In Ehrenburg's novel, *The Life and Death of Nicolai Kurbov,* Tsvetayeva provided the model for the heroine, who is known as a naïve and misguided counter-revolutionary. On his side, Ehrenburg had always been a little put off by Tsvetayeva's mixture of arrogance and lack of practicality, and many years later would write, in his *First Years of Revolution,* of the distaste aroused in him by her Moscow flat as covered in tobacco ash and dust. Perhaps she guessed his reaction. He saw her, without recognizing her true spirit, as someone who could be mocked as a 'romantic monarchist'. For all his early kindness, she did not express a wish to meet him again when she was planning to return to Berlin the following year.

Tsvetayeva's life was soon far from domestic. In spite of Alya's touching childhood accounts of life together in the small forest-side hut, Marina knew that it was only in Prague that she would find her own place. As early as 2 November 1922, there is a letter to Anna Teskovà, who was President of the Prague Czech-Russian Society, agreeing to give a poetry reading and asking to know about the rest of the programme.

* Pasternak, too, differed from Tsvetayeva: he saw a lumbering power in the person of Lenin, whom he had heard speak in December 1921; and he admired Trotsky, whom he had met in 1922. As he later had the eponymous hero of *Dr Zhivago* say: 'A grown man must clench his teeth and share his country's fate.'

She had become a friend of the critic Mark Slonim, and was thought of as one of the most important poets to have gone into exile.

At first Tsvetayeva made few friends among Czech intellectuals, but she did meet the important Russian prose writer Alexei Remizov; and, as Vladimir Nabokov recalls in *Speak, Memory* spent some days hiking about the hills of Prague with him in the spring of 1923. Over the next year, Tsvetayeva gradually established herself at the centre of Prague literary life even before finding a pied à terre. By November 1923, the poet Vsevelod Khodasevich (whom she had known since she was sixteen) and Nina Berberova (two other former habitués of the Pragerdiehle café in Berlin, who had often sat at the same table with Tsvetayeva) moved to Prague. An extract from Khodasevich's diary gives an impression of the intimate and frequent intellectual encounters Tsvetayeva enjoyed at that time with Roman Jakobson and others, including Khodasevich himself and Mark Slonim:

> November 19. Tsvetayeva.
> November 20. R. Jakobson.
> November 23. Tsvetayeva and R. Jakobson.
> November 24. R. Jakobson.
> November 25. R. Jakobson, Tsvetayeva.
> November 27. R. Jakobson.
> November 28. Tsvetayeva.
> November 29. R. Jakobson, Tsvetayeva.
> December   1. R. Jackobson.
> December   5. the Jakobsons.
> December   6. departure for Marienbad.[104]

With characteristic sharpness Berberova has analysed her impressions of Tsvetayeva at this time. She saw her as someone who deliberately assumed the role of a misfit, and refused to acknowledge it as a disability, and she mistook Tsvetayeva's proud courage for arrogance. When Tsvetayeva wrote (in her poem 'Praise to the Rich') of taking up her position 'among the tramps and outcasts' of the world, it was no romantic game. Poetry was her only means of sustaining her self-respect. Nina Berberova resented the implied slight in

Tsvetayeva's insistence (in so many poems) that she had no
wish to be like the rest of humanity. What she missed was the
genuine envy Tsvetayeva always accorded beautiful women.

Nina Berberova herself had a rare beauty and part of
Tsvetayeva's behaviour in her presence was a kind of showing-
off closer to wooing than any declaration of superiority. On
one particular occasion, Tsvetayeva's provocative and exhila-
rating conversation aroused in Berberova an uneasy sense of
danger. The sexual element in this behaviour became explicit,
when Tsvetayeva pulled the light bulb from its socket, and
half-jokingly kissed and tickled the reluctant Berberova.

In contrast to the rich and beautiful, Tsvetayeva looked
weary; and although she was handsome, she was in no ordinary sense pretty. She had an arched nose and two deep lines
now divided her reddish eyebrows. Her chubbiness had altogether vanished, and she had the figure of an Egyptian boy, with
a thin waist and a generally aristocratic leanness, her ankles
and wrists being particularly delicate. Her hair, always golden-
chestnut in colour, was now beginning to turn prematurely
grey, which increased the pallor of her face, and made the
green of her eyes even more arresting.

Tsvetayeva did not repudiate fashion out of affectation, as
many of her acquaintance assumed. She simply refused to
imitate an elegance that was beyond her means. She wore
second-hand clothes, and gave very little thought to their
appearance. Altogether she was rather puritanical in her habits,
and her attitude towards dress was part of that puritanism.
She went to bed late and got up early. Cigarettes were her
only luxury and she preferred them strong and masculine.
When she worked, all she needed was a mug of black coffee
and a cigarette. She never felt the need to leap up or walk
about the room, but sat at her desk as if she were nailed to
it. There she muttered and tried out words for their sound;
sometimes writing with amazing speed; sometimes writing
out many alternative lines, one after another, never crossing
out those that were rejected. She always used a simple wooden
penholder and a thin school nib, and as she worked, she literally dug the point of her pen into the notebooks in which she
preferred to work.

Tsvetayeva's genuine dislike of the 'good houses' of the

Russians came from her childhood, and her distaste for the pressures of ordinary everyday life was at its most intense when she contemplated the soulless search for amusement of those who had no work to do – hence the paradox of her great poem 'Praise to the Rich' written in 1922 (and published, in Seryozha's magazine). At the same time, Tsvetayeva herself had, as she admits in the poem, been brought up very much as one of the privileged. Her rejection of the rich people around her was tinged with bitterness, for her pride made their condescension unacceptable.

> And so, making clear in advance
> I know there are miles   between us;
> and I reckon myself with the tramps, which
> is a place of honour in this world:
>
> under the wheels of luxury, at
> table with cripples and hunchbacks . . .
> From the top of the bell-tower roof,
> I proclaim it: I *love* the rich.
>
> For their rotten, unsteady root
> for the damage done in their cradle
> for the absent-minded way their hands
> go in and out of their pockets;
>
> for the way their softest word is
> obeyed like a shouted order; because
> they will not be let into heaven; and
> because they don't look in your eyes:
>
> and because they send secrets   by courier!
> and their passions   by errand boy.
> In the nights that are thrust upon them they
> kiss and drink under compulsion.
>
> and because in all their accountings
> in boredom, in gilding, in wadding,
> they can't buy me,   I'm too brazen:
> I confirm it, I *love* the rich![102]

Tsvetayeva still felt protective towards Seryozha and was happy, initially, simply to see the family reunited. She backed all his projects, and made no demand on his contribution to the family finances. Nevertheless, as early as the beginning of 1923, friction had begun to develop between herself and her husband. During the years they had lived apart, he had changed. He was no longer able to furnish Tsvetayeva with that 'monstrous trust and understanding' she needed. Nor did he wish to enter her internal world; he was even angry and uncomprehending when she invited him to do so. Worse, Tsvetayeva had to face the fact that he had begun to feel her natural make-up was altogether in opposition to his. They drew away from one another, even while they shared the same living space.

Much of what she objected to, when she reflected upon Ehrenburg (in a correspondence with the Berlin critic Alexander Bakhrakh which Tsvetayeva initiated on 19 June 1923) betrayed her growing resentment at the way most men treat women with 'a living soul':

> That's how it is with women. Always with women. Or rather that's how men are always towards women. . . . I did not want to be a dear child, I did not want to be a romantic monarchist or a romantic, I just wanted to exist, to be; and *he* forgave me existing.

Seryozha wanted a cheerful uncomplicated life with a certain frivolity. The Pragerdiehle café-life in Berlin, which Tsvetayeva despised (even while dominating it) would have suited him better than her stern dedication. Sharply as Tsvetayeva described Seryozha to Bakhrakh, however, she continued to pay tribute to his basic nobility (though unquestionably she regarded it as a form of 'sick goodness'), and it was mainly because he could no longer give her the kind of attention she needed that she began to look for it elsewhere.

Tsvetayeva began to write to Bakhrakh, after reading his extremely favourable review of her poetry. Initially, Tsvetayeva wrote carefully and with formal elegance, yet even her first letter was an unusual gesture, for she took little interest in critics. By the second letter, Tsvetayeva must have

known that she wanted something more from Bakhrakh than
a literary correspondence. He was personally unknown to her;
for that very reason, as she suggested, 'everything was possible. An unknown man is the one from whom you can expect
anything. He doesn't yet exist.' Tsvetayeva created the new
relationship delicately, even as she described her own tentative
feelings. Observing how young was the voice in Bakhrakh's
letters, she commented: 'Immediately that makes me feel
tenderness towards you. And at the same time, make me feel
a thousand years old.' Tsvetayeva was thirty – that is, ten
years older than Bakhrakh – but the gap between them was
clearly one Bakhrakh was as eager to overcome as she was.
He wrote back without any sign of embarrassment and
Tsvetayeva began to acknowledge a claim upon him even as
she assured him that she was not possessive.

Bakhrakh wrote back tenderly, touched by the intimate
thoughts she had revealed to him, and it was in this context
that Tsvetayeva declared her continuing, desperate need for a
miracle of trust, and understanding. It was a demand Bakhrakh
encouraged and the correspondence grew in intimacy. Writing
about their relationship years afterwards, Bakhrakh
complained, as others had, that Tsvetayeva had imagined him.
The letters suggest otherwise.

Tsvetayeva's interest was not at first sexual. She makes this
very clear in her letter of 14 July 1923:

> I want you (you are twenty) to be seventy years old –
> and at the same time a seven-year-old child – because I
> don't want to think of *any* age. I don't want to think of
> counting, I don't want to think of fighting. I don't want
> to think of barriers. I don't know who you are, I don't
> know anything about your life. I can therefore be
> completely free with you because I am talking to a spirit.

Two days later she spelled that out:

> I am too old for love. That's a matter for children, and

not because I am thirty. When I was twenty,★ I said exactly the same thing to Mandelstam, the poet whom you love best.[104]

In the same letter, Tsvetayeva actually rejected Bakhrakh's offer of love, claiming wisely that he could not possibly love her whatever he might think, and refusing to allow him to delude himself. Bakhrakh for his part was flattered by the attention of so remarkable a figure and his letters encouraged Tsvetayeva to respond to his infatuation.

Moreover, it was at his invitation that she considered a visit to Berlin. In a letter of 25 July, Tsvetayeva asked whether he would be able to get permission for her to stay there, and how much she would have to pay for such permission. She also inquired about where she could live, and touchingly betrayed her own anxiety about moving round big cities where she always felt blind, stupid and helpless. There are hints of other hopes in the same letter, where she declares that, much as she is afraid of the city, she is not afraid of any development their relationship might take: 'I am afraid of everything that happens by day and I am not afraid of anything that happens by night.'[105]

Sporadic civil disturbance prevented Tsvetayeva from going to Berlin, but there was no question of her refusing to do so in order to keep Bakhrakh as an ideal and remote figure, about whom she could fantasize. Every occasion in these letters when Tsvetayeva recalled her relationship with Mandelstam indicated exactly the kind of relationship she wished to begin with the young critic.

In the following month, August 1923, there was a breakdown in postal services between Berlin and Prague, and Tsvetayeva feared Bakhrakh had decided to end their correspondence. In her anxiety she said as much – 'I wrote you twice and I didn't receive an answer'[106] – and drew back to her ealier, more formal style of writing, in order to inquire, with dignity, whether the letters ever reached him.

During the month of August, as Bakhrakh's silence

★ Tsvetayeva was actually twenty-three at the time of her affair with Mandelstam.

continued, Tsvetayeva suffered all the torments associated with the ending of a real love affair. Her journal shows the depths of her misery at this time, recording her loneliness and boredom without the interchange of letters she had come to depend upon. She felt as nervous and feverish as if she had been deprived of a drug, and she tried to make sense of what might have happened between them. And ironically, as if foretelling what would most often be said about her, on 17 August she noted:

> As if it wasn't enough that I never saw you with my eyes or heard you with my ears – on top of *that*, the unheard voice of the letters has to fall silent! After that I'm told I *imagine* people![107]

Throughout August she continued to yearn for information from people who knew Bakhrakh in Berlin, and when she did meet someone who knew him, she could not resist asking for his address, not because she needed it but simply to assure herself that Bakhrakh really existed. As Tsvetayeva began to resign herself to the thought that he had fallen in love with someone else, and that this was why he had stopped their correspondence, a letter came that made clear that the whole misery had been an accident of the post.

That August was in every way a difficult month. The Efron family had arranged to send Alya to Tshebova, a small town in Moravia on the German border, where there was a good Russian boarding school. At first, Tsvetayeva was reluctant to let her go, and it was Seryozha who insisted both on the separation and the education. Parting from her daughter was only made possible for Tsvetayeva because Alya had changed from a precocious little girl, eager to imitate her mother in every way, into a disappointingly 'ordinary little girl'. Alya (who recorded this incident in her memoirs) showed no sign of resentment at this description. It was Tsvetayeva who found the change in her daughter painful, and she said as much in one of her letters to Bakhrakh:

> Alya . . . now plays with dolls and treats me with profound indifference. . . . Oh, God must indeed want

to make me a major poet, otherwise He would not thus deprive me of everything.[108]

It was difficult, nevertheless, to pack Alya off to her gymnasium. Seryozha and Alya went ahead, and Tsvetayeva at first planned to spend the time from August onwards in Prague where she had rented a room on the high hill in Smixove, in which she had already begun to taste new freedom. However, she felt she had to introduce Alya to life in her new school, and this she did with a certain impatience at the loss of two weeks; she was also still suffering from the supposed snub from Bakhrakh. Paradoxically, she wanted to be needed, but not by her family. Still less did she want to be simply and functionally necessary as a mother.

While Tsvetayeva was in the forests around her daughter's new school, she was at her most superstitious, feeling that Fate was storing up something enormous and terrible for her. While she was walking about on her own, she heard a woman and the barking of a dog, and when she saw a hunchbacked beggar woman with a bag on her shoulders, she identified the old crone with Fate. Accordingly, she offered all that she had with her, including all of Alya's things, her own shoes, bread and clothes, to be put into the old woman's bag. The woman kissed her hand like a mad creature. Still Tsvetayeva only half believed that the woman was a supernatural visitation, and a brief inquiry revealed that 'Fate' had three children and a husband. Nevertheless, Tsvetayeva sensed that something momentous was about to happen.

It was not Bakhrakh who concluded the love-affair-by-post. It came to an end when Tsvetayeva fell in love with another, altogether real person present in Prague. When this happened, she knew she must write and admit her new involvement. She did so in September 1923:

Gather all your strength and courage in your hands and listen. Something has ended. The most difficult part is over, now I have said that. I love someone else.[109]

It is very clear from the following letter that Bakhrakh had written back in some indignation, for Tsvetayeva had to amplify her earlier words:

> You have not understood my letter. You didn't read it carefully. You didn't take in my tenderness, nor my care for you, nor my human pain.[110]

Nothing could make plainer that it was not Bakhrakh's indifference to Tsvetayeva that led to the conclusion of their relationship. Nor does it seem that either of them intended that that relationship should exist only in their imaginations.

For all the tenderness she continued to feel for Seryozha, Tsvetayeva's own passionate sexuality had only found expression in her love affair with Sophia Parnok. Konstantin Rodzevitch, the man of whom she had written to Bakhrakh, satisfied her desires completely.

In Prague in 1923, Rodzevitch was thought by many to have been a White oficer. He had, in fact, served with the Red Navy for a time, but (accurately) judged that things would go better for him in *émigré* circles if he allowed the impression to stand that he had fought on the White side. Although his father, Boris Kazimirovich, had been a general in the Tsarist army, after the Revolution his son served on a ship in the Bolshevik military flotilla on the Dnieper. After being captured by the White Army, sentenced to death, then reprieved, Konstantin was persuaded to join the Whites. A haphazard way of forming an allegiance, it was in many ways typical of the man.

Yet he did not give the impression of weakness. He was a man of good manners and great charm, demonstrating almost eighteenth-century courtesy; well-dressed, witty in speech, there was nothing 'soulful' about him. He took a fastidious pride both in his clothes and his person, and he had a flattering, caressing manner with all women, always enjoying considerable success with them.

All this Tsvetayeva found irresistibly attractive. What ensnared her above all else was the way that he treated her as an object of sexual desire, rather than as a celebrated poet. It was his natural mode with all women, but it was new for her. At the very start of their relationship, he found it easy to speak 'those great words than which there is nothing simpler' without any self-consciousness and Tsvetayeva wrote to Bakhrakh that it was like receiving the offer of love for the first time in her life. She was used to casting herself in the maternal, protective role; perhaps she had once found it safer, perhaps even with Mandelstam it was a genuine preference. Now, with Rodzevitch who was known as a ladies' man, she was risking an altogether new kind of relationship. She could not resist what she described in her letter to Bakhrakh of 29 September 1923:

> For the person who loves *me* – the woman in me is a gift; but the person who loves *her* creates a debt I can never repay.

Without any literary pretensions himself, Rodzevitch was well aware of Tsvetayeva's eminence. It did not alarm him. He enjoyed dealing with strong women. He had some talent for drawing, and one or two of the sketches he made of Tsvetayeva at this period are remarkably honest; however, a painting on wood made at the same time shows a completely idealized, unlined face, with hair untouched with grey. Tsvetayeva was not repelled by the flattery. On the contrary, she found the attention given to her physical person pleasingly unfamiliar.

Initially, Rodzevitch had been a friend of Seryozha, whom he had met in Prague when they were both students at the university. However of Rodzevitch's relationship with Tsvetayeva, which lasted from September 1923 to 12 December of the same year, Seryozha knew nothing, and if he found that friendship with her husband made him uneasy, Rodzevitch overcame his guilt. While the love affair lasted, it was a mutual passion, *'un grand amour'*, as Rodzevitch liked to call it.

Tsvetayeva loved Konstantin not only for his good looks and charm, but also for some greatness of soul that no one else imagined in him. Rodzevitch had no such aspirations, and once he was conscious of being in some way admired beyond his merits, he did not enjoy it. He began to feel her power as something 'overwhelming'. In his opinion, love was intended to be a pleasure, and her devouring hunger alarmed him: 'I couldn't bear the tension. I couldn't live up to the hero she thought I was. I couldn't live up to the myth.'[113]

The love affair lasted only a few months. In the 'Poem of the Mountain', Tsvetayeva wrote of how, in October 1923, the lovers walked together up a hillside in Prague and made love. Their first encounter took place with all the tumultuous passion she describes:

> How far from schoolbook Paradise
> it was so *windy* when
> the mountain pulled us down on our
> backs. To itself. Saying: Lie here![114]

It was a cold winter but the lovers were too passionately concerned with one another to care. Tsvetayeva ironically gave the initiative to the mountain rather than Konstantin, yet for once, as the much more experienced lover, he was almost certainly the first to put out his hand to her.

Something of the daily quality of their relationship is brought out in a lyric from the long cycle of 'Poem of the End', in which she described their favourite breakfast shop, where they often took an undistinguished cup of coffee together, regarded as regulars by the knowing waitress. It was a relationship that depended upon Tsvetayeva's having a separate base in Prague, but this was essentially a perch, not intended as a home. Tsvetayeva wrote there as fiercely as ever. Nor did her love affair close her in upon herself.

At the height of their love, in November 1923, Tsvetayeva received a letter, 'an epistolary howl', from Andrei Bely, begging her to find a place for him in Prague and expressing his longing to be near her. Occupied as she was, Tsvetayeva answered at once with the offer of a room next to her own in Smixove, and news that she had spoken to Slonim, who assured her that Bely would receive a Czech stipend of 800 crowns a month. Her letter was not only practical but affectionate. She promised Bely that they would eat dinner together; that there would be other friends; and that her own loving care was always ready.

Nevertheless, the room she had arranged was never to be

occupied. Nor was Slonim's offer of a stipend taken up. In November 1923, Bely returned to the Soviet Union. He set out without even waiting for a reply to his letter to Tsvetayeva, as if he had forgotten his impulsive cry for help. And indeed he probably had.

There were many reasons for the break in Tsvetayeva's affair with Rodzevitch but no question that it was at his insistence. He claimed to find it unbearable to continue betraying his friend Seryozha. He also claimed political necessity: he was preparing to engage in active politics, and had to disengage himself from Tsvetayeva in order to commit himself decisively to the Left. Whatever his motives, Rodzevitch subsequently went off to marry Moussa Bulgakova, the daughter of a famous theologian and well able to provide all the bourgeois comfort Tsvetayeva could not. Tsvetayeva had this in mind in her poem-cycle 'Poem of the Mountain' when she spoke of him returning from the delirium of the love among the pine trees to 'the gentle mercies of domesticity'. In that sequence of lyrics she jeers at the horrors of suburban life, and imagines plots of land being developed on the mountain itself by middle-class, married 'shopkeepers on holiday'.

In great misery, she turned back to Seryozha, confessing the affair with Rodzevitch and expecting emotional support. Instead, he was deeply wounded at the discovery, which had come as a great shock. Far from offering help to Tsvetayeva, he drew into himself and his great dark eyes grew even more bitterly unhappy. In the early spring of 1924, Seryozha wrote to his sister in Moscow:

> It is bad for me in Prague. I live here as if under a hood. I know very many of the Russians here, but I warm to few of them. And yet in general I get on well with people! I feel terribly warm towards Russia. How soon will it be possible for me to return? Not in the sense of how soon will it be *safe*, but how soon will it be morally possible? I am prepared to wait another three years. I fear that my strength will not last longer.[115]

For the first time in their relationship, he considered parting from Marina, and he put the possibility to her even before

Rodzevitch had brought her affair with him to a decisive close. Seryozha's suggestion filled Marina with such dismay that she could not sleep and she began to lose weight. She was unable to imagine life without Seryozha, and for his part, he felt uneasy about leaving Marina to the mercy of a man whom he now saw as a small-time Casanova.

Seryozha was physically weak at this time and the discovery of Tsvetayeva's deception made his life repulsive to him. It took away his purpose. Even though they had grown apart, Tsvetayeva had always been the important figure in his life, whose needs he was happy to satisfy, and to whom he had thought himself essential. The extent of her passionate involvement with Rodzevitch made it impossible for him to see himself any longer as a necessary prop to her existence, and that winter, he decided to live full-time outside Prague in the village, even though it meant travelling twenty miles a day.

For her part, in January 1924, Tsvetayeva turned to Bakhrakh, not only to explain that her love affair with Rodzevitch was over, but to assess the damage to herself. Not for the first time, she reflected on how much easier she had found it to *love*, than to *be loved*. For her, it had been possible only with children, old men, poets and (however briefly) with Rodzevitch.

> To be loved is something of which I have not mastered the art. . . . Dear friend, I am very unhappy. I parted with the ability to love and to be loved at the very height of my love. I didn't part from it, I was torn away from it. . . . I cannot love myself, because I love; and don't want to, because I love him. I don't want anything apart from him. And he will never be there again. . . . This is the first such parting in my life, because he wanted everything, he wanted life, he wanted a simple life together. That is something which no one who had loved me before had ever even thought of. . . . I, who started loving from the moment I opened my eyes, declare I never met anyone like him. With him I was *happy*. I never thought that could happen to me.[116]

In the same letter, Tsvetayeva bitterly commented that she

had desperately longed for a son by Rodzevitch. That passionate desire she felt God had denied her, and after their affair ended, she was unable to see any baby without feeling the bitterness of having that desire unfulfilled. Tsvetayeva's misery led her to feel for a time that she no longer had any existence.

She minded Rodzevitch's choice of a successor, whom he married within the year, although she knew that Moussa Bulgakova could offer him a simple, structured home. She was a less attractive woman than Tsvetayeva but less demanding emotionally. It hurt Tsvetayeva to think that Rodzevitch had rejected her because he could not live up to her and was unwilling, like Seryozha, to live in her shadow. It augured ill for her future, if the very greatness of her poetry was to bring loneliness and rejection in its train. This foreknowledge of her own isolation led to her bitter identification of poets with Jews.

> Ghetto of the chosen. Beyond this
> ditch. No mercy!
> In this most Christian of worlds
> all poets are Jews.[117]

Meanwhile, Seryozha looked forward to 1925 with dread. He was torn between his desire to continue at the university and the necessity of earning a living. Paris, he saw clearly, would offer more chance of work; at the same time, he was reluctant to leave for Paris because it would mean discontinuing his studies. A measure of Seryozha's gloomy spirits at this time was his reflection upon the waste of all his efforts, which he described in a letter to his sister written in the autumn.

He did not, however, sink into self-pity entirely. He began to take an interest in bringing together writers who were still in Russia and those who had gone into exile, and setting up a small journal in which they could appear side by side. Through his sisters, he solicited articles about the Vakhtangov Studio and the famous actor and producer Vsevolod Emlevich Meierhold. He also asked his sisters to talk to Voloshin and Antokolsky to see if they would agree to send poems for his

magazine. The work helped but, nevertheless, he continued
to feel that everyone in Moscow had forgotten him, and now
bitterly regretting his White sympathies, he feared that they
would make his return impossible.

Tsvetayeva began her own recovery very much more
quickly. She began to work again, transfiguring her misery
into two of her greatest poem-cycles: 'Poem of the Mountain'
and 'Poem of the End'. In June 1924 she noted that 'Poem of
the End' was completed, and although she adds 'but the end
in me – how much earlier!' she does not sound spiritually at
an end, however much her own misery was exposed in her
writing. She must have known she had written her finest
poetry so far.

It is in 'Poem of the End' that Tsvetayeva gives a profoundly
moving description, not only of her own pain at Rodzevitch
ending their affair but of the entire relationship. In the first
lyric, Rodzevitch appears almost dapper, almost unnaturally
courteous.

> A single post, a point of rusting
>   tin in the sky
> marks the fated place we
>   move to, he and I
>
> on time   as death is
>   prompt   strangely
> too smooth the gesture of
>   the hat to me
>
> menace at the edges of his
>   eyes   his mouth tight
> shut   strangely too low is the
>   bow he makes tonight
>
> on time?   that false note in
>   his voice, what
> is it the brain alerts to and the
>   heart drops at?

under that evil sky, that sign of
   tin and rust.
Six o'clock. There he is waiting
   by the post

Now we kiss soundlessly, his
   lips stiff as
hands are given to queens, or
   dead people thus

round us the shoving elbows of
   ordinary bustle
and strangely irksome rises the
   screech of a whistle

howls like a dog screaming
   angrier, longer: what
a nightmare strangeness life is
   at death point

and that nightmare reached my waist
   only last night
and now reaches the stars, it has
   grown to its true height

crying silently love love until
   —Has it gone
six, shall we go to the cinema?
   I shout it! home![117]

In Lyric 4, she draws the society in which Konstantin and she could move about, almost invisibly, together: a degraded, money-grubbing society, without scuples, like a licentious party.

Throughout Lyric 6, the dialogue between the two lovers has the sound of words edged indelibly on the memory. Konstantin cannot deny his love for Tsvetayeva, but he loves her 'in torment', 'drained and driven to death'.

   —And now a last request.
   —Of course. Then say nothing

about us   to those who will
    come after me. (The sick
on their stretchers talk of spring.)
—May I ask the same thing?

—Perhaps I should give you a ring?
    —No. Your look is no longer open.
The stamp left on your heart
    would be the ring on your hand.

So now   without any scenes
    I must swallow, silently, furtively.
—A book then? No, you give those
    to everyone, don't even write them

books . . .[118]

It is as they walk alongside Prague's beautiful river that the
greatest lyric of the sequence (Lyric 8) exposes the whole of
Tsvetayeva's misery without any attempt to claim a dignity
she cannot feel:

Last   bridge   I won't
give up or take out my hand
this is the last bridge
the last bridging between

water   and firm land:
and I am saving these
coins for death
for Charon, the price of Lethe

this   shadow money
from my dark hand I press
soundlessly into
the shadowy darkness of his

shadow money it is
no gleam and tinkle in it

coins for shadows:
the dead have enough poppies

This bridge

Lovers for the most
part are without hope: passion
also is just
a bridge, a means of connection

It's warm: to nestle
close at your ribs, to move in
a visionary pause
towards nothing, beside nothing

no   arms no   legs
now, only the bone of my
side is alive where
it presses directly against you

Life in that side
only, ear and echo is it: there
I stick like white to
egg yolk, or an eskimo to his fur

adhesive, pressing
joined to you: Siamese
twins are no nearer.
The woman you call mother

when she forgot
all things in motionless triumph
only to carry you:
she did not hold you closer.

Understand: we have
grown into one as we slept and
now I can't jump
because I can't let go your hand.

and I won't be torn off
as I press close to you: this
bridge is no husband
but a lover: a just slipping past

our support: for the
river is fed with bodies!
I bite in like a tick
you must tear out my roots to be rid of me

like ivy   like a tick
inhuman   godless
to throw me away like a thing,
when there is

no thing I ever prized
in this empty world of things.
Say this is only dream,
night still and afterwards morning

an express   to Rome?
Granada? I won't know myself
as I push off
the Himalayas of bedclothes

But this dark is deep:
now I warm you with my blood, listen
to this flesh.
It is far truer than poems.

If you are warm, who
will you go to tomorrow for that?
This is delirium,
please say this bridge cannot

end
          as it ends[119]

As Tsvetayeva tried to recover from the pain of her rejection, letters from Pasternak continued to be of central importance to her. She needed to know that he was glad to have her send him both her poems and everything else that mattered to her. And it was a saving joy to receive a letter from him on 14 June 1924: 'What remarkable poems you write. . . . How painful that at the moment you are greater than I am. . . . You are a disgracefully great poet.'[120]

Letters, however, were not to be her only hope of happiness. At about the same time that she received Pasternak's glowing praise, she began to take up less characteristic pursuits: knitting, and other handicrafts, at which she was not skilled, but enthusiastic. Tsvetayeva had become pregnant again. Rumours abound that the child was not Seryozha's – Tsvetayeva certainly carried it with as much joy as if it were the child of Konstantin that she had so much longed for – but the child was eventually born thirteen and a half months after the affair ended and it seems unlikely her former lover would have risked renewing their relationship.

Like her mother before her, Tsvetayeva had always longed for a son, and was now convinced that she carried one in her womb. She felt that great importance attached to this pregnancy, and began to prepare for the child in a new way. She consulted doctors, collected second-hand children's clothes from among her acquaintances and made inquiries to her new-found friend Anna Teskovà about the best maternity hospital in Prague. She had given up her room in Prague when Rodzevitch abandoned her, and did not now intend to tire herself by travelling into the city, even though Horni Mokropsy increasingly bored her, and the muddy village paths were particularly exhausting.

When, in the summer holidays of 1924, Alya arrived in Prague with the beginnings of a tubercular lesion on her lung, Tsvetayeva reacted fiercely to the discovery of her daughter's illness, which she feared might infect the child in her womb. Alya was hurt both by the response and by overhearing Tsvetayeva declare that secondary education was of no use to girls. Indeed, from this time onwards Alya's life became more and more subservient to the needs of her mother (and soon to the needs of her young brother). And even though her good health reasserted itself, and she was able to work inexhaustibly for the whole family from that year until her departure for the Soviet Union in 1937, very little further attention was given to her education. She acquired some French, however, from Tsvetayeva.

At eleven, Alya was a poignantly beautiful child with wise eyes and a face framed by thick hair. All her early years had been possessed by her mother. They had faced every hardship in their lives (in the poet Konstantin Balmont's words) 'like two sisters', giving one another love and courage. Now she knew herself rejected without being freed. It is surprising that, in later years, she was able to recall the moment without bitterness.

Tsvetayeva at first wished to name the child she was expecting after Pasternak, whose love, throughout her life in Czechoslovakia, had sustained her self-respect. She had created another imaginary, almost legendary presence, who was with her all the time, demanding, exhausting, compelling her to continue her work – or sometimes preventing it, of whom she had written in 1923 (before her affair with Rodzevitch):

> But you hinder me from writing. Yes, you. This burst open like a dam – poems for you. I recognize such strange things in them. I am tossed as if by waves. You are *exhausting* in my life. My head becomes tired; how many times a day do I lie down, sprawl on the bed, *capsized* by all the cranial, intercostal dissonance – of lines, feelings, illuminations, and simply of noises. Read through and check. Something appeared, swelled up, and does not want to cease – and I am unable to put a stop to it. Can a *person* cause such things to happen?[121]

By 1924, Tsvetayeva's poetry had begun to find wide acceptance both in *émigré* magazines and in Moscow itself. Nevertheless, she spent most of the year withdrawn from the literary world as she prepared for the birth of her child, her pregnancy making her reluctant to face Prague society. When Anna Tesková invited Tsvetayeva to give a reading in Prague, the latter wrote, on 5 December 1924, 'I don't know whether I'll manage it on the 14th – train trips are difficult for me, and I don't have a suitable dress.' However, she missed the liveliness of Prague, even though she avoided gatherings of people, and so she invited Anna to visit the Efron family in their country home:

> We'll go for a walk – the surroundings here are marvellous; if there is rain or snow we'll sit inside and talk. I'll read poems to you. By the way, you will meet my husband and daughter.

Tsvetayeva gave birth to a son at home on 1 February 1925, a Sunday, at midday. It was a simple enough birth, though not a short one. Tsvetayeva wrote to Anna Teskovà that 'They said I comported myself well – in any case, without a single scream.' The quiet satisfaction of this assertion was not proud. She was glad to pay the necessary price of pain, and recollected the words of a friend who had helped with the delivery: 'It was *meant* to be painful.'[123]

Her pride lay in the fact that the child was a son. Her original intention to christen him Boris, after Pasternak, brought thunderous objections from Seryozha. Perversely, Tsvetayeva did not persist with her preference when Seryozha finally sighed and gave in. Instead, the child was named Georgy, after the patron saint of Moscow, whose reputation as the protector both of wolves and cattle particularly appealed to her.

Seryozha did not find that the birth of a son attenuated his own misery, and he showed little interest in the baby. He felt insecure and ill, and only ten days after the birth, he set off for Paris on a short visit to look for a job.

After his departure, Tsvetayeva declared herself to be so happy, so absorbed in her son that she could hardly bother to take care of her health. At a time when all upper-class women were encouraged to spend weeks lying in to recover from childbirth, she was soon sitting up in bed, and coping well enough; though she had not yet found a maid, and the woman who brought in the charcoal was leaving at the end of the week. As Seryozha was usually away at the library all day, his absence does not seem to have depressed her. The whole organization of the house depended upon Alya.

The fact that they were contemplating hiring a maid did not mean that the financial circumstances of the Efron household

had improved. Tsvetayeva had to write to Anna Teskovà to
beg her to send a simple washable dress:

> All winter I have been living in the same woollen one,
> which is falling apart at the seams. I don't need a good
> one – it is not for a public appearance – just something
> simple. I cannot hope to buy and sew something now;
> yesterday I had to pay 100 crowns to the midwife for
> three visits; a few days ago I gave 120–150 crowns to the
> charcoal dealer for fuel for ten days, then there is medi-
> cine, sanitation! There is no point even thinking about a
> dress. But I would very much like something clean. Even
> a snake must sometimes change its skin. If it is too big,
> never mind – it can be altered at home.
>   I bought a pram for 50 crowns – almost new,
> wonderful; at the same time I bought a bed and a huge
> arm chair – some Russians were selling it off before their
> departure.[124]

This letter was written (like so much of Tsvetayeva's poetry
at this time) at 3.30 in the morning, when everyone else was
alseep and Tsvetayeva had her only chance of time to herself.

Tsvetayeva had been invited several times to give poetry readings in Prague, but postponed them again and again. Hence,
Anna Teskovà decided to visit her. Tsvetayeva was so glad to
see her, and so delighted to find someone she could talk to
about literature, that she forgot to provide either food or tea
for her guest.

   Her absorption in her son is the key to such an uncharacter-
istic lack of hospitality. No doubt Seryozha, already painfully
aware of being moved closer to the edge of Tsvetayeva's life
than he could bear, found his mood darken as he perceived
this new obsession. Tuberculosis, which often recurred when
his spirits began to fail, took hold of him once again. By July
1925, he was all bone and huge mournful eyes, having lost
many kilos in weight. He felt caught in a trap, and his
depression made him long to leave for Paris. At the same time,
his disease made it essential for him to enter the Zemgorska
sanatorium, and he was far too ill to organize himself the

family's departure to Paris. By September 1925, his conviction that a move to Paris presented his only chance of making a life for himself reawakened Tsvetayeva's protective loyalty.

And so Tsvetayeva began to arrange to leave Czechoslovakia and her friends, to move to yet another country for the third time in three years. As Seryozha was too ill to travel with them, it was impossible for her and Alya to take all their belongings on the journey, and Tsvetayeva arranged to store a large basketful with Anna Teskovà. Tsvetayeva was, in any case, unconvinced of the wisdom of the move, and liked the idea of leaving things in Prague for a possible return.

Their passports were arranged by Mark Slonim, and Tsvetayeva managed to raise enough money to buy tickets for herself, Alya and Georgy, now affectionately called Moor, a pet name that is variously spelled but having always the soft, purring sound of a pet animal. The train journey filled Tsvetayeva with terror, largely on account of her young son. Now without money for even the barest necessities she could not imagine how she was to deal with his food. 'He eats four times in twenty-four hours and everything needs to be warmed for him. How is this to be done? One cannot light a spirit lamp,'[125] she wrote to Anna Teskovà. Nevertheless, she arranged to leave some time after 20 October 1925.

However much Tsvetayeva feared the journey to come, she did not regret leaving Vshenory. The last year and a half had been a period of great isolation, as she described in a letter of 19 July 1925 to Boris Pasternak. Far less lofty in style than those that preceded it, this letter essentially told him about her lonely life and the spiritual poverty of it, although she was also frank about her material hardship. Even in her loneliness, she continued to take great joy in her son Georgy, and to work furiously on her poem 'The Pied Piper', which she was was not to finish until she reached Paris.

Vshenory, near Prague
19 July 1925

Dear Boris,
The first really human letter from you (the rest are Geistbriefe), and I am flattered, inspired, raised on

high. You have just deemed me worthy of your rough draft.

And here is my rough draft, in brief: for eight years (1917–1925) I have been *consumed* by the daily round. I am that goat, whose throat they are constantly slitting and never quite slitting enough. I myself am that brew that bubbles ceaselessly (eight years) on my primus. My life is a rough draft, by comparison with which – oh, you should look! *my* rough drafts are the whitest of white sheets. I despise myself for the fact that at the first call of life's everyday necessities (1001 calls a day) (N.B.! life's everyday necessities – one's debt to other people), I am torn away from my notebook, and NEVER go back to it. I have a Protestant's sense of duty, compared with which my Catholic – no, my Khlyst [Flagellant] love is a thing of nought.

Do not think of me as living abroad. I live in the country, with the geese and the pump-houses. And do not think: the country: an idyll. No, it means one's own two hands, and not a single gesture for oneself. I do not see the trees. A tree waits for love (attention), and rain is important to me in so far as the washing does or does not dry. Day: I cook, wash, carry water, look after Georgy, (he is five and a half months; a *miracle*), study French with Alya; have another look at Katerina Ivanovna in *Crime and Punishment* – that is me. I am furiously embittered. I have been bubbling in the cauldron all day. I have been writing my poem 'The Pied Piper' for over three months. I have no time to *think*: my pen thinks. Five minutes in the morning (time to sit down a little), ten minutes in the afternoon; the night is mine, but at night I can do nothing, I am unable to; a different kind of attention; life unlike itself but beside itself and nobody to listen to, not even the noises of the night, since the landlords lock the exit door at eight in the evening, and I have no key (all my doors are entrances; a yearning for an exit. Understand?) Boris, for a year I have been living, in effect, locked up. You at least have snatches of pavement between your house and the publisher's, and between one publisher and another. I live in a hollow, choked up with hills: the roof, a hill; on the hill, a cloud. A hulk.

I have no friends. Here they don't like poetry; and what am I apart from – not poetry, but apart from that, *from which* it is made? an inhospitable hostess, a young woman in old dresses. . . .[126]

However, the thought of leaving Prague made Tsvetayeva anxious. The city itself enchanted her. She loved the legend of the Golem, that seventeenth-century monster of stone created by Rabbi Löwe to defend the Jews of Prague against their enemies,* and she particularly admired the statue of the knight of Karlov's Bridge, which was supposed to represent a boy guarding the river. To Tsvetayeva, he was a symbol of fidelity – above all, fidelity to himself. She wrote to Anna Teskovà:

I would passionately like to have a picture of him. Where can I get one? There isn't one anywhere. I want an engraving to remember him. Tell me everything you know about him.[127]

Even as Tsvetayeva continued to make the necessary plans for leaving, she secretly imagined that the family would soon return to Prague, and went so far as to plan in some detail where they would live, determined this time to find somewhere in the suburbs where it would be possible to walk and talk with her friend Anna. She insisted that she hated Paris, as much as anything else because it was too much admired already. As the day of their move drew inexorably closer, she tried to comfort herself with the thought that it would be easier to make a living for the family there, and, in moments of optimism, hoped she would find new friends. Certainly she had few of them in the village of Vshenory, in which she felt all her emotions slept. But for all her confusion, in reality she had no choice but to leave.

* It had to be destroyed, partly because it became disobedient, and partly because the feeling grew that its creation was blasphemous. The shattered pieces remain in an upper room of the Alte Neue Synagogue.

By 26 October, a hitch in their plans threw Tsvetayeva into another kind of panic. They were due to leave on the 31st, and money she had been expecting from friends in Paris had not arrived. The flat in Vshenory was soon to be occupied by incoming tenants; Seryozha was still in the sanatorium; and there was no one to help. She wrote off at once to Anna Teskovà, asking her to put in a word with a certain Madame Yurchinova (the pen name of Anna Yevekova, a Czech writer), begging a loan of 1000 crowns and promising to pay it back by 15 November. In the same letter, she offered to send Alya round to Teskovà's house, in case the latter could think of any other possibility of raising money. All she could offer as a guarantee of payment was her monthly Czech maintenance money.

On 28 October a telegram arrived from Paris saying that no money could possibly reach her before the date of their departure. So Alya was despatched to Teskovà's house, and returned with enough money to make the journey possible. Tsvetayeva wrote with gratitude that 'the money will save us all': certainly it had been very much touch and go.

To live with the prospect of a departure that might or might not happen was to put oneself in a state of suspense, and Tsvetayeva found this particularly intolerable. Now, with the loan arranged, and with a mixture of hopes and fears that made this departure as harrowing as any she had undertaken, she set off for Paris with her two children, and so left behind the city in which she had lived so intensely, and which she loved more than any other outside the Soviet Union.

Part IV

Paris

8

Fame and poverty

1925–1927

Paris did not open to Tsvetayeva as Prague had, even though her fame preceded her among the many Russian *émigrés*, for whom the city had always offered the most graceful European alternative to their homeland. As an adolescent, she had found the Parisian bustle intoxicating; now city traffic filled her with panic. In any event, it was not to the beauties of Paris that she found herself delivered.

On 31 October 1925 Marina Tsvetayeva arrived from Prague with her nine-month-old son Moor and her twelve-year-old daughter Alya, to stay with Moor's godmother Madame Kolbasina-Chernova. (She had once been Tsvetayeva's friend and neighbour in Prague.) The Chernovas had three rooms in Clamart, a working-class neighbourhood, and the whole family lived in great poverty. But Madame Chernova was fond of Tsvetayeva; her daughters knew and admired her poetry; and all of them did their best to let their guests share their meagre life equally. It was an act of considerable generosity to give up one of their three rooms.

Tsvetayeva knew this, but nevertheless found the lack of space and the noisy street outside oppressive, and the lack of any privacy tormented her. The room she occupied was often invaded by other people, who not only chattered among themselves, but expected her to take part in the conversation. Even Tsvetayeva found it impossible to ignore the social necessity of talking about matters of no interest to her. Like Seryozha

in Prague, she felt she had stepped into a trap, as she explained
in a letter of 30 December to Anna Teskovà:

> There are four of us [Seryozha having arrived by then]
> crammed into one room. I cannot write at all. I think
> bitterly that even the most mediocre journalist has a
> writing desk and two hours of quiet. I don't – not a
> minute: I am constantly surrounded by people in the
> middle of conversations which divert me from my note-
> book. I think almost with joy of my job in Soviet Moscow
> – on that job I wrote three of my plays; *An Adventure,
> Fortuna* and *Phoenix* – 2000 lines of poetry.[128]

She found the world around her ugly, the block in which
they lived reminding her of some novel about London slum
life. It looked out over a canal, and it was impossible to see
the sky for the numerous chimneys. She hated the smell of
soot and the continuous thunder of lorries. There was nowhere
to walk, not so much as a bush anywhere close at hand, the
only park was forty minutes' walk away.

Mark Slonim, in his memoir, rebuked Tsvetayeva for the
way she harped on her poverty, but she rarely complained
about people who helped her in the awkward chores of daily
living. She was always grateful to women with strengths in
these areas in which she herself felt feeble. Above all, she had
learned to love and trust 'those who knit your jumpers and
look after your children'. She remembered with affection the
Chirikov family who had helped to mother her newly born
son in Czechoslovakia (Chirikova was an actress), and also her
Czech friend, Anna Andreyevna, whose maternal nature led
Tsvetayeva to call her a 'mother animal'. She spoke lovingly
of another village friend, Katya, who had once carried Alya
on her back up the difficult slopes of Vshenory.

In Paris, Tsvetayeva feared that she would not find the same
protection, and she began to write of Chernova as if she were
a landlady. Yet Tsvetayeva did, at least, have a real desk,
which was given to her by Olga (one of the Chernov daughters), and despite all the domestic pressures, she found the
opportunity to use it. It was with the Chernovs that she
finished 'The Pied Piper'[129] – writing and rewriting it, even as

she cooked Moor his porridge, and dressed and undressed and bathed him as she had in Vshenory. The one-hundred-page epic, *The Pied Piper*, transforms the familiar story of the cheating burghers of Hamelin exuberantly with new frenetic rhythms, touching the death of the children at the end into magical lyricism.

On 4 December, Tsvetayeva again wrote to ask Teskovà to intercede with Madame Yurchinova, this time to beg a dark dress that would enable her to go out in more interesting company. She had begun to be asked out, and she was ashamed of her shabbiness in Paris, as she had not been in Prague. Depressed as she was by her surroundings, she could not face the grand world, and people began to think her stand-offish. Begging, too, embarrassed her, and she particularly asked Teskovà not to mention her request to Seryozha who was still in Czechoslovakia: all her letters to him were reassuring about life in Paris. In the event, Seryozha, who arrived in Paris in late December 1925, found that, within about six weeks, his wife had become a celebrity.

Tsvetayeva was asked to give a poetry reading, and though it was postponed from January 1926, it finally took place a month later, and was widely advertised in all the Russian *émigré* papers, as far afield as the Berlin daily newspaper *Rul*. She was booked to appear with the soprano Tsunelli and the violinist A. Mogilevski, but there was no question about their relative importance. Her reception at the packed hall was tumultuous, and confirmed her position as one of the most important poets of the emigration.

Irina Kotting, a poet who attended that reading, wrote a poem the day after in which she described herself wandering aimlessly in the rain, barely escaping being hit by cars, because she had been so overwhelmed by Tsvetayeva's great voice. *Rul*, in Berlin, also described the reading as a personal triumph.

The applause did more than give Tsvetayeva's spirits a much needed boost; it established her as a literary celebrity in the Russian community in Paris. However, it was only with difficulty that Seryozha, still much in need of comfort and affection, could take pleasure in her success, and the Efron family certainly needed money more than fame. Their practical affairs remained precarious, and over the next year, they moved from their initial perch to a series of flats in the south-western suburbs of Paris. There was no possibility of affording a place in the centre of Paris, even if Tsvetayeva had not felt uneasy there: 'In a city square I am the most pitiable creature, like a sheep that has found itself in the middle of New York.' And so, as late as September 1926, and for all her grand acquaintance now included Bunin and his circle, Tsvetayeva was still hoping to return to Prague, still dreaming of finding somewhere near the city centre, so that she could enjoy all that Prague had to offer. She was so bound by the children and her need for money that she realized that a whole flat would be out of the question but she conjectured in a letter to Anna Teskovà, 'Would it not be possible to find two rooms with Czechs who loved Russians and were not too strict about tidiness?' and considered a brief return visit to try and persuade the Czech authorities that she had not changed her domicile permanently, and so they should continue her regular stipend of 1000 crowns a month. The threatened reduction of this stipend by half would have made Tsvetayeva altogether dependent upon the charity of her friends.

Her correspondence with Pasternak, however, took on a new intensity. The ecstatic note Tsvetayeva sounds in all her letters to Pasternak might well have alarmed an alien spirit. From the letters Pasternak wrote to her in return, it is clear that his infatuation was by now equal to her own, and had begun to affect his relations with his wife, Zhenya. On 20 April 1926, he wrote begging Tsvetayeva to decide the course of their relationship within a year.

Look about you, and in what you see and hear discover your answer; only let it not be guided by your desire to see me, for you must desire this knowledge knowing how much I love you. Send me your answer as soon as possible. If you don't stop me, I will come now.

It was Tsvetayeva who backed away from such involvement, as she mentioned in a letter to Anna Teskovà many years later: 'In the Summer of 1926, after reading my "Poem of the End", B. was madly drawn to me, wanted to come and join me – I restrained him: I feared total disaster.'

Pasternak was later to be grateful for her refusal to let an earthquake destroy his life along with her own.

In April 1927, the Efron family settled in Meudon, where a number of other Russian exiles, then as now, clustered together. Their new address – 2 rue Jeanne d'Arc – appealed to Tsvetayeva. At that time, Meudon was an attractive enough suburb with pleasant hills and parkland in and around it. The Efron flat was only a fifteen-minute train ride from Paris, and there was the luxury of a garden for Moor, although the Efrons were to share the house with another family. Tsvetayeva was delighted at the prospect of the move, and was able to make fun of the disapproving French landlady of her previous flat, who demanded that the cupboards should all be sensitively before they left.

In Meudon she found congenial neighbours who were to remain loyal to her for the rest of her life – notably, Elena Izvolskaya, the daughter of a Russian statesman, once ambassador to France. Herself a translator of poetry, Izvolskaya's impressions of Tsvetayeva at that time are sensitively detailed. She described her as

> neither elegant nor pretty: thin, pale, almost emaciated . . . altogether not beautiful, but *icon-like*. She worked and wrote and gathered firewood and fed scraps to her family. She washed, laundered, sewed with her once slender fingers, now coarsened by work. I well remember those fingers, yellowed from smoking; they held a tea pot, a cooking pot, a frying pan, a kettle, an iron, they threaded a needle and started a fire. These very same fingers wielded a pen or a pencil over paper on the kitchen table from which everything had been hastily removed. At this table Marina wrote – verse, prose, sketches for entire poems, sometimes she would trace two or three words and some particular rhyme and copy it many, many times. . . . Watching [her work] was like a naturalist observing the growth of a blade of grass, a leaf,

a stem, the hatching of fledglings in forest nests, the
metamorphosis of a chrysalis into a butterfly.[130]

Seryozha was becoming more and more involved with a
political movement in which Tsvetayeva had little interest.
The Eurasian movement had been started by Peter Suvchinsky
the musicologist who, with his wife Vera, was a near neighbour, and there were a number of supporters living close
by, including Elena Izvolskaya. The essential ideal behind the
movement was that the Soviet Union belonged both to Europe
and to Asia. Among the *émigré* community, supporters were
thought of as having Bolshevik sympathies, even though their
chief, perhaps grandiose, hope was of reforming (if not over-
throwing) the Soviet regime. Whatever Tsvetayeva's own
political sympathies, the extension of their circle of Paris
acquaintances, which followed on Seryozha's involvement in
the movement, was to be very important to her.

The critic D. S. Mirsky (Prince Dmitry Svyatopolk-Mirsky,
later a Communist) was at this time a member of the group
and a contributing editor of its magazine *Mileposts*. Tsvetayeva
– who had been hurt by not being included in his anthology
of Russian lyrics, and had been described by him as a 'slovenly
Muscovite' – found him now an unexpected ally. Vera Suvchinsky, herself a great admirer of her poetry, claims to have
effected this dramatic change in Mirsky's attitude to
Tsvetayeva. However, she was less patient with her as a
person. They had first met in Clamart, in late 1925, when
Moor was barely nine months old. Then, Tsvetayeva's refusal
to wear her glasses had struck Vera as an absurd sign of her
inability to come to terms with the outside world, but she did
admire the poet's walk – 'like a she-goat'. This is no compli-
ment in English, but the Russian *kozochka* is. Marina's walk
was light-footed, angular and determined in spite of her hard
life.

In the spring of 1926, following her triumphant poetry
reading that February, Mirsky invited Tsvetayeva to
accompany him on a visit to London with the hope of laun-
ching her in England with a poetry reading. In the event, there
was no reading. These were Tsvetayeva's first free weeks in
the eight years since the Revolution. After an unpleasant and

cold Channel crossing, she found that she loved London: the river, trees and children, the dogs, the cats and 'the wonderful fireplaces and the wonderful British Museum'. Ecstatically, she wrote as much in a week as would have taken her a month and a half in her usual domestic circumstances.

Tsvetayeva spent one night with Mirsky in London. He reported to Vera Suvchinsky that she had appeared, rather to his surprise, in his bed, and that he had been struck by her boyish beauty when undressed. Whether or not Vera Suvchinsky is right in saying that he found the experience unsatisfactory, neither of them attached much importance to it.

When she returned to Paris from London, Tsvetayeva found that generous friends had made another break possible, and she and the children spent that summer with Vera Suvchinsky near the seaside, at St Gilles in the Vendée, while Seryozha remained in Paris. Tsvetayeva's looks improved as soon as she was able to shed the ugly clothes her poverty imposed on her. She tanned easily, as she had in the Crimea so many years before, and though she was still not a lover of sea bathing, she loved to lie in the sun. She also took great pleasure in the increasing health and strength of her son Georgy, now about eighteen months old, and delighted in everything he did. Vera found her attitude towards Georgy infuriating. Once, the child was standing in such a way as to block the sunlight from reaching Vera's body. Vera asked him to move. Tsvetayeva, teasingly, reproached her: 'You can't ask *him* to get out of the sun. Look at him! He *is* the sun. . . .' This hyperbole irritated Vera, but then she found much to criticize in Tsvetayeva's behaviour as a mother. She saw, for example, how Alya was neglected while Tsvetayeva gave all her love to her young brother. Alya showed no desire to compete for the loss of her mother's attention, but instead became more stolid, and less complaining than ever.

Tsvetayeva's time at St Gilles was, however, far from completely idyllic. Sometimes it was so cold and windy that everyone had to wear winter coats. Then, although she acknowledged the grandeur of the ocean shore and the sea itself, she felt no fondness for it:

What can I do with the sea? Look at it. That's not enough

for me. Swim? I don't like the horizontal position. . . . I love the vertical: walking, a mountain, I love the sense of power that results. Before the ocean, I am a spectator: as if I were sitting in a box at the theatre. . . . Besides that, the sea either intimidates or makes one grow soft. The sea resembles love too much. I don't like love (that is always a question of sitting and waiting for what love will do with me). I love friendship: a mountain.[133]

All through that summer of 1926, Tsvetayeva's letters to Anna Teskovà came from St Gilles where, in spite of the proximity of beach and sea, she still longed for Prague. She knew herself to be a guest in St Gilles, and Tsvetayeva hated being a guest because of the expenditure of courtesy it entailed. When she looked at a postcard from Prague, she saw in the very trees an invitation to return.

However, by June 1926 Tsvetayeva was beginning to abandon her plan to return to Czechoslovakia. There were practical considerations – for instance, the rent for the house in Meudon had already been paid until the middle of October, and the money could not be wasted – but more significant was the necessity of putting the emotions of 'Poem of the End' and 'The Mountain' behind her. Perhaps it was healthier, now that Rodzevitch had married, to imagine that the city of Prague no longer existed.

Tsvetayeva mentioned the marriage of her lover casually in a letter to Pasternak of 10 July. Now she began to ask proudly what she still hoped for in her relationships with men. Her analysis was grim, as she probed for an understanding of the reasons why she had never inspired the kind of passion she longed for. As a sex, she sensed, men preferred Eve to Psyche, and for all her power to fascinate, she had never found any-one to love her more than anything else in the world. This was not only because she was too spiritual, but because there was something in her that made her more of a guest than a host.

People shoot themselves for the mistress of the house, not a guest . . . I do not doubt that I shall be the most promi-

Marina with her daughter Ariadna (Alya), *c.* 1917

Marina and Alya *c.* 1925

Sergei Efron and Marina Tsvetayeva

Top left: Osip Mandelstam, poet,
1891-1938

Left: Anna Akhmatova, poet

Top right: Boris Pasternak, poet,
1890-1960

nent woman in the senile memoirs of my young friends – but I never counted in the masculine present.[134]

In another letter, written on 21 June, Tsvetayeva evaded a detailed analysis about Pasternak's new poem 'Lieutenant Schmidt' as he was later to find difficulty in responding to her 'Pied Piper'. She had many literary problems. Mirsky was in trouble with the *émigré* critics, for his defence of Tsvetayeva's poetry as well as Pasternak's. Many of them were actively hostile, and the most vitriolic of all was Zinaida Gippius. There was an element of rivalry between the two women, although Gippius was too arrogant to admit a comparison. For example, in 1926 she wrote a letter in her capacity as one of the editors of *Contemporary Notes*: 'The poems of Tsvetayeva are of course a matter of the taste of the editorial board, but having them on the same page with mine, such a conjunction is in undoubtedly bad taste. Don't you agree?'[135]

Pasternak's admiration for Tsvetayeva continued unabated, increased indeed by her integrity in refusing to praise 'Lieutenant Schmidt'. In a letter to Maxim Gorky in 1927, Pasternak tried to enlist his powerful support for the 'huge talent of Marina Tsvetayeva and her unhappy, unbearably twisted fate', and offered to do or write anything that would help her to the Soviet Union. Gorky's refusal to help caused an angry breach between Pasternak and the playwright/ novelist, even though Gorky's intentions were far from villainous. He and his wife had known both Marina and her sister as children, and Gorky was still on friendly terms with Anastasia. However, compared with Pasternak, he was both less impressed by Tsvetayeva's work and had a much shrewder idea of the dangers she would face if she returned to the USSR.

In her letter to Pasternak, Tsvetayeva mentioned something that had hurt her much more than the jealousy of the *émigré* critics. Vladimir Mayakovsky was a poet for whom Tsvetayeva had always felt and expressed unstinting admiration, an admiration which, of course increased her unpopularity in *émigré* circles, where no Soviet poet was acceptable. So to read in a reprint of an article what Mayakovsky had advised Soviet booksellers was all the more painful:

. . . The bookseller must bend the reader a little more. A Komsomolka comes in with the almost definite intention of buying, say, Tsvetayeva. To this Komsomolka, [female member of Soviet organization for young people] one should say, blowing the dust off the old book jacket: Comrade, if you are interested in gypsy lyricism, might I be so bold as to suggest Selvinsky? The same theme but what treatment of it! So manly! . . . Try reading this book of. . . .

Hurt though she was, Tsvetayeva bore no grudge, and did not modify her own critical opinion of Mayakovsky's worth. He was a fine poet, even if she no longer idolized him.

Tsvetayeva once declared that she had encountered only two people who were her equals in strength: Rilke and Pasternak, though her contact with Rilke was to be entirely a matter of correspondence. Although, in her childhood, Marina had once met Rilke's mistress in a fairy-tale castle, it is an imaginary meeting she writes of in her essay 'Your Death', and their correspondence began only six months before he died. Nevertheless, it was heartfelt and reciprocal. The initial contact between the two poets came in 1925 through Pasternak. Rilke had sent his old friend Leonid Pasternak a letter for his son and had already read some of Tsvetayeva's poetry. On 9 June 1926, Rilke sent Tsvetayeva a long, beautiful elegy that he dedicated to her, which includes:

Waves, Marina, we are sea, the depth, Marina, we are sky.
Earth, Marina, we are earth, we are a thousand springs,
larks that are thrown by their new song past the border of sight.
We begin in joy, but soon are overwhelmed
Our sudden weight distorts the song downwards to a lament
But is it a lament? Perhaps a new joy for what lies beneath us
Even gods below want to be praised, Marina.
Gods are so innocent, they wait for praise like schoolboys.[136]

In response, Tsvetayeva emphasized that her ardour was 'a kiss without lips', and declared her sense of him as 'poetry incarnate'. A few weeks later, he sent her a copy of *Vergers*, a volume of poems he had written in French, which was inscribed:

Marina: voici galets et coquillages ramassés récemment à la française plage de mon étrange coeur . . . (J'aimerais que tu connaisses toutes les étendues de son divers paysage depuis sa côte bleue jusqu'à ses plaines russes.)[137]
(*Marina: some sea-shells and flints*
Just picked at the French coast.
I wish you knew the whole of its view, which varies
From its shore of blue to its Russian prairies)

Of all those with whom Tsvetayeva had intense relationships through correspondence, Rilke most unambiguously confirmed her spiritual conviction that poetry offered immortality, not in the banal sense of finding admiration in posterity, but through the holy strength of the act itself, and they shared a religious awe before the miraculous richness of the world. Yet even he, as she wrote to Pasternak, failed her to some degree. She found he lacked ordinary humanity towards his grown-up married daughter of his Saxony first marriage; he had no interest in his grandchildren; and (unfairly) she suspected his interest even in her poetry when she discovered the difficulties he now had with the Russian language. That he had once been able to read Goncharov without a dictionary only made it worse, as she exclaimed to Pasternak:

In this, I saw him for a moment as a foreigner. That is, I saw myself as a Russian, and him as a German. Humiliating. There is a world of certain solid values (even low ones are solid in their lowness) about which he, Rilke, ought not to know – in any language. I have nothing against Goncharov, as part of the history of Russian literature in a particular quarter-century. But on Rilke's lips he loses too much. One should be more charitable.[138]

Three days later (29 May 1926), Tsvetayeva decided not to write any more to Rilke. She declared it not only fruitless, but disconcerting to the point of putting her off her writing. As much as anything else, Rilke's coldness was painful to her, because he didn't need her letters. Her pride, as she confessed to Pasternak, was wounded.

> I am not a lesser one than he (in the future), but I am younger than he. By many lives. The depth of a stoop is the measure of height. He bowed deeply to me – perhaps deeper than . . . it's not important. And what did I feel? His *height*. I knew it before, but now I know it first-hand. I wrote to him: 'I shall not belittle myself; that would not raise you any higher (nor make me lower!); it will only make you *more alone*, on the island where we were all born – all like us. . . .' O Boris, Boris, heal, lick clean the wound. Say why. Prove that everything is so. . . . Don't lick it clean; *burn it out*! 'I tasted little honey' – remember? What's honey?!
> I love you. The fair, the donkey-carts, Rilke – all this goes into you, into your vast river (not a sea!). I so miss you. Just as if I saw you only yesterday.
>   M. Ts.[138]

In relation to Rilke, Tsvetayeva's withdrawal sprang from her misjudgement of the difficult, almost reclusive nature of the poet to whom she was writing. Fired by her excitement at being in close touch with him, she began to declare a passion he found unwelcome, and overstepped a significant boundary in her letter of 2 August 1926.

> Rainer, I want to come to you . . . Don't be angry, after all it's *me*, but I want to sleep with you. Simply to fall asleep and to sleep. . . . And nothing further. No, there is something; to bury my head in your left shoulder, my arm on your right one and nothing else. No, something else: to know in the deepest sleep that you are there. And also to hear the sound of your heart. And to kiss the heart.[139]

Even if at this time Rilke had not been already mortally ill with leukaemia, he would have taken fright at her tone, which

was not only physically demanding but alarmingly possessive. (She demanded the right to be considered the only poet
to represent Russia for Rilke.) Although he wrote back
without reproach, she sensed the change in his feelings, and
even wrote him a sad card inquiring 'whether he still loved
her?'

Rilke himself had only six months to live, and when he
died, Tsvetayeva broke into a passion of grief. Later she was
to write a great poem, 'New Year's Greetings' in Rilke's
honour. As she wrote on New Year's Day 1927:

> Boris, he died on the 30th December, not the 31st. Yet
> another of life's blunders. The ultimate trivial vindictive-
> ness of life – against the poet.
>
> Boris, we shall never travel to Rilke. That town is no
> more.[140]

After describing a recent dream of an ocean liner, which she
was sure meant that Pasternak would come to visit her, and
remembering London with a certain nostalgia, she returned to
consider what was impossible for her in relation to Rilke.

> Do you see, Boris; the three of us together in real life –
> nothing would have come of it anyway. I know myself;
> I couldn't have *kissed* his hands, I could not have kissed
> them – even in front of you; almost not even in front of
> myself. I would have strained and snapped, would have
> crucified myself, Boris, because it would have been, after
> all, still *this* world. Boris, Boris! How I know the other
> world. Through dreams, through the air of dreams,
> through the disencumberment, the vital urgence of
> dreams. How could I not know this, not love it, be hurt
> by it! The other world, only understand: light, illumi-
> nation, things *differently* illuminated – with your light,
> with mine.
>
> *The other world* – so long as this expression exists, so
> will the people. But this is not about peoples.
>
> His last book was French – *Vergers*.
>
> He tired of the language of his birth. . . .
>
> He tired of omnipotence, wanted apprenticeship,

grasped at French, the most thankless of languages for poets; he managed it, once more he managed it; and tired at once. It turned out that the problem was not German, but human. The craving for French turned out to be a craving for the angelic, for the other-worldly. In the book *Vergers* he let out the secret in angel-language.

You see, he is an angel; I invariably feel him over my *right* shoulder (not my side).[141]

Her letter concluded with an impassioned plea to the angelic Rilke to visit her often in her dreams.

This is a measure of the dullness that now filled her daily existence. Seryozha still spent some time working on his literary magazine, but most of the energy he had went into his work for the Eurasian movement. Tsvetayeva found the ideals behind it worthwhile enough, but she saw that Seryozha was exhausted and knew his health was deteriorating again. (He may well have developed some new debility since he now took arsenic every day as part of his treatment.) Moreover, the finances of the family were extremely shaky in spite of money given to Tsvetayeva by Salomea Halpern and others. As Tsvetayeva put it:

We are devoured by coal, gas, electricity, the milkman, the baker. For several months, we have been eating only horsemeat and then the cheapest cuts of it. . . . Everything that is three francs fifty a pound – that is, the heart, the liver and the kidneys of course – rather than horsemeat at seven or eight francs a pound.

Tsvetayeva hid the fact from Seryozha that the family was eating horsemeat, but to her surprise, when he did find out, he enjoyed the idea of eating horses' hearts, seeing in it a link to Genghis Khan and his Eurasian inheritance.

Had Tsvetayeva lived by herself, the 1000-franc-a-month contributions of Salomea Halpern and other friends would have made such hardship unnecessary. However, she had two children to support and, moreover, had to raise tuition fees for Seryozha to train as a cameraman, though, as it turned out, the only money he ever earned from the film industry was by working as a film extra.

In the summer of 1927, Tsvetayeva's sister Anastasia, who had been staying with Gorky in Sorrento, came to visit Marina in Paris. Both had changed, though Marina was still slender enough to look like a Roman youth to her sister, who observed mainly the new darkness around the light green eyes. Marina's style of dress had, of course, altered, too. She now wore a grey housewife's apron instead of the colourful kaftan of Koktebel, and had learned to crochet – not only scarfs, but even large blankets. Anastasia found that, as Alya had grown, she had begun to resemble her father, and that her eyes were now also too huge for her face. Two-year-old Moor, on the other hand, looked like neither parent. He had a large frame – 'a little giant' Anastasia called him – and they had to buy him clothes meant for six-year-olds. Anastasia noticed at once that Marina showed a deeper love for her son than for her daughter.

Little as she could afford the extravagance, Marina had bought a good cut of veal to celebrate her sister's arrival, and had roasted it in her honour. Unfortunately, Anastasia had become a vegetarian, and so, although the Efron family enjoyed the rare dish themselves, they were unable to share it with their guest.

The following day, the two sisters went to Versailles. Anastasia observed with surprise that, after years in Paris, her sister was still afraid of traffic. At first, there was a natural constraint between the two women, and it was only at Versailles, as they walked about the small quiet town, that the two of them gradually relaxed and began to talk about their own lives. By the evening, Marina was lying on the couch that served as her bed, chain smoking and talking as eagerly as in the old days. She read her sister a recently completed poem and described what she was trying to do in it: it was to be like a fairy tale, taking off from what happened when she went to bed after drinking black coffee, which she described as flying off somewhere while not quite asleep. And yet, as she explained how her days were used up by trips to the market, dragging herself home again with the shopping, it was clear that Marina no

longer coped cheerfully with her everyday worries. In the
chaos of the flat in Boris and Gleb Street, she had looked
stronger than she did now in these small new rooms, dressed
in an apron, by a gas cooker, in a foreign city. It is possible
that what seemed like fatigue in Anastasia was also the first
onset of illness.

Anastasia in turn told of her friendship with Gorky, and
Tsvetayeva was so grateful to hear of it that she wanted to
write and thank him. Not wanting to hurt her sister, Anastasia
rather exaggerated the warmth Gorky felt towards Tsvetayeva's own work.

Only a few days after this conversation, Alya and Moor fell
ill with scarlet fever. Anastasia postponed her return to
Sorrento – in part because she did not want to worry Gorky
with the threat of infection, since his daughter had died of the
disease in 1906. Her decision was fortunate. Marina soon
needed help badly. As the two sisters struggled to nurse the
sick children, they drew closer together; and when the children
slept, Marina confessed freely that she now felt that her life
was stifled by Seryozha's obsession with his friends in the
Eurasian movement. All she wanted was to be left alone to
write. She rarely had the chance in the daytime, and the
evenings made no difference to her, because her strength had
faded by then. Marina frankly admitted that Alya was being
denied education because Marina could not cope without her
help. Even though Seryozha had found a little work with a
publisher, Marina was the main breadwinner for the family.
And Moor had to be looked after. If she could only get some
work done, Marina felt, she would brighten up and even be
glad to talk to people.

Anastasia tried to suggest that her sister might find more
peace in Russia, but Marina was too weary even to consider
it seriously. She might play with the idea of going off alone
to Easter Island or somewhere else remote and primordially
innocent, but although she felt nostalgic for the birch-covered
hills of Tarusa, she insisted it was only for *places* that she felt
longing. As Anastasia recalled in her memoir, Marina asked:

Do you still love *people*? I long ago gave up loving
anything – except animals and trees. . . . Alya is at a

difficult stage. She is *very* talented, very intelligent. But completely different from me. Moor – he is *really* my son! He's wonderful. [142]

To Anastasia, however, her young nephew was altogether less out of the ordinary than Alya. She remembered well how, at Moor's age, Alya's precocious intelligence had sparkled at everything. Moor was neither precocious nor talkative, and it was hard to see why Marina saw herself in him so fiercely.

Gradually, Moor began to recover, though Alya remained ill. Then, just as the family seemed to be returning to normal, Marina herself went down with scarlet fever. At the age of thirty-five, this was a serious matter. Marina had a high fever, and for some days, it was by no means clear that she would survive the illness, as she tossed in delirious pain. It is difficult to see how the family could have managed without Anastasia's help since there was no money to hire a nurse. Seryozha (immune to the disease, in spite of his own physical frailty) could not abandon the only work he had found, and although Alya was back on her feet, Moor still needed attention.

As Marina gradually recovered enough to get out of bed, Alya was still pale and even Moor had grown thin, and it was time to prepare for Anastasia's departure. Anastasia continued to beg the family to return to Russia. Marina's reply was to give her a present of oranges, an unbelievable extravagance, just before the train left the station. The last memory Anastasia had of Seryozha was of his narrow face, his hat raised, and huge kind eyes.

9

'No one needs me here'

1927–1934

Though now in her middle thirties, Tsvetayeva could have been taken for twenty-three. She had never really looked her correct age: as a child she had looked far older than she was; now she looked younger. Her clothes, too, were more suitable to a younger person, many of them having been gifts. But her illness had left her spiritually weakened. She remembered her own delirium; but she did not remember Alya suffering a serious illness. All she recalled was the child's sore throat, whereas her own sickness, which left her unable to sleep for the pain in her limbs, stayed in her memory as the gravest of her life. She was left weakened and bald, with only a child's light blue cap to hide her head, which had been shaven on medical instruction.

Perhaps as a means of escape from the prison of suburban poverty she felt closing round her, she reverted to her plans of returning to Prague. Her dislike of Paris was becoming fierce. She longed for Prague, a city she had never really broken away from. By December 1927, she was writing to Anna Teskovà:

Soon it will be Christmas. To tell you the truth, I am so exhausted by life, that I feel nothing. Over the years and years (1917 to 1927) my mind and my soul have grown blunt. I have made a surprising observation: it is for feelings one needs time and not for thought. . . . A single example: when I am rolling one and a half kilos of fish in flour I can *think* . . . but I can't feel; the smell interferes, the *fish* interferes – each fish separately out of the whole one and a half kilos of them.[143]

Tsvetayeva continued to work on proofs of her book of poems *After Russia*, which, while unquestionably her best book to date, was never to receive the recognition of her earlier work. And aside from her poor health and the usual financial pressures, new anxieties disturbed her. Critics of the supporters of the Eurasian movement in the Russian *émigré* press had begun to declare that the movement was receiving huge sums of money from the Bolsheviks. However distant from the movement Tsvetayeva felt herself to be, she was as much shaken by the accusation as if she had been accused of receiving Bolshevik money herself. She was all the more indignant as she could not see how anyone receiving such sums would have had to take on menial work as Seryozha had – acting, for instance, as a bit-player in early films for forty francs a day, of which he had to spend five on fares into Paris, and seven on meals.

There were other pains. Her old lover Rodzevitch and his wife had settled in Paris, and were now part of the same circle as Seryozha and Marina; indeed, they were close neighbours. Tsvetayeva wrote to Anna Teskovà of the unwelcome, easy friendship she had struck up with Madame Rodzevitch: 'We go to the cinema. We buy presents together. I for my family, she for him.' On New Year's Day in 1928, a party was held at Tsvetayeva's flat at which presents were distributed. Among the guests were Konstantin and Moussa Rodzevitch, and most of the others were members of the Eurasian movement. Tsvetayeva felt that she had nothing in common with the people who shared the ideals of the movement, and more and more, her exile seemed boundless. She was even an exile inside her own home. In the letter to Anna Teskovà describing this sad New Year, she wrote: 'In every group I am an alien, and have been all my life.'[144]

In 1924, in one of her finest poems, 'An Attempt at Jeal-

ousy', she had written of Rodzevitch's marriage with a fine
flow of pride, jealousy and hurt:

> How is your life with the other one,
>   simpler, isn't it? One   stroke of the oar
> then a long coastline, and soon
>   even the memory of me
>
> will be a floating island
>   (in the sky, not on the waters):
> spirits, spirits, you will be
>   sisters, and never lovers.
>
> How is your life with an ordinary
>   woman?   without godhead?
> Now that your sovereign has
>   been deposed (and you have stepped down).
>
> How is your life? Are you fussing?
>   flinching? How   do you get up?
> The tax of deathless vulgarity
>   can you cope with it, poor man?
>
> 'Scenes and hysterics   I've had
>   enough! I'll rent my own house.'
> How is your life with the other one
>   now, you that I chose for my own?
>
> More to your taste, more delicious
>   is it, your food? Don't moan if you sicken.
> How is your life with an *image*
>   you, who walked on Sinai?
>
> How is your life with a stranger
>   from this world? Can you (be frank)
> love her? Or do you   feel shame
>   like Zeus' reins on your forehead?
>
> How is your life? Are you
>   healthy? How do you   sing?

How do you deal with the pain
  of an undying conscience, poor man?

How is your life with a piece of market
  stuff, at a steep price.
After Carrara marble,
  how is your life with the dust of

plaster now? (God was hewn from
  stone, but he is smashed to bits.)
How do you live with one of a
  thousand women   after Lilith?

Sated with newness, are you?
  Now you are grown cold to magic,
how is your life with an
  earthly woman, without a sixth

sense? Tell me: are you happy?
  Not? In a shallow pit. How is
your life, my love? Is it as
  hard as mine with another man?[145]

The confidence of that poem sprang from the conviction
that she had mattered as fiercely to Rodzevitch as he had
mattered to her. Vera Suvchinsky, who had stayed in touch
with Rodzevitch since their friendship in the Twenties,
strongly doubted this when I questioned her in 1975, but her
attitude to Tsvetayeva as a woman has already been noted.
The general opinion of those who knew both Tsvetayeva and
Rodzevitch at the time was that he seemed to be coping very
well without her. Tsvetayeva guessed as much and was hurt
by it.

However, when I visited Rodzevitch himself in his tiny,
meticulously neat apartment in Paris in 1975, he gave unexpected support for Tsvetayeva's belief in the continuation of
his love. Fifty years afterwards (years in which he had moved
his belongings many times, to fight both in Spain and the
Resistance), he still had a collection of memorabilia he treas-
ured. There were photographs of Marina taken in the

Twenties, and a painting on wood that he had made himself, a copy of a photograph that he has made more life-like by illuminating the wonderful green of her eyes. Perhaps most convincing was his confession that his present wife was still jealous of the intensity of his feelings for Tsvetayeva – so much so that he only liked to talk about the affair when his wife was out, as she was on the afternoon we met. Still, to Tsvetayeva, four years after her relationship with Rodzevitch had ended, to be hurt by daily confrontation with the fact of his own enjoyment of a domesticity that Tsvetayeva herself, for all her efforts, could never offer, remained hard to bear.

Among the friends at that New Year's Day party was Vera Suvchinsky, who continued to have great admiration for Tsvetayeva's poetry and little sympathy for the personality that produced it. Vera was shocked by the Efrons' living conditions. She could not understand how anyone could neglect either her person or her flat to the degree that Marina did. She found the stench repellent, and later recalled with aristocratic disgust the layers of grease in the kitchen. She was also convinced that Tsvetayeva's attitude to Alya was totally selfish.

If the truth be told, Vera was much more sympathetic towards Marina's handsome, soft-natured husband. Herself an inordinately beautiful woman who had always found men ready to fall in love with her, Vera had a natural arrogance that Tsvetayeva dealt with as best she could. One of the ways she did so was by carrying out a series of practical jokes that recall her impish treatment of Nina Berberova in Prague. Once, when Vera arrived for dinner, Marina greeted her at the door with a half-skinned rabbit, which she brandished in Vera's face, laughing.

Part of Tsvetayeva's depression at this time came from her continuing poor health. Although her hair had grown back well after her recovery from scarlet fever, she had had a series of abscesses, which had to be lanced and treated with hot compresses. Her financial anxieties, too, worsened in January 1928 when it looked as if her Czech maintenance would stop. Her only hope seemed to lie in finding subscribers for her new book of poems *After Russia*. The plan went badly. The editor she had looked to for help had left what she considered to be her publishers, and could not be found. It turned out he had contracted the book without the knowledge or consent of the firm. And even as she absorbed these practical problems, she began to sense how little enthusiasm remained for her work among the *émigrés*.

In her gloomiest moments, she considered returning to the Soviet Union, but it was only half in jest that she wrote to Anna Teskovà that the letters U S S R contained no feeling of old Russia. The thought of going to a country *without vowels* appalled her, as if it were a country without *voice*. In any case, she doubted if the Soviet authorities would let her in. Already she had begun bitterly to assess the situation in which 'in Russia I am a poet without books; here I am a poet without readers'.

In addition, even though in March 1928 a few old friends (among them Boris Pasternak's father Leonid) had taken out subscriptions, *After Russia* (though promised) had not yet been officially released. The publisher was still sitting on it, and Tsvetayeva commented wryly, 'In Russia, we used to have such coachmen: they sleep, while the horse pulls. But sometimes they sleep and the horse also sleeps.'[146]

Meanwhile, Tsvetayeva had recently had another brush with death. The son of a friend had just died of tuberculosis of the intestines. He had been only twenty-eight years old, and had not realized he was in any danger. She was especially affected, not only by his youth, but by the deluding, cheerful dream he had the night before his death. The funeral itself shocked her because French custom does not allow gravediggers to cover the coffin with earth until the relatives have left. She herself remained stubbornly beside the grave nevertheless, and it was with some difficulty that she and the young man's mother managed to persuade the gravediggers to fill in the hole in their presence. It was a long, sad business – the shovels were small – yet she stood there stubbornly for an hour and twenty minutes with snow underfoot so that a mother would not have to watch her son being buried without a friend at her side.

As she grieved, she must also have been thinking of her own isolation. Once, in a moment of complete frankness, Tsvetayeva spoke to Mark Slonim of her complete loneliness as a woman. She mourned the absence of a great love: 'I have

lived forty years, and never had a man who loved me more
than anything else in the world.'[147]

As spring came to the Paris of 1928, Tsvetayeva began to
feel an old longing to escape the daily round of responsibilities
of her family life. In Meudon, the horse chestnuts were turning
green, and as Tsvetayeva observed the leaves ruefully, the
contrast between the gradual onset of spring in Paris and the
violent joy with which it was greeted in Russia reminded
her both of her lost youth and of her own homesickness.
Nevertheless, about this time Tsvetayeva had a stroke of unexpected good luck. A visitor arrived from Russia to stay with
the family and offered to pay for her lodgings by helping in
the house. For the first time in ten years, Tsvetayeva had spare
time.

So it was that, in that year, Tsvetayeva came to make friends
with an eighteen-year-old boy, Nikolai Gronsky, whose father
was one of the editors of the *émigré* paper *Latest News* and
whose mother was a sculptor. The young man had some talent
for poetry, and was eager to spend long hours walking with
Tsvetayeva in the woods and over the hills near Meudon.
His love for mountains rather than the sea coast made him
particularly congenial to her, and certainly she and her young
hiking companion were more than friends. One of the passages
in Tsvetayeva's letters to Georgy Ivask, (the Estonian critic
with whom she began a correspondence in 1933), that refers
to her friendship with Gronsky admits as much:

> You are right. He was of my race. How did you know
> about our friendship and its battlefield (for the friendship
> was a battle), in the royal woods of Meudon. . . . He was
> my *physical* companion – a creature of the mountains, not
> a creature of the sea.[148]

Whether or not they were lovers is irrelevant; the degree
of Tsvetayeva's emotional involvement did not depend upon
sexual contact. That she *was* deeply involved emotionally with
Gronsky can be seen from the intensity with which she awaited
him that summer on the Atlantic coast. At the beginning of
August she had gone with her family to the Villa Jacqueline
at Pontaillac (near Royan) where there was quite a community

of Russians on holiday, including Peter and Vera Suvchinsky. The Efrons had a visiting Russian house guest who dealt with the chores and looked after Moor, and for once, it felt like a real holiday for Tsvetayeva. She remained there until the end of September, even though Seryozha had to go back to Paris much earlier on 'Eurasianist matters'. This was also a time of temporary financial respite, partly through the proceeds of a poetry reading given in June, but mainly through generous gifts from Salomea Halpern and D. S. Mirsky.

Tsvetayeva enjoyed the sunshine, but the real reason she stayed on was her obsession with the young Gronsky, who had promised to join her. What she wanted was to set up a new 'we', as she put it to Anna Teskovà, and she needed time to develop that relationship. They had often been alone in Meudon, but there had been no chance for a bond of the strength she needed to form in Paris.

Gronsky agreed to join her on the first of September, but when Tsvetayeva went joyfully down to meet him on that day, he was not at the station. Bitterly disappointed, she returned to find a letter from him, apologizing for his broken word and explaining that he had been obliged to stay behind for the sake of his family.

This was not a casual excuse. Gronsky was the only child of two people who felt their exile cruelly, and he was the main thread that held their lives together. He had always known as much, but he discovered it literally when he went home to bid them farewell on his way to Pontaillac. There he found his mother on the point of leaving his father, so he placed his suitcase across the door and began to try and talk his mother out of her decision. Six hours later, he was able to return to his own garret, knowing that his mother had agreed to stay, but he was never to join Tsvetayeva by the ocean, and she knew instinctively that the opportunity would not present itself a second time. His failure to visit her that summer marked a decisive end to the development of their relationship, yet she was far too generous in spirit to press him to change his mind. She did not want to 'tear at the soul of an eighteen-year-old boy', and so although the friendship between them continued for a time after that summer, Gronsky gradually drifted away from her, as she knew he would. The strongest

sense of what his young affection had meant to her in the
summer of 1928 comes out of her lyric, written many years
later:

> Because once when you were young and bold
> you did not leave me to rot alive among
> bodies without souls or fall dead among walls
> I will not let you   die altogether
>
> Because, fresh and clean, you took me
> out by the hand, to freedom   and brought spring leaves
> in bundles into my house   I shall not
> let you be grown over with weeds and forgotten.
>
> And because you met the status of my
> first grey hairs like a son   with pride
> greeting their terror with a child's joy:
> I shall not let you go grey into men's hearts.[149]

Whatever Nikolai's parents may have feared in Tsvetayeva's
relationship with their son, *Latest News* remained one of the
few papers interested in publishing her poetry, although
editorially they preferred to print her earlier work. This
Tsvetayeva found ironically amusing: 'It isn't the *Latest News*!
In 1928 they take poems from 1918!' Since they only wanted
early poems she was forced to write to Anna Teskovà and ask
for the manuscript of her earlier poems which was in the
safe-keeping of Mark Slonim, then still based in Prague. She
preferred to write to Teskovà rather than directly to Slonim,
because she felt he might (however well-disposed towards her)
be very slow about sending the poems. Her welcome as a
contributor to *Latest News*, however, was soon to end.

In 1928 Mayakovsky visited Paris, and Tsvetayeva's admiration for his poetry was now to bring her into conflict with
her last supporters among the emigrant community. Even
before she had discovered his low opinion of her work two
years before, their personal relationship had never been a close
one. But she often recalled meeting him on a deserted Moscow
bridge on one of the last days before her departure. She had
asked him then what she should say to people abroad, and he

had answered, 'That the truth – is here.' Tsvetayeva often thought of his words, and of the sight of him as he strode away. She even wondered in later years what would have happened if he had shouted, 'Come off it, Tsvetayeva! Give it up! Don't go!' Would she have stayed in Russia? It seems unlikely that any plea could have overcome her need to rejoin Seryozha at that time. Yet the memory of his words to her recurred, damagingly, in an exchange that was to become celebrated.

Mayakovsky gave a reading at the Café Voltaire in Paris in November 1928, and at the end, Tsvetayeva was asked, 'What can you say about Russia after Mayakovsky's reading?' To this she replied, remembering their earlier encounter, 'Strength is over there.' Her words, and their context, were reported in *Eurasia*.

The 'strength' to which she referred was the strength of poetry, as well as the strength of spirit that she found missing in the *émigrés* who surrounded her. Yet the *émigrés* chose to interpret her remark politically. Even on those terms, however, the contrast between 'truth' and 'strength' hardly justified the way in which her words were taken as praise for the Soviet regime. *Latest News* (which, by now, played a very important part in the economics of the Efron family) refused to continue to publish her. Ironically, the poems that were due to appear next were those in praise of the White Army (*Swan's Encampment*), but Tsvetayeva was now counted as a Bolshevik by the entire editorial board.

Tsvetayeva met Mayakovsky for the last time in the early spring of 1929. He had been asked by a group of Communists in a suburban district of Paris to appear before an audience of French workers. One of the organizers was a friend of Seryozha's. Tsvetayeva introduced her husband to Mayakovsky, who at once asked Tsvetayeva to translate his poems into French for him because, as he very well saw, few people at the gathering would otherwise have understood them. Tsvetayeva agreed. Mayakovsky read his poems in Russian, and explained their content briefly. Then Tsvetayeva had the difficult task of rendering them spontaneously into French. She also acted as interpreter for questions from the hall and for Mayakovsky's replies. The listeners were less interested in poetry than in the life and concerns of the working class in the Soviet Union, but Tsvetayeva was willing to perform this task without irony because of her love and admiration for Mayakovsky as a poet.

At about this time, Tsvetayeva began work on a long article about the Russian artist Natalya Goncharova, who was living in Paris. Tsvetayeva found Goncharova a remarkable person, although she had little understanding of the way she painted. She was older than Tsvetayeva by fifteen years, but there were many similarities between them – for instance, Goncharova's complete indifference to public opinion, and her liking of solitude. The fact that she was the great-granddaughter of Pushkin's wife, whose beauty had led to his fatal duel, lent her an additional fascination. Indeed thought preoccupied Tsvetayeva in her essay more sharply than the artist's work. Tsvetayeva sat and made notes in the artist's presence as she tried to arrive at an understanding of the innermost workings of what she admired most in Goncharova: her 'enormous I'. While she was writing her description, the artist was working on illustrations for Tsvetayeva's poem *A Peasant*.

As in so many of her friendships, however, Goncharova began to draw away as Tsvetayeva became more and more deeply involved with her. In April 1929, even as Tsvetayeva noted with admiration Goncharova's calmness, she recognized the beginnings of a familiar unease. As she wrote to Anna Teskovà: 'I am always ashamed to give more than the other person needs (i.e. more than he can take!)'[150] That trait in her character, which Rodzevitch had feared and which Mark Slonim described as 'a single naked soul', had frightened away yet another friend.

Tsvetayeva wondered if any of her friendships could last. Even Slonim's loyalty she felt was qualified. On one occasion when she sat as a guest at a literary gathering, Tsvetayeva watched him with a pretty blonde on one side and a brunette on the other, neither of whom had the slightest idea about literature, and felt herself humiliatingly ignored. For his own part, Slonim was anxious for Tsvetayeva, for he could see that Seryozha was a sick man, as well as a hopelessly weak one, a born loser. Slonim's main response to Tsvetayeva's continued affection for the man was respectful bewilderment, and certainly Seryozha's fatal mix of naïveté and idealism was soon to prove destructive. Rumours had long circulated that Seryozha was not only a Communist, but also an agent of the NKVD. When they reached Tsvetayeva's ears, she simply refused to believe them – even when Professor Nikolai Alekseyev (one of the founders of the Eurasian movement) and several other members of it publicly declared that Seryozha was a Bolshevik. In reaction, Tsvetayeva decided that Alekseyev was a scoundrel; her chief emotion was pain for Seryozha, and with fierce loyalty, she insisted that he was the only moral force left in the Eurasian movement.

However, Seryozha had always longed to serve some cause greater than himself, and just as he had once been misled by dreams of loyalty to join the White Army, he had been casting about for some time in search of an equally lofty ideal. For a time, the Eurasian movement had seemed just such a possibility, but this did not last. When, finally, he threw in his lot with Communism, he gave himself up as unreservedly and fanatically to it as he had served earlier causes. That he had begun to do so now seemed beyond belief to Tsvetayeva, and was a measure of how far they had grown apart. For some years, it had not been easy for Seryozha to preserve his own sense of dignity: he was always seen as 'the husband of Marina Tsvetayeva' and, worse, a financially dependent husband. His own interest in literature had dwindled; and it was years since he had written anything himself. Slonim commented, 'I never noticed any common views and aims. They went their different ways.'[151] Yet Tsvetayeva felt her husband's misery sharply. When publication of the magazine *Eurasia* was suspended, she understood his disappointment as well as his lifelong desire to yoke himself to some burden forever beyond his strength.

All her love, however, was now turned towards her four-year-old son Moor. The child, although cheerful, was very conscious of being Russian, and Tsvetayeva concluded that this was why he found it difficult to make friends. She herself still dreamed of the countryside round Vshenory: the river, the plums, the fields, everything that was so much more like true countryside than the suburb just outside Paris in which she lived. She longed for geese and goats, and even for the sound of a smithy. Being in Paris had no value to her, since she could not enjoy the life of the city. She was cut off from museums and concerts, and trapped in an area that had nothing to offer her. It was not only Moor who felt cramped by a sense that there were people in the houses around them in Meudon whose disapproving looks from the windows followed the Efrons' every move.

In August 1929 Tsvetayeva began to organize a poetry reading in Prague. She was quite proud of her Parisian wardrobe (having been given several good dresses) and Anna Teskovà found her a house in which to hold the performance. She sent Alya to Brittany for two weeks to stay with friends and arranged to take Moor with her to Prague.

With everything apparently arranged, it is surprising to find that, by 30 September, Tsvetayeva's plans had changed once again. An invitation had come to give a reading in Brussels. At first, this did not involve a cancellation of the Prague performance, and Tsvetayeva planned to go straight on there from Brussels. She continued to occupy herself with arrangements for the sale of tickets for the Prague reading. She thought she could probably muster an audience of 300 people, and was alert to the possibility of selling autographed copies of her books at a side table.

On 26 October 1929 Tsvetayeva was in Brussels, where she gave a performance to a small, poor and extremely right-wing Russian colony. Only a hundred people gathered to hear her, and as a result she made no more than 50 French francs. As a financial venture, this was disastrous, since the cost of travel, passports, visas and living expenses, had come to more than 400 francs. The only advantage Tsvetayeva derived from the journey was the chance to walk about Brussels, which, reminding her of Prague, she loved for the quietness and the antiquity. Later she was able to visit Antwerp and Bruges.

Tsvetayeva sent Anna Teskovà the famous picture of the little boy of the Brussels fountain, and continued to assure her that she wished to come to Prague to read. Nevertheless, she had to put off the possibility until January. The main reason for this was a crisis in the mental and physical health of her husband. Seryozha was no longer earning any money at all, he was dispirited and extremely thin, and pulmonary tuberculosis had reasserted itself. There was medical assistance to be had, but to pay for it the entire family was living on credit. A visit to Prague was not to be thought of. What was essential was that Seryozha should be moved from Meudon, which was in a hollow and particularly damp.

Along with this new call upon her resources, Tsvetayeva had to face the possibility that her Czech maintenance would end in 1930, and so deplete her income disastrously. She had little enough to show for a year of very hard work. She had been writing a long poem about the civil war, *Perekóp* ('Terracotta' or 'Baked Earth'), but it fell awkwardly between the two *émigré* camps: those on the right wing found it leftist, or 'advanced' in form; those on the left found it 'right wing' in content. It seemed unlikely to produce any money.

Seryozha was told that he had to go into a sanatorium for three months, and any further thoughts of a trip to Prague would have to be postponed until after that. On 23 December 1929, Seryozha left Meudon for St Pierre-de-Rumilly in the Haute Savoie. Fortunately Tsvetayeva's friends helped out, chiefly Salomea Halpern. Moor was also in extremely poor physical condition, and had been sick for a week with a high temperature and severe pains in his stomach. The state of Tsvetayeva's own health may be guessed from the fact that she had written nothing whatsoever for a month and a half. With Seryozha's departure, she began to think she might begin again, but even to name what she might undertake threatened bad luck.

In April 1930, Vladimir Mayakovsky killed himself. An obituary of the Soviet poet, contemptuous in tone, written by the *émigré* critic A. Levinson, was published in the French newspaper *Les Nouvelles Littéraires*, and many well-known French and Russian writers and painters wrote in to protest against it. On 12 July, a counter-protest appeared that asserted that Mayakovsky had never been a great Russian poet, and this bore the signatures of (among others) Nina Berberova, Ivan Bunin, Zinaida Gippius and Vladislav Khodasevich. Tsvetayeva attached her signature to neither declaration. Her attitude was to be expressed in her magnificent cycle of seven poems to Mayakovsky.

Grief at Mayakovsky's suicide, and her quarrel with the *émigré* community, together with Seryozha's illness and her anxieties over money, brought Tsvetayeva to the edge of a breakdown. On 21 April 1930, she wrote to Anna Teskovà, 'The person writing to you is under attack.' She continued to work for her family's survival, and yet she knew very well that she had begun to take a kind of spiritual leave of absence from them. It was not a question of love. The family had all her heart, but the heart, she felt, expanded at the expense of the soul. No one was clearer than Tsvetayeva about the falsity of the usual opposition made between the desire to work for fame, and the desire to write for money. For herself, as she knew, 'I write because I can't help writing.' Yet she was no longer ashamed to write for money. There were to be no more aristocratic refusals to accept anything more than presents, as in the days of her early publication in Petersburg. Now she would accept money, readily:

Money, my dears. As much as I can get.
Money enables me to go on writing. Money is tomorrow's
    poems.
Money is my ransom from the hands of editors, publishers,
    landladies, shopkeepers, patrons; it is my freedom,
                                and my writing desk.

That desk was the taskmaster of Tsvetayeva's soul, and for the rest of her life she submitted to its discipline willingly and without respite.

DESK
My desk, most loyal friend
    thank you. You've been with me on
every road I've taken.
    My scar and my protection.

My loaded writing mule.
    Your tough legs have endured
the weight of all my dreams, and
    burdens of piled-up thoughts.

Thank you   for toughening me.
   No worldly joy could pass
your severe looking-glass—
   you blocked the first temptation,

and every base desire
   your heavy oak outweighed
lions of hate, elephants
   of spite   you intercepted.

Thank you for growing with me
   as my need grew in size
I've been laid out across you
   so many years   alive

while you've grown broad and wide
   and overcome me. Yes,
however my mouth opens
   you stretch out   limitless.

You've nailed me to your wood.
   I'm glad.   To be pursued.
And torn up.   At first light.
   To be caught.   And commanded:

Fugitive. Back to your chair!
   I'm glad you've guarded me
and bent my life away
   from blessings that don't last,

as wizards guide sleep walkers!
   My battles burn as signs.
You even use my blood to set out
   all my acts in lines—

in columns, as you are a pillar
   of light. My source of power!
You lead me as the Hebrews once
   were led forward by fire.

> Take blessings now from me,
>   as one put to the test, on
> elbows, forehead, knotted knees,
>   your knife edge   to my breast.[153]

'Her life was a heroic one. Every day she performed some act
of bravery. These acts were out of loyalty to the only country
of which she was a citizen: poetry.' So Pasternak spoke of
Marina Tsvetayeva to Alexander Gladkov after her death.
Certainly the ordeal of remaining the sole prop of her family
was a duty that continued to exhaust her.

At the end of 1929, when Seryozha's tuberculosis had flared
up so seriously that he had gone into a sanatorium in the
Haute Savoie, he was expecting to stay three months. He
was eventually to be there for eight. In the summer of 1930,
Tsvetayeva and the children went to stay close by – not in the
village, but in a small chalet with a huge barn at the base of
the mountain. Seryozha was living in a Russian boarding house
set up inside a fifteenth-century castle, and Tsvetayeva was
able to see him every day. Sometimes she visited him, and at
other times he was strong enough to walk over and visit
them. Once a week, she walked with Alya and Moor to the
neighbouring small town to buy vegetables and meat for the
week. Time passed as if in a dream. Fortunately, the Russian
branch of the Red Cross, who looked after refugees in need,
was paying all Seryozha's medical expenses.

The summer was rainy, and the woods were damp, rather
like those in the Taiga. Everything was covered in ivy and
blackberry brambles. There were streams under foot that
might well have been beautiful had there been sunshine. But
Tsvetayeva's thoughts were not on the riches of nature. She
tried to work, particularly on a French translation of her poem
A Peasant (which was not to prove time well spent), and on
the poems to Mayakovsky, which she hoped to publish in *The
Will of Russia*.

On 9 October 1930, the family returned together from the
Haute Savoie to Meudon, to a situation in which work of any
kind was increasingly difficult to find. Indeed, there was no
longer much if any hope of work for Seryozha. It was almost
impossible to find employment in a factory even for the

completely fit, and although Seryozha had gained about ten pounds, he was still a sick man and he dared not tax his strength. Meanwhile, the family continued to live on credit. There was not even enough money for the one franc fifteen centimes fare into the centre of Paris, and Tsvetayeva had already sold off all the beautiful silk dresses of which she boasted only the year before to Anna Teskovà.

Stubbornly, Tsvetayeva finished translating *A Peasant*, but despite the illustrations by Goncharova, who was at that time very well known in Paris, her effort was altogether wasted. No one wanted the book. Altogether, it had become impossible to turn any of the work done over the previous two years into hard cash. *The Will of Russia* would not take her long poem about the White Army, *Perekóp*; *Contemporary Notes* refused even to answer her letters. Tsvetayeva felt unwanted by all her Parisian acquaintances; there was no one to whom she could go without having to arrange an appointment in advance. She recalled bitterly how, before she went to join Seryozha in the Haute Savoie, no one called at the flat except the gas man and the electrician. Only Elena Izvolskaya continued to come and visit her. Even more hurtful than her estrangement from Russian *émigré* society (which had never really accepted her) was the cooling off Tsvetayeva sensed in Goncharova. Not that Goncharova was unwelcoming if she called, but Tsvetayeva was very conscious that the artist never visited her. Even her family, she felt, 'was interested in anybody except me, and at home – dirty dishes, hamburgers. . . .'[155] There was no one to whom she felt important, as she wrote to Anna Teskovà on 26 February 1931: 'No one needs me here.'

The Czech stipend, on which the whole family depended, stopped coming through in 1931 for several months, and by September they were seriously behind with the rent, with no way of finding the money for the next quarter. In her eagerness to earn something, she accepted Mark Slonim's invitation to write an article for the first number of the *New Literary Newspaper*. In her innocence, she wrote about a new Soviet children's book that she found admirable by comparison with the literature of her childhood. It was a hopelessly naïve thing to do. The editors refused the article, because they regarded it as axiomatic that children's books under a Soviet regime could only be propaganda. Tsvetayeva was surprised at their attitude. She had imagined that, by avoiding the use of the word 'Soviet', she could somehow make what she said apolitical. In 'A Poet on Criticism', she had said: 'My task is to hear true. I have no other,'[156] but it was no longer possible to write of things as she saw them, however truthfully, and have that truth accepted outside the political divisions of that time. The emigrant community had hardened its own line, and there was no question of it respecting the task Tsvetayeva had imposed upon herself.

Financial anxieties were not the only drain upon her energies. The imposed 'family togetherness' was also crippling: 'I am always in someone's company, never alone,'[157] she complained to Slonim. Worst of all was the responsibility of keeping house. As she wrote to Anna Teskovà on 31 August 1931: 'For the poet, everything is a blessing . . . except being overburdened with ordinary life.'[158] It was not a question of the energy consumed by the daily chores in themselves – she was far from domestically fastidious – nor was it a matter of feeling reduced to the role of an ordinary Meudon housewife. What made it impossible to give up her days happily was the pressure of abandoned poems and unanswered letters.

It was Tsvetayeva's habit to send Anna Teskovà New Year's greetings, in which she often assessed her own spiritual state. Tsvetayeva's stocktaking was bleak indeed at the opening of 1932 – so bleak that she felt almost too fainthearted to send off the four pages covered in small handwriting, and was tempted to cast them into the stove. By 31 March 1932, Tsvetayeva was reduced to moving the whole family to Clamart, where she had been able to find a much cheaper flat. It was cramped and Tsvetayeva had to sleep in the kitchen to make room for her desk and her books. Heating, too, was a problem, but gradually they settled in.

Tsvetayeva began to vex herself continually with the question of where she ought to live. Everything seemed to be pushing her towards a return to the Soviet Union. In 1931, Prokofiev had visited Tsvetayeva because he wished to set some of her poems to music. Perhaps, after all, she would be welcome if she returned. And yet, part of herself did not

believe that: 'Here I am unwanted, and there I am *impossible*.'
Tsvetayeva knew enough of what was going on to sense why.
'Go to Russia? . . . there my mouth would not only be closed
because my works would not be published, but they would
not let me even write them.'[160]

Her health was deteriorating through undernourishment;
she was anaemic and losing her hair. One of Tsvetayeva's four
remaining literary outlets, *The Will of Russia*, ceased publication on losing its subsidy from the Czech government. There
were months when the whole family had only the five francs a
day Alya earned by knitting, and they could not have survived
without the generosity of friends such as Salomea Halpern and
Mark Slonim; the latter also tried to organize a group of people
who would undertake to make regular contributions. Mirsky,
too, helped.

On 11 August 1932, Tsvetayeva was in a small bookshop
near the Clamart forest. There she saw five volumes of Dumas'
Joseph Balsamo, a book she had been given by Voloshin twenty
years earlier. She did not have the eight francs necessary to
buy them, but she went home remembering her youth. Her
thoughts wandered to Voloshin living in Russia, and that
evening she remarked of the Bolsheviks and their treatment
of writers: 'Voloshin, for example, from their point of view
is a clear counter-revolutionary and yet they have given him
a pension of 240 roubles a month and, I am *convinced*, without
his applying for it.'[161] A friend of hers idly inquired whether
Voloshin was still alive, and Tsvetayeva, horrified, assured her
that he was.

But only five days later, Tsvetayeva read in *Pravda* that
Voloshin had died at Koktebel. Superstitiously, she noted that
the hour of his death was the very moment (noon) when she
had been trying to strike a bargain for the volumes of *Balsamo*
in Clamart. Soon afterwards, Tsvetayeva began to write her
memoir of Voloshin. Her intention was to present him as a
man, dedicated like herself, as much to defending Soviet
writers from White detractors as White writers from the Soviet
authorities – that is, a genuine humanist.

She had never more deeply missed the support of her old
friend. Sitting writing at her desk in Clamart, she recalled him
whenever she looked at the plate with the lion's head on it she

had carried with her from Moscow all those years ago; and thought longingly and sadly not only of Akhmatova but other women poets she had known, notably Cherubina de Gabriac who had died two years earlier in Turkestan. Thinking of the women poets that Voloshin had befriended, it seemed to her as if all poems written by women had in some sense been written by the same woman. She expressed this in her memoir about Voloshin: 'By one and the same one – a *nameless* one.'[162] Tsvetayeva felt in herself the force of that anonymous and powerful creature.

Tsvetayeva's spirit is not easily caught in photographs. Her gestures are remembered more than her features: her incessant smoking, loose-limbed gait, the movements of her boyish figure. She herself thought talking about looks in her case was foolish since her appearance was irrelevant. She had none of the grandeur of a woman who is beautiful, or who exacts the kind of devoted service that Anna Akhmatova was able to command. Yet the changeability of her face from day to day was itself a mark of resilience. She had no strong bones to support an impassive face; every change of mood showed on it. Hers was often the face of a driven creature, sometimes an impatient one, but never (except in the posed 'pretty' photographs of the early Twenties) static. She could look weary, standing on the cobbles of Clamart one day in 1933, staring towards her son with her hair unkempt and her dress like that of a poor gypsy; and then appear ten years younger at the seaside in the summer of 1935, her hair loose and longer, and sunlight erasing the harsh lines from nose to mouth.

By the Thirties, Tsvetayeva's personality was marked by a stern absence of self-pity and a proud contempt for human beings who thoughtlessly took solace from ordinary pleasures, particularly good food. In fact many of her poems written in the middle of that decade poked fun at the gourmet's pleasure in food. Before D. S. Mirsky left for the Soviet Union in 1932, he had often been irritated by her refusal to take any interest in the quality of the meals he had offered her, but by now Tsvetayeva ate anything and had no favourite foods. This had prompted Mirsky to complain: 'All you do is talk! You don't care what you eat. One might as well give you hay.'

Tsvetayeva's harshness was in part a justification of her own inability to manage to perform everyday chores briskly. She explained her asceticism in correspondence with the Estonian critic Georgy Ivask, who began to write to her in 1933.

I'd never throw away the tiniest piece of bread. A crust in a dustbin is a monstrosity. . . . So people here think I am mean, but I know it is something else. Undemanding, as were my father and my mother; she did not sink to a favourite dish (– generally – a Protestant and a Spartan!) Didn't ever suspect there might be some particular food which was disliked. [164]

Meanwhile, for the first time in her life, she turned from poetry to write prose memoirs of some of the poets to whom she had been close in the past. These included the one on Maximilian Voloshin, begun after the news of his death in 1932, and another about Bely who died in 1934. As she wrote to Anna Teskovà from Clamart on 24 November 1933:

I write almost no poems, and this is why: I cannot limit myself to one poem; they come to me in families, cycles, like whirlpools and even maelstroms in which I am inevitably trapped – and it's a question of time. I cannot write my current prose pieces and poems both at the same time; could not even if my time were my own. I am a concentric. And no one, anywhere – they forget I am a poet – will publish my poems. Not a line. 'No one, anywhere' means *Latest News* and *Contemporary Notes* – there's nowhere else. [165]

She added: 'Emigration has made a prose writer out of me.'

In 1934 Tsvetayeva was overcome by grief at the death of Nikolai Gronsky, who had been accidentally killed by an underground train. Although Tsvetayeva had stopped seeing the young man well before he died, his father, who was still on the editorial board of *Latest News*, asked her to write a note about his son's poetry. In the six years between the end of their intimate relationship and Gronsky's death, she had met

Nikolai only once, in the spring of 1931, and then casually. Her invitation to resume their friendship had never been pursued by him, but nevertheless, she felt his death painfully. She undertook the commission from his father readily enough, and if she overstressed his merits as 'the first *real* poet' to appear in the emigrant community, there was nothing exaggerated in her poignant memory of his beauty. She was particularly moved by the sculptures that Gronsky's mother had made of her son: first as a ten-year-old, then when the boy was sixteen, and finally she had sculpted a full-length statue of the young man sitting, head slightly tilted, with his hands in his pockets.

When her essay on Gronsky was rejected by *Latest News*, she felt deliberately humiliated, but as she admitted in a letter to Vera Bunina, both the Gronskys were genuinely dissatisfied by the intimate tone of her article. Offended as she was, she recognized that Nikolai's father was in a state of nervous collapse, one that was so severe that he had to be taken to a sanatorium. And she knew that, whether the doctors called it acute neurasthenia or depression, for him Nikolai's death felt like the end of everything.

To honour her grief for Nikolai, she gave an evening performance. Possibly through stress, she lost her voice two days beforehand, but the hall had been rented and the reading advertised, so she could not cancel. The audience listened attentively, but Tsvetayeva could feel that the work did not reach them. Perhaps they disliked her certainty that she knew Nikolai far better than his parents. It is in her own poems for him, *Epitaph*, that we feel Tsvetayeva's unhappiness, and her unwillingness to accept the usual consolations.

> And I won't exchange you for sand
> and steam. You took me for kin,
> and I won't give you up for a corpse
> and a ghost: a here, and a there.[166]

Tsvetayeva was badly in need of kinship. Her own family relationships were beginning to collapse.

10
The question of return
1934–1937

Homesickness

Homesickness!   that long
exposed weariness!
It's all the same to me now
where I am   altogether lonely

or what stones I wander over
home with a shopping bag to
a house that is no more mine
than a hospital or a barracks.

It's all the same to me, captive
lion   what faces I move through
bristling, or what human crowd will
    cast me out   as it must

into myself, into my separate internal
world, a Kamchatka bear without ice.
Where I fail to fit in (and I'm not trying) or
where I'm humiliated   it's all the same.

And I won't be seduced by the thought of
my native language, its milky call.
How can it matter   in what tongue I
am misunderstood by whoever I meet

(or by what readers, swallowing
newsprint, squeezing for gossip?)
They all belong to the twentieth
century, and   I am before time,

stunned, like a log left
behind from an avenue of trees.
People are all the same to me, everything
is the same, and it may be the most

indifferent of all   are these
signs and tokens which once were
native   but the dates have been
rubbed out: the soul was born somewhere.

For my country has taken so little care
of me that even the sharpest spy could
go over my whole spirit and would
detect no native stain there.

Houses are alien, churches are empty
everything   is the same:
But if by the side of the path one
particular bush rises

          the rowanberry . . .[167]

By 1932 Sergei Efron had joined the Union for the Repatriation of Russians Abroad, a pro-Soviet organization whose
avowed aim was to arrange for exiled Russians to return to
the Soviet Union. Alya had joined too, and Tsvetayeva knew
that both of them longed to go back to Russia. Seryozha's
application for a passport, however, was not at first successful,
and Tsvetayeva was positively relieved he couldn't go. For
her own part, she was determined not to return. In a letter
written to Salomea Halpern in 1933, she declared, 'I am
definitely not going; this would have meant separation, which
for all our bickering, would be hard after twenty years of
being together.'
   As well as her sister Anastasia being in the Soviet Union,

Tsvetayeva also had friends there, Pasternak and Ehrenburg, although in a letter to Georgy Ivask written from Clamart on 4 April 1933, Tsvetayeva rejected with contempt her old closeness to Ehrenburg for the way in which he fell, spine-lessly, under first one influence then another. She was not a woman who would have understood how to bend or compro-mise, or even be quiet. She was not likely to avoid unwelcome attention in Stalin's Russia. As Pasternak was to muse after her death, she

> was a woman with a practical masculine mind; at once decisive, and indomitable. In her life she had been impetuous, avid and almost rapacious in the way she strove for finality and certainty, in her work. Yet she was helplessly impractical in daily life.

At the decisive moment several voices that might have been raised in warning were silent. Ehrenburg had visited Paris on several occasions, though his encounters with Tsvetayeva were rare. When they did meet, he was as impatient with her as he was with the Russian community about her, however different she felt herself to be from it; and he ridiculed her insistence on refusing to relinquish the old calendar, and celebrating the advent of the New Year on 13 January. But he was sorry to see how hard her life was, and how little chance her sick husband had of finding work. Well as he knew the dangers that might greet them in the Soviet Union, he may have genuinely thought that their situation could not be any worse there than in Paris.

When Ivask probed Tsvetayeva's feelings towards the Bolsheviks, knowing that a good part of the distrust the *émigrés* felt about her sprang from their awareness of her involvement with the Eurasian movement, Tsvetayeva's obstinate reply makes plain that she would never be forced into a political position she did not hold:

> . . . I think you mean that my hatred against the Bol-sheviks is too feeble for the *émigrés*' taste? I'll answer; it's *another kind* of hatred. They hate because their estates have been taken away, I – because Boris Pasternak is not

allowed to go to his beloved Marburg, and I to my native Moscow. As to the executions, my dear – all executioners are brothers; the recent execution of that Russian [Gorgulov who assassinated President Paul Doumer of France], with a *legal* trial and the defence counsel in tears, or the shot in the back by the Cheka, I swear it's all the same foulness, to which I do not submit *anywhere*, as I don't to any organized violence, in whoever's name it might be done.[169]

The information about the vast scale of political murder in the Soviet Union of Josef Stalin was not yet known; on the contrary, unexpected acts of generosity (such as were shown to Voloshin) were continually being brought to her attention.

The loss of Ehrenburg's friendship counted much less with Tsvetayeva than the gradual falling-off there had been in her correspondence with Pasternak. It was not that Pasternak had forgotten his friendship with Tsvetayeva, or that his admiration for her poetry had diminished. On the contrary, he had a remarkably sharp understanding of her personal qualities as well as her greatness as a poet. Some idea of how he saw her can be gained from a poem dated in 1928 and first published the following year, in which Tsvetayeva's particular virtue is seen to be the acceptance of the truth of things as they are; a casual affirmation, which renders to everything that has happened its own beauty.

> You were so right, turning your pockets out
> in front of me, to make me poke and rummage.
> I understand now: mist does not make spring –
> Any true fact is like a morning in March.

However, unlike Ehrenburg, Pasternak's knowledge of what was happening all over the Soviet Union had driven him to the very edge of madness. He had been in a miserable state of mind since the beginning of the Thirties, when he had done some travelling to gather material for a book about collective farms in the new countryside. On those journeys, he found so much unimaginable calamity everywhere that 'the mind could simply not take it in. I fell ill. For a whole year I couldn't sleep.' It is all the more remarkable, that when (after so many years' planning) the two poets met in Paris in 1935, Pasternak failed to warn either Tsvetayeva or her family of the dangers they would face on returning. He was to feel guilty about that omission for years after her death. Yet it is hard to be as harsh upon him as he was on himself.

Pasternak arrived in Paris in June 1935 as a delegate to the Communist-sponsored Congress of Writers in Defence of Culture. He was ill and unhappy; a frightened man, who knew exactly what had been happening in the USSR after the murder of Kirov (which served as a pretext for Stalin's purges) and could not speak of it. He might well have avoided a meeting with Tsvetayeva altogether, if she had not herself appeared impetuously at his hotel. Even so, and although they met several times afterwards during his stay in Paris, he remained withdrawn, and it was in part a rage at failing to make real contact with him that prompted Tsvetayeva's harsh letter after his departure. And yet the contrast she draws in it, between her own willingness to endure human claims upon her strength and Pasternak's instinctive self-preserving withdrawal from them, is a true one and crucial to understanding the shape of Tsvetayeva's life.

By 1935 Tsvetayeva was in poor health, ill-fed, and isolated. In letters to her Czech friend Anna Teskovà, she was working through a painful assessment of the way life had begun to close in upon her. She was weary of her thirteen years of exile, in which she had coped with the daily necessities of shopping and cooking, while acting as the main support of two children and a husband rarely free from tuberculosis. The essential paradox of Tsvetayeva's nature was that she was *not* a ruthless woman, even though her own daughter was to write: 'She was able to subordinate any concerns to the interests of her work. I insist, *any*.'[171] Tsvetayeva was sustained by an endurance she herself said she had learned from her own mother.

And yet she certainly showed less comprehension of Pasternak's situation than he did of hers. Pasternak arrived sick with the knowledge of purges unmentioned in the West. A large delegation of anti-Fascist writers were happy to attend the congress, among then Heinrich Mann, André Gide, Henri Barbusse, Bertolt Brecht, André Malraux and Louis Aragon (as well as Ehrenburg, of course). Pasternak's presence, along with that of Isaak Babel, had been particularly requested by a group of French writers who had approached the Soviet ambassador in Paris, although neither writer had originally been included in the Soviet delegation. Both of them therefore arrived in Paris by air, after the congress had already begun its work.

There is no doubt that Pasternak was in a state of acute anxiety. He had been forced to leave his wife behind, and tried to explain to Tsvetayeva how they had had to put him force-ably on an aeroplane. Sleep eluded him throughout his stay. At one point he had an opportunity to whisper to Tsvetayeva, who was part of the audience, 'I didn't dare not to come: Stalin's secretary came to see me, and I was frightened.'

However, Tsvetayeva had no way of understanding the nature of the menace. Although Pasternak could hardly explain to the congress the reasons for his mental disturbance, he did speak about his illness in his address and said very few words about poetry. André Malraux, who introduced him, presented him as 'one of the very major poets of our time', and acted as interpreter for Pasternak's speech. Pasternak received a prolonged ovation. Nevertheless, there was a terrible irony in his description of poetry as 'an organic function of the happi-ness of men endowed with the blessed gift of rational speech', at the very moment of his fear that all that was bloody-minded and irrational in human nature was being let loose in his own country.

When Tsvetayeva, dressed in unsuitable and extremely poor clothing, came to his hotel, and approached him while he was standing with other members of the Soviet delegation, it is to Pasternak's credit that he welcomed her warmly and proudly, and introduced her to the other members of the delegation as 'one of our major Russian poets'. After that initial meeting, Tsvetayeva and Pasternak met a number of times in the corri-dors of the hall where the congress was being held, and spoke to one another of the poems they had written most recently. Pasternak also had the opportunity to go to Tsvetayeva's house and got to know her son and daughter as well as her husband. Of Seryozha, Pasternak said he was 'a sensitive, charming, utterly steadfast man, whom I came to love as my own

brother'. Pasternak wrote this in 1967, when all the facts of
Efron's life were available to him; and certainly 'steadfast' is a
surprising adjective to apply to Efron's political principles. As
a reflection of Seryozha's loyalty to Tsvetayeva, however, it
was entirely just, and for Pasternak that may have been the
most important consideration.

Pasternak was well aware that Tsvetayeva's family wanted
to return to the Soviet Union; by now, Seryozha, Alya and
Moor were all sympathetic to Communism as an ideal.
Pasternak could see the terrible life that Tsvetayeva had to live
in Paris and the impossibility of her functioning there much
longer. Nevertheless, when Tsvetayeva asked Pasternak his
opinion, he could not bring himself to warn her. As he wrote
somewhat euphemistically in *Novy Mir* in 1967, 'I did not
know what to advise her, and was too much afraid that she
and her remarkable family would find life hard and unsettling
in Russia. The tragedy that befell the whole family was
infinitely greater even than I had feared.'

Pasternak knew exactly how unhappy being an exile made
her, and he was not only thinking of her poverty. In *A Captive
of Time*, Olga Ivinskaya quotes some lines of his in which he
clearly had Tsvetayeva in mind:

> A distant foreign land. Foreign rain
> Pouring down our hats, in ditches,
> And turned into an oak by sheer forlornness
> The poet stands, a stranger, like Pushkin's miller.[172]

He must already have known that Tsvetayeva would have
lacked any sense of how to survive in Stalin's Russia: she could
not have mastered the elementary essential of keeping her head
down. Yet she would have been forlorn indeed in Paris
without her family.

In a letter to Anna Teskovà of 2 July 1935, Tsvetayeva
makes it clear that Pasternak need not have blamed himself as
bitterly as he did. He had spoken of himself as unwell and on
the edge of a nervous breakdown; probably he hardly realized
Tsvetayeva's state of mind at all. Certainly what she said to
Anna Teskovà in that letter suggests as much: 'I will write

about the meeting with Pasternak, (there *was* a meeting – and what a non-meeting) when you answer me.'[174]

When Pasternak left Paris, he was too ill to return to Russia immediately, and spent two days with the Lomonossoff family in London before catching a boat to Leningrad. Tsvetayeva was incredulous that he had not taken a train through Germany to visit his mother, who lived in Munich. The letter that follows shows how little she understood what Pasternak had been through. She had no idea of the pressures upon him, or she could not have suggested, so cruelly, that he ought to 'think less' about himself.

Late October 1935

Dear Boris,

I have put everything aside in order to answer at once.

About you: one cannot, it is true, judge you as a person. . . .

I shall never, for the life of me, understand how one can go past one's mother on a train, past twelve years of waiting. And you should not expect your mother to understand. It is the limit of my comprehension, of human comprehension. I am the opposite of you in such things. I would drag the train *myself* to meet her (although perhaps I would have the same fears, and would have as little pleasure in it). One observation of mine is appropriate to *all* who have been close to me – and there have not been many of them – they have been infinitely softer than me. Even Rilke wrote to me: '*Du hast recht, doch Du bist hart*'. [You are right so you are hard.] And that upset me, for I could not be otherwise. Now that I can take stock of the past, I see that my apparent harshness was only the form, the contours of reality, an essential barrier of self-defence – defence against *your* softness, Rilke, Marcel Proust and Boris Pasternak. For you would withdraw your hand at the last moment and leave me alone to face my own humanity – long after I had made my exit from the family of men. Among you superhumans I was *merely* a human. I know that yours is a superior race, Boris; and it is *my* turn to put my hand on my heart and say: 'It is not you, but I, who is the proletarian.' Rilke died without summoning his wife, his daughter or his mother. Yet they *all* loved him. He was concerned for his *own* soul. When my time comes to die, I shall have no time to think of my soul (of myself). I shall be fully occupied: have my future pall-bearers been fed? Have not my relatives ruined themselves arranging it all? And at best – the most egotistical possibility – I hope they haven't plundered my draft work.

I have only ever been myself (my soul) in my notebooks and on solitary roads (which have been rare), for all my life I have been leading a child by the hand. I no longer had anything left for 'softness' in dealing with people. I could manage only social intercourse, service, *useless* sacrifices. A *mother-pelican* is evil because of the system of sustenance that she creates. There you have it.

About *your* softness: you buy yourself off with it. With this hygienic cotton wool you stop up the openings of the wounds that you yourself inflict. Oh you are kind! If you meet somebody, you are *incapable* of being the first to stand up or clear your throat in preparation for good-byes. You could not thus 'give offence'. You go out 'for some cigarettes' and disappear for good, turning up in Moscow, on the Volhonka, No. 14 – if not further. Robert Schumann *forgot* that he had children, forgot the date, forgot names, forgot facts. He merely asked about the older girls – whether or not they all had such wonderful voices.

But now for your justification: only *such* people can do *such* things. Goethe, too, was one of your kind. He did not go to say goodbye to Schiller, and for X years he did not go to Frankfurt to see his mother. He was saving himself up for *Faust* Part Two or some such thing. And then at the age of seventy-four he fell in love and decided to get married – no longer taking care of his (physical) heart. For in everything you are squanderers. . . . For you cure yourselves of everything (of yourselves, of the aweful superhuman in yourselves, the divine in your-selves) with the simplest medicine – love. . . .

I myself chose the world of superhumans. Why should I grumble?

★

. . . If your mother forgives you, then she is the mother
in the medieval poem – do you remember? – the hero
ran, and his mother's heart fell from his hands, and he
tripped over it: 'Et voici le coeur lui dit: 'T'es-tu fait mal,
mon petit?'

Well, Boris, be healthy. Think less about yourself. I shall
pass on your greetings to Alya and Seryozha. They
remember you with great fondness, and they wish you –
as I do – good health, good writing and good rest.
    Regards to Tikhonov if you see him. . . .

M. Ts.[175]

Tsvetayeva had begun to feel old – and out of touch. In the
eyes of the twenty-year-olds around her now, she was, she
felt, no more than an eccentric old lady, in whom they took
no interest. She, who had always attracted the young and lived
in their excitement, felt altogether excluded.

For Tsvetayeva, human compassion always transcended
political and economic theories. 'Anything that is being hurt
regains its innocence. It gathers all of its forces and straightens
out,' she had written in 1924, in a part of 'Terrestrial Indications' published in *The Will of Russia*. And now she drew
back from Seryozha and Alya's political commitment, not
from an abstract principle, but out of a distrust of such principles. Alya's enthusiasm for Communism was genuine, but
at the same time, its psychological sources were easy to guess.
She had long since turned eagerly to her father, and was only
too willing to find in the ideals of Communism a replacement
for the absolutes she had once seen embodied in her mother's
worship of Art.

For Tsvetayeva, this defection was less painful than her
gradual realization that Moor's loyalty to her was far from
absolute. The only person to whom Tsvetayeva could hope
to feel truly necessary was her ten-year-old son, and she
worried all the more since the limitations on his intelligence
were now clear enough. He was neither a thinker nor an
idealist, but she still longed for him to do something worthwhile with his life. However, he did not understand her, and
was impatient with her way of feeling. He had always been a

difficult child, and Slonim now found him rude and spoilt, and it upset him to see how uncomplainingly Tsvetayeva adored her son. Yet even she began to worry anxiously about the way he was developing. She hated the way he repeated the commonplaces of ideology learned from his father and sister. She recognized that Seryozha and Alya believed in them passionately; when she heard the same phrases from Moor, they sounded smug and unthinking. Clearly, she could not turn to him for support or understanding. Yet in trying to decide what was the best thing to do, his interests were those she put first.

Tsvetayeva's feeling that Moor was of paramount importance was demonstrated in an unlikely context. Some time in 1935, she made the acquaintance of the American heiress Natalie Clifford Barney, who held a celebrated literary salon at 20 Rue Jacob. Barney's own writing talents were modest, but she passionately believed in one particular cause: the power of love between women. She herself had appeared as a character in many novels (notably Radclyffe Hall's *Well of Loneliness*), and it is unsurprising that she should have inspired Tsvetayeva to write a remarkable essay: 'Letter to an Amazon'. During her time as an emigrant, however, Tsvetayeva had not experienced any lesbian involvement on a par with her relationships with Sophia Parnok and Sonya Holliday, and she wrote the essay mainly to analyse the quality of her own responses. For all the beauty of love between women (which in Tsvetayeva's view was not opposed by God), she had come to feel that female nature itself defeats the power of any long-standing affair – not through the need for a man, but through the universal desire for women to have children. Tsvetayeva's sociological observations may seem irrelevant today; they are, in any case, most revealing about her own choices. She was a woman whose own obsessive love for her son was stronger than any other passion she felt; indeed, it can be said that her longest love (that for Seryozha) was a close approximation of a maternal love. The most significant sentence in her essay is that where she declares that only pathological women find that they do not love their children more than their lovers.

Tsvetayeva feared for Moor's future whether she took him to Russia or whether they continued to live in exile. Certainly his prospects in France were poor. Tsvetayeva looked around at other young people who were trying to make something of their lives in exile and could see only a dead end for him. Seryozha and Alya encouraged her to see there were far more genuine hopes for him in the family's return. Anastasia, whom Tsvetayeva loved, was once again in Moscow, and they reminded her of the fine writers who remained there. Tsvetayeva also knew that she would find it hard to support herself and Moor on her own. The small income that came from the job Seryozha now had (which Tsvetayeva took to be some clerical work for the Union for the Repatriation of Russians Abroad) would cease when he returned to the Soviet Union himself, and *Latest News* had no more space for her work.

Nevertheless she hesitated, but this had nothing to do with the terrors that Pasternak could have whispered to her. Tsvetayeva's reasons for not wishing to return were peculiar to herself. She thought of the newly rebuilt Moscow as an asphalt lake with loudspeakers and huge advertisements. She feared the Soviet educational system in which, after school hours, children were pressed to join Pioneer groups and spend little time with their families. Tsvetayeva, who might have been expected to see in this the opportunity for women to work outside the pressures of domestic life, could only see in it the threat of losing all contact with Moor.

She knew instinctively that she would be incapable of 'singing a welcoming address to the great Stalin', but her inability to do so had nothing to do with any knowledge of his crimes. She regarded him simply as the chief figure of a banal church, to which she knew she could give no worship.

The choice had to be made, but still she hesitated, to such a point that her old superstitious nature reasserted itself and she wrote to Anna Teskovà, 'Do you know, dear Antonovna, of a good fortune teller in Prague? It seems I can't manage without a fortune teller.'[176] There was no way in which she could use her reason to think the situation through. And this was not surprising. There was so much information she did not yet have.

Tsvetayeva's belief in poetry was her only certainty as she tried to decide which course of action to take. Yet the claims she made in that extraordinary, brilliant, often inconsistent essay, 'Art in the Light of Conscience', were very different from those usually made for poetry. Though she called it 'holy', she took as an example a poem by Pushkin that she felt to be deeply blasphemous – 'Feast during the Plague' – which fascinated her with its vision of the plague as 'the proper name and visage of *evil*', whose power the poet feels so strongly that he is seduced by it.

The lyric poet betrays himself by song, and always will, for he cannot help making his favourite (his double) speak in his own, poet's language.[177]

At a time when poets were eager to put their art to the service of humanity or the cause of the people, and in any event to commit their talents to a fight, Tsvetayeva coolly maintained that anyone who so wished to serve 'should join the Salvation Army, or something like that – and give up Poetry'.[178] Poetry was outside the control of the will, and approached the immoral condition of dreaming. For her, 'The condition of creation is a condition of being overcome by a spell. Until you begin, it is a state of being obsessed; until you finish, a state of being possessed.'

'Art in the Light of Conscience' concludes with Tsvetayeva's most deliberate comment on her own moral role even while those around her (and, in her own family, both Seryozha and Alya) were hurrying to throw themselves into the service of a cause they felt to be more noble. She knew the limits of her service.

To be a human being is more important, because more needed. The doctor and the priest are more needed than the poet because they are at the deathbed, while we are not. Doctor and priest are humanly more important, all the rest are socially more important. (Whether the social is itself important is another question, which I shall have the right to answer only from an island.) Except for parasites, in all their various forms, everyone is more important than we are.

And knowing this, having put my signature to this

while of sound mind and in full possession of my faculties,
I assert, no less in possession of my faculties and of sound
mind, that I would not exchange my work for any other.
Knowing the greater, I do the lesser, this is why there is
no forgiveness for me. . . . Only such as I will be held
responsible at the Judgement Day of Conscience. But if
there is a Judgement Day of the Word, at that I am
innocent.[179]

By 1936 Seryozha was earning a small amount of money that
came out of a special Soviet government fund for secret agents.
Of this Tsvetayeva suspected nothing. All she knew was that
she was very often left alone in the house, while Seryozha
and Alya were out together at meetings, which, Tsvetayeva
believed, were part of Seryozha's work to promote the return
of Russian citizens to the Soviet Union. She was absolutely
unaware of the pressures that were being brought to bear on
him. Yet he had already been asked to prove his devotion to
Moscow in some significant way in order to make visas for a
return possible. Since these were matters he could not discuss
with Tsvetayeva, the emotional gap between them widened,
and increased her perplexity. Even when her husband and
daughter were home, her own lack of interest in their concerns
made her feel that she was living with strangers.

It would have been easier to bear her loneliness if Moor had
returned her love, but the boy deeply resented his poverty,
and blamed the continuation of family exile on his mother's
political obstinacy. And she continued to live under the threat
of Seryozha's and Alya's impending departure, feeling all the
while drawn in their wake. As she wrote to Anna Teskovà
on 29 March 1936, 'I'm already not living here.'[180] Moor's
performance at the private school he attended, too, was disappointing, though Tsvetayeva blamed the French school
system, with its emphasis on cramming. She felt that Moor
was entitled to a better education than he might have received
at a free school, because her own father had so often sent
students abroad at his own expense.

One of the few new relationships to develop in these bleak
years was that with Vera Bunina. Tsvetayeva had been living
in Clamart when she first wrote to Anna Teskovà in

November 1933 of her reactions to the award of the Nobel Prize for Literature to Ivan Alekseyevich Bunin. She was particularly critical because she found 'Gorky . . . greater and more humane, more original and more needed. Gorky is an era, and Bunin is the end of the era. But *of course* it is all politics, *of course* the King of Sweden couldn't pin a medal on Gorky the Communist!'[181]

Tsvetayeva did not like Bunin, finding him cold, cruel and smug. Towards his wife, however, she felt warmly. Vera Bunina was a friend of Tsvetayeva's half-sister Valeria, and it was possible for Tsvetayeva to share with Vera a whole lost world of pre-Revolutionary Russia. Vera had been a pupil in art history under Tsvetayeva's father and their acquaintance dated from that period, though they only became close friends in Paris. Tsvetayeva's dislike of Bunin himself made it all the easier to sympathize with Vera's situation. Bunin, notoriously, had a young mistress called Galina Kuznetsova, who travelled everywhere with the family, and Vera had chosen to endure the situation calmly. Tsvetayeva found Vera's continuing love for Bunin altogether admirable, and quickly recognized that Vera understood herself to be indispensable and stayed with Bunin for that reason, like a mother.

Bunin was altogether a flirtatious gentleman. Meeting Alya at a poetry reading, he teased and joked with her, and finally invited her for dinner. Tsvetayeva's reaction on hearing this was tinged with jealousy. She noted that Alya had behaved without embarrassment, and wondered whether that was the secret of women's success with men. Not for the first time, she lamented how listlessly she had been loved, and reflected how, instead: '*Spirits* like me, *souls* love me; poets, lonely old men, dogs, eccentrics. . . .'[182]

In was in 1935 that Tsvetayeva drew closest to Vera Bunina, but as in all her relationships, she showed anxiety over the least imagined slight. On 10 January 1935, for instance, she wrote of her doubts about Vera's desire to see her, and mentioned gossip in the editorial offices of *Latest News* that Bunina had no intention of seeing her again. Her relief at discovering that Vera was not annoyed with her was profound.

From the letters to Bunina, we gather a good deal of information about Tsvetayeva's financial circumstances between

1935 and 1937. Despite the importance of the emotional relationship to Tsvetayeva, this did not preclude her making use of Vera's connections, and frequently borrowing money. It was to Vera she explained the difficulty she had in raising the fees for Moor's schooling, and complained (not altogether honestly) about the number of readings she had to give in 1935. She even mentioned that she had needed a contribution towards those fees from V. V. Rudnev, an editor of *Contemporary Notes* – a fact she mentioned, no doubt, to encourage further financial assistance. Tsvetayeva's letters to Bunina were often roundabout ways of eliciting money from her powerful friends; and the reason she usually made the payment of school fees the chief need was because it was easier to plead for luxury than for money for food. Even though so many letters to Bunina were about money, their relationship remained highly charged on Tsvetayeva's side, though she resolved not to be carried away as often as she had been in past infatuations. Tsvetayeva wrote to Vera with remarkable percipience of her own self-restraint in not allowing her passionate nature to get out of hand:

> I also know that I could have loved you a thousand times more than I did but, thank God, I stopped myself at *once*. . . . You represent perhaps the first sensible action of my life. . . . My God, what torture that would have been! (For me; for you.) I would have lived from meeting to meeting, letter to letter. Meetings would have been postponed, letters would have failed to arrive – or would have arrived, but the wrong ones (always the wrong ones, only you yourself write the *right* ones). Vera! Thank God I love you a thousand times less than I know I could have.[183]

She had sent a copy of her essay 'Mother and Music' to Vera, who enjoyed it. Tsvetayeva was very eager to know whether she had liked the portrait of her mother, 'Mother herself', by which she meant Vera's sense of her mother's personality, and declared her own knowledge: '*I owe her everything.*'

In June 1935 Tsvetayeva planned to go with Moor to La

Favière in Vat, where a garret and part of a garden only four minutes from the sea (and belonging to Baroness Ludmilla Sergeyevna Wrangel, a second cousin of Tsvetayeva's) were theirs for the whole summer. Tsvetayeva still needed 430 francs for two return tickets, but was unable to get any more money out of V. V. Rudnev. So even as Moor developed a stomach-ache (which, as she feared, presaged appendicitis), she went on writing out tickets by hand for a poetry reading arranged for an evening in June. And she gave the reading even though her fears for Moor were confirmed.

They made the trip to La Favière for his convalescence, and while he was recovering, she dedicated herself to him absolutely; her life centred only on his pleasure. She gave him the only room with a pleasant view from the window, and stayed outside in the sun with him all day even though she could never work outdoors. After he went to bed, she sat alone in the kitchen, listening to strangers' voices. Some of them rose from the settlement of Russian *émigrés* in the pine forest close by, but there was no way in which any member of the Efron family could now be accepted by that community.

That summer by the sea she could work only after the chores of the day were done, in the kitchen luminous when the door was open, and stopped up like a bottle when it was closed; with no table and failing energy. Yet the summer had been a most necessary rest, which would have been paradisial for someone to whom writing was not a necessity. She found herself longing to be like other people, who could treat summer as a chance to take a rest from their work; whereas for her, rest was her work, and when she could not write, she was simply unhappy.

That autumn, in Paris, the friendship with Bunina faltered, and over the following year the two women drifted apart, without quarrelling. There is a note from Tsvetayeva dated 26 October 1936 in which she thanks Vera for greetings conveyed to her through Khodasevich, but this attempt to revive their acquaintance failed.

Tsvetayeva's situation required urgent decisions. She eagerly questioned writers such as Malraux who had returned from the Soviet Union. He was enthusiastic about the life there, though when Mark Slonim asked him, in Tsvetayeva's pres-

ence, about the freedom allowed to writers, Malraux answered, 'Right now is not the time for that.'[184]

Another poetry reading trip to Belgium in 1936 had produced money enough for Tsvetayeva to clothe Moor. Yet,
once again, further signs of Moor's developing character
distressed her. He was ill-mannered and showed no signs of
natural kindness; he thanked the woman who daily set his
food before him as 'if he was barking'. Tsvetayeva half-
jokingly called him 'a savage', but without much of a smile.
She had become aware she was pitied for his rude behaviour
towards her.

She had wandered about Brussels a little, looking for a place
where she might live, alone and without friends, since it was
possible to live well there much more cheaply than in Paris.
However, the plan would only be a fantasy so long as she
could not leave Seryozha, and he was tied to Paris. May was
the month in which they had met for the first time in Koktebel,
twenty-five years before, and Tsvetayeva was still moved
when she recalled that early meeting. Her husband's life,
however, was now developing quite separately from hers.

Early in the summer of 1936 the young poet Anatoly Steiger
initiated a brief, but highly emotional attachment. Tsvetayeva
had only met him briefly before that, though she knew of him
through his sister Alla Golovina, whom Tsvetayeva regarded
with some contempt as a literary hanger-on. Steiger was a
close friend of many of Tsvetayeva's old enemies, and it is by
no means clear why he turned towards her, but she responded
to the gift with all the desperate warmth of a passionate nature
starved of affection. He was consumptive, had been seriously
ill for a long time and was suffering from the loss of a lover
who had recently deserted him. Between August and
September 1936, he was recovering from an operation in a
Berne hospital, and it was from there that he sent Tsvetayeva
a book of his poems. In response to his first letter, she wrote
not one but many; every few days a letter went off, together
with poems composed to him, which celebrated her joy at
finding someone with a genuine need of her affection.

The unhappiness in Steiger's original letter was genuine, and
he was grateful to receive an instant response to it. Tsvetayeva,
however, wrote him long, difficult letters, with detailed

analyses of the nature of sickness and writing and love. She believed that, in this way, she could harness her own spiritual strength to rouse in him the will to live. Predictably, as he grew stronger, he drew away from her. And the pain she felt then was real enough, though only a faint increase of a continuing disappointment.

Tsvetayeva returned to her translation of Pushkin's 'Feast in Praise of the Plague' of which she had written so magnificently in 'Art in the Light of Conscience' and her extraordinary essay 'My Pushkin'. In the middle of her own wilderness, she heard that Anna Teskovà's mother had died, and Tsvetayeva wrote to offer what help she could. It was a difficult letter – she was afraid of being superfluous in the face of great loss – but she comforted herself with the thought that no human voice could be anything else.

Tsvetayeva reached the end of 1936, ill with flu, and only just able to cope with producing a New Year's tree and presents for Moor. Seryozha and Alya were too concerned with their own plans to return to the Soviet Union to be much interested in her old-fashioned New Year's celebration.

When Alya received her visa to return to the USSR in March 1937, she began to pack at once. Everyone helped. Seryozha spent a great deal of money buying suitable clothing, but Tsvetayeva was too numb with grief to inquire into where so much money was coming from. It was almost as if Alya were getting married, and all their acquaintances contributed towards her 'dowry'. Everything she was given was of the best quality – a fur coat, linen, sheets, a watch, suitcases, cigarette lighters – all the worldly goods she had lacked all her life. Tsvetayeva walked to the Marché aux Puces (the famous Paris flea market) and there bought her a gramophone; she also presented her daughter with her own silver bracelet, a brooch, a cameo and a cross.

Alya departed cheerfully. She was dressed entirely in new clothes, and looked very elegant in the crowd that had come to see her off, like a bride setting out on her honeymoon. As the train left, Tsvetayeva felt a great sadness. She had seen off other friends and knew enough to realize that the euphoria might not last long. As several months passed with no letters from Alya she worried desperately. However, when they finally did come, the first letters were, beyond measure, reassuring. Alya had gone to live with Seryozha's sister, and was studying English with Tsvetayeva's sister, Anastasia. She was earning some money, and had every prospect of earning more with her illustrations. Altogether, she sounded very satisfied with her situation. Tsvetayeva comforted herself with the hope that her daughter had made the right decision.

On 14 June 1937 Tsvetayeva went to visit the World's Fair which was being held in Paris, and looked with particular attention at the Soviet and the German pavilions. In the Soviet display, Tsvetayeva thought she could discern something that represented *life*, whereas the German art appalled her. The distinction was not entirely false, but neither was it a true instinct – after all, 1937 was the very height of the Stalinist horror under Yeshov (Chief of the Secret Police 1936–1938). But Tsvetayeva was trying very hard to understand how her daughter and her husband could give their devotion to any ideology, and was relieved to find she could at least share their horror of Fascism. To herself, she admitted that both pavilions were full of idols.

Cheerful letters continued to arrive from Alya, who was expecting to begin work very soon on a journal, and was being well paid for freelance work meanwhile. Tsvetayeva began to wonder if the Soviet system was not humane and decent after all. Not that all the news from Moscow was good. Alya wrote that Sonyechka – the beautiful girl Sonya Holliday to whom Tsvetayeva had been so attached in the spring and summer of 1919 – was dead. Tsvetayeva was overwhelmed with grief, which she tried to assuage by beginning to work on a tribute to her memories of that period.

For the whole of the summer Tsvetayeva's mind went back into that Moscow of 1919, as she tried to recreate the life she had shared with her young friends of the Vakhtangov Studio. She spent the whole summer writing a lengthy memoir about that time of starvation and freezing cold, her love for Pavel Antokolsky, her infatuation with Sonyechka and her friend-ship with Volodya. She wrote of those who had made their way south to join the White forces, at the same time as she contemplated a return to the USSR – a signal mark of her characteristic lack of worldliness. She may, in any case, have been still hesitating. Tsvetayeva could have had no idea how soon there would be a decisive turn in events, a change that would make it impossible for Seryozha to remain in Paris.

11

'It was all unstoppable, unchangeable, fatal'

1937–1939

Just how closely Seryozha was involved in the murder of Ignace Reiss is difficult to establish. His gentle, weak character makes him an unlikely choice for a central role, yet he was certainly receiving money from 'special' Soviet funds marked for espionage, he had already agreed to arrange for other people, presented to him as traitors, to be put under surveillance, and he was under pressure from the NKVD to offer evidence of the genuineness of his commitment. While there is no doubt that the NKVD were ultimately responsible for Reiss's murder, one piece of evidence offers a decisive link between Seryozha himself and the assassination.

Reiss had been a spy for the Soviet Union for twenty years, mainly in Germany, but after Hitler came to power, he and his wife spent most of their time in Paris. He had access to official funds from which he was able to pay German Communists who had had to flee from the Third Reich. It was in this way that he first came to help Gertrude Schildbach – and Schildbach was the key link that led back to Seryozha.

She had arrived in Paris in 1934 as a bona fide refugee. Reiss paid the rent for her apartment and used it occasionally for meetings, without involving her in the NKVD in any other way. Reiss had known Schildbach since 1917, and thought her far too unstable emotionally to be trusted as part of his network.

In August 1936, after the trials of the Old Bolsheviks –
Grigori Zinoviev, Leo Kamaneev, I. N. Smirnov and others
– had ended with the death sentence for all sixteen defendants,
there were many important defections from the NKVD in
Europe. Among these was Ignace Reiss, then in Paris, who
had the courage to compose an open letter of protest to the
Central Committee of the Communist Party and return his
Order of the Red Banner, awarded for services to the party
since 1919. Reiss calculated that the letter would take a week
to reach the Central Committee through embassy channels,
and he and his wife made for Lausanne, well aware of their
peril.

Meanwhile orders began to arrive, demanding the return of
many NKVD agents to Moscow. Those who accepted the
orders did so for mixed reasons. Even if some of them
suspected that they were returning to be shot, those with
families still in the Soviet Union dared not refuse to return,
for by 1937 relatives paid with their lives for every political
error in the family.

In Lausanne, on the morning of 4 September 1937, Reiss
and his wife met Gertrude Schildbach in a café and were given
a box of poisoned chocolates by her. Other agents had been
placed in the café to make sure that Schildbach did not break
down and warn Reiss of his danger, but despite any reluctance
she may have felt, she did not do so. One of the reasons she
did not was a young man called Rossi (an NKVD agent) who
had made love to her. She was, however, deceived by him,
for he was also the lover of another girl, Renata Steiner. Both
Schildbach and Steiner worked for the same organization as
Seryozha, and in the case of Renata Steiner, Seryozha himself
had recruited her.

It was Rossi who hired the getaway car from the Cassina
garage on 2 September, and although Madame Poretsky
(Reiss's wife, who survived) claimed that, when Rossi came
to fetch Renata, Efron was among those in the car, Seryozha
was certainly not among the killers. The French police
interrogated him extensively and released him for lack of
evidence, but most of his friends knew he was implicated and,
with the exception of Vera Suvchinsky, held him to some
degree responsible.

Vera had been seeing a good deal of him because they were
a part of the same Communist group, and she was emphatic
that there was no change in his behaviour in the week
following the murder. She was just on the verge of giving
birth, and Seryozha took her to the maternity hospital on 20
September. However, it is hardly likely that he was still
ignorant of the Reiss murder two weeks after the event. Her
reluctance to believe in his involvement is, however, understandable. She had always been fond of him.

His own wife was altogether incredulous. Tsvetayeva had
come to accept Seryozha's commitment to the Soviet cause,
but she had no idea that the money he had begun to receive
every month came from the NKVD. When orders from
Moscow forced him to take flight abruptly, she was stunned.
The very suddenness of his departure was a blow in itself, but
it was followed immediately by close questioning by the
French Sûreté. This she found altogether bewildering, and
even her interrogators quickly grasped that she was totally
ignorant of espionage, politics and her husband's activities.
She had no idea who Seryozha's 'contacts' were, nor of his
role in the Union for Repatriation of Russians abroad, and
rejected any possibility of Seryozha's involvement in a murder.
Her answers were altogether wide of the mark. Since she did
not understand the thread of their accusations, she replied with
quotations from Corneille and Racine. At length the police
began to have doubts about her sanity and let her go without
much difficulty.

For days afterwards, Tsvetayeva sobbed violently. She now
knew, of course, that Seryozha had been taking money from
funds earmarked for espionage but she could not believe in his
guilt. Even his sudden return to the Soviet Union did not
convince her. She had seen enough to know that, once
Seryozha's name had been given to the French police, he would
have been useless to the NKVD – and many people in that
situation had been recalled to the USSR.

Whatever she might protest, however, the *émigré*
community made up its mind decisively, and Tsvetayeva knew
her isolation from them was now to be complete. She was
numb with terror and loneliness. However, on the very day

that Seryozha left for the Soviet Union, she wrote to Anna Teskovà without mentioning her situation.

The likeliest explanation for this was Tsvetayeva's old fear that things become more true when they are put into words. When her daughter Irina had died, she had gone around for three weeks unable to talk about it to anyone, unable to tell anyone that the death had happened. Explaining her behaviour to Vera Suvchinsky in Paris, she said that she had felt as if, by telling someone, she would have made the death final. Here, too, in the face of losing Seryozha (who remained a fixed point in her life), she feared to write or speak of it.

From this point on, Tsvetayeva felt she had no choice except to return to the Soviet Union. She no longer had Seryozha's small stipend, and since his exposure, the *émigré* community were more likely to hound her to death than contribute to her support.

Mark Slonim met Tsvetayeva in October of that year and was distressed to see how she had suddenly aged and dried up, even though she was only forty-five. It was the first time Slonim had seen her cry. Moor was not there, and Slonim afterwards remembered her saying quietly, 'I should like to die, but I must live for Moor's sake. Sergei and Alya don't need me any more.'[185]

During that winter, between November 1937 and February 1938, Tsvetayeva could bring herself to write nothing. Even to write a letter to Anna Teskovà took more stamina than she could muster. She wrote postcards instead. 'I am not up to writing anything more,' she excused herself.

It was only in May 1938, when Czechoslovakia was menaced with German invasion – which Tsvetayeva felt as a personal threat – that she was roused from her own misery. Outraged as the great powers signed at Munich in September and German tanks moved into Prague in October, she began to think day and night about Czechoslovakia. As she wrote to Teskovà:

The whole of Czechoslovakia is one huge human heart beating just as mine does. . . . The deepest feeling of disgrace I feel is for France, but it was not the *real* France that was responsible for this betrayal! In the streets and the squares is the whole of the real France. . . .[186]

Tsvetayeva's insistence that it was the people on the street who were the 'real France' marked a change in her political hopes. For the first time in her life, Tsvetayeva rejoiced to see Communist demonstrations in the streets against the government. For the first time, too, she read leftist newspapers. In a postscript to a letter to Anna Teskovà of 24 September, she wrote:

I am now ashamed to live. Everyone now is ashamed to live. Since one cannot live in shame. . . . Have faith in Russia!

Tsvetayeva's personal isolation was now total. The press had taken up the Reiss affair in the early part of 1938 and almost all the Russians she knew in Paris treated her as a criminal. (Salomea Halpern was an exception, but in that year she was living in London.) Tsvetayeva's Russian neighbours forced her to leave her home and move to a cheap hotel at 13 Boulevard Pasteur. It was there she received her first letter from Seryozha.

As a result, on 15 June 1938 she honoured his request to raise a memorial stone to Seryozha's parents and brother in the Montparnasse cemetery. To do so produced absurd problems. The person who had bought the plot in the first place had signed in the French style – 'Effront' – and since this spelling was entered and confirmed in all consequent documents, the director of the cemetery would not permit her to correct the name to 'Efron' on the gravestone. There were other problems – with the date, and the Cyrillic script – but Tsvetayeva seemed to have drawn renewed energy from Seryozha's letter, and set to work enthusiastically to ensure that the modest memorial was correctly erected.

Soon, too, a postcard from Prague declared that Anna Teskovà was at least still alive. Tsvetayeva wrote back at once, sharply nostalgic for the time, thirteen years before, when she and Moor and Alya had left Prague for Paris. She had begun a poem cycle of protest against the invasion, and asked Anna Teskovà to send her a book of the legends of Prague, and repeated an earlier request for a photograph of the famous statue of the Knight of Prague to help her do so. In the same letter, Tsvetayeva, who had never before been emotionally attached to precious goods, asked to be sent a necklace of smoky coloured crystal from Prague, which she was to treasure to her death. It reached down to her breast, and the beads were cut in the old-fashioned style so that they were all the same shape and size. In addition, she, like others, tried to buy Czech goods wherever possible. She even bought an enamel jug for her ink, because it had 'MADE IN CZECHOSLOVAKIA' on it.

Perhaps it is strange that Tsvetayeva should have reacted with so much more intensity towards the fall of Czechoslovakia than towards any other comparable political event. She herself said about it: 'I think that Czechia is my first such grief. Russia was too great and I was too young.' Tsvetayeva suspected of hypocrisy all those who mouthed regrets and did so little. She had no wish to belong to the society of women who, to keep up appearances, muttered their horror at the ill-treatment of the Jews and, afterwards, turned out to be having affairs with members of the anti-Semitic Black Hundreds. Everywhere around her was cowardice and complicity, and she felt completely alone in her indignation.

In 1938, a good deal was going on in Russian *émigré* circles. There were plays by Mark Aldanov and Nina Berberova in the theatres as well as several important poetry readings, but Tsvetayeva's name was to be found nowhere. She was altogether an outcast. Strangely, her own emotional response to the invasion of Czechoslovakia restored some shadow of her former strength, and she was able to write to Anna Teskovà that she did not feel so preoccupied with her own loneliness. The poems that she wrote for Prague at this time rose from her agony of hatred at the violation of the country in which she had felt most happy:

> What tears in eyes now
> weeping with anger and love

Czechoslovakia's tears
Spain in its own blood

and what a black mountain
has blocked the world   from the light.
It's time – It's time – It's time
to give back to God   his ticket.

I refuse to be. In
the madhouse   of the inhuman
I refuse   to live.
With the wolves of the market place

I refuse   to howl,
Among the sharks of the plain
I refuse to swim   down
where moving backs make a current.

I have no need of holes
for ears, nor prophetic eyes:
to your mad world there is
one answer: to refuse![187]

In referring to the ticket she wishes to return to God,
Tsvetayeva was thinking of the gesture made by Ivan Karamazov in Dostoevsky's *The Brothers Karamazov*, when he
refused the possibility of salvation if it had to be bought with
the suffering of a single child.

Tsvetayeva was now seriously debilitated by cold – almost
delirious with it. Dreams of Prague filled her days with
longing. She managed to produce a Christmas tree for the
thirteen-year-old Moor; they exchanged Christmas presents.
But there was a bleakness between them. Perhaps the best
news for Tsvetayeva in 1939 was a telegram of greetings from
Alya on New Year's Day.

However, by 31 May 1939, the decision to leave for the
Soviet Union had been made, although Tsvetayeva told very
few people about applying for a visa. She could not take much
with her, and besides, money was short and she had to sell
many things. She spent a long time sorting out her notebooks.

The rest of her time she used to sew on Moor's buttons. At the beginning of June 1939, she went, with Moor, to say goodbye to Mark Slonim, whose house was one of the very few in which she was still received. They were to leave in a few days, and it was with great sadness that Tsvetayeva and Slonim recalled the altogether carefree days they had once spent together in Prague. Tsvetayeva read to him her latest poem, 'The Bus', which Slonim found particularly brilliant, both in language and humour. It was a long poem, of great virtuosity, as can be seen in its opening lines:

> The bus jumped, like a brazen
> evil spirit,   a demon
> cutting across the traffic
> in streets as cramped as footnotes,
> it rushed on its way   shaking
> like a concert-hall vibrating
> with applause.   And we shook in it!
> Demons too.   Have you seen
> seeds under a tap? We were
> like peas in boiling soup,
> or Easter toys dancing in
> alcohol.   Mortared grain!
> Teeth in a chilled mouth.
>
> What   has been shaken out   someone
> could use for a chandelier:
> all the beads   and the bones
> of an old woman. A necklace
> on that girl's breast. Bouncing.
> The child at his mother's nipple.
> Shaken without reference
> Like pears   all of us   shaken
> in *vibrato*, like violins.
> The violence shook our souls
> into laughter, and back into childhood.[188]

Moor listened and looked bored. Tsvetayeva confided to Slonim her anxieties about what she would find in Moscow and whether her work would be published. At this, the yawning Moor showed some interest and rebuked her: 'Really, Mama, you won't believe it, but everything will be splendid!' Tsvetayeva and Slonim talked until midnight, even though Moor tried to hurry his mother away. She lingered on, reluctant to go. At last they said goodbye on the landing, and then Slonim sadly and silently watched them enter the lift. As it began to move, their faces dived down beneath him and disappeared from his sight, and he had a premonition it would be for ever.[189]

Moor was too excited to be sensitive to his mother's feelings, but he was interested enough in his own. A plump, good-looking boy of fourteen, he was very keen to buy himself something smart to wear even though Tsvetayeva had to struggle simply to keep them both alive.

There was at least one letter from Seryozha during Tsvetayeva's final months in Paris, and in it, he complained of nothing more than a nostalgia for the French cinema. Tsvetayeva, perhaps as a result of this unexpected comment, began to visit the cinema more often than usual, and it became one of her few pleasures. Through the last weeks, Tsvetayeva wore her Czech necklace continually, almost as if it had magical protective properties. A journal entry of 23 April 1939 recorded a dream of magical power from which Tsvetayeva woke comforted.

Dream 23 April '39: I walk up a narrow mountain track. Landscape of St Helena: on the right, a precipice; on the left, a sheer rock face. Nowhere to turn. Down the track towards me – a lion. A huge one. With a face that is huge even for a lion. I cross myself thrice. The lion lowers itself on to its stomach and creeps past between me and the precipice. I walk on. Down towards me – a two-humped camel. Also larger-than-life, larger-than-camel, unusually tall even for a camel. I cross myself thrice. The camel steps over me (I under the arc of the tent-stomach). I walk on. Down towards me – a horse. It cannot fail to knock me over the edge, for it is hurtling at full speed. I cross myself three times. And the horse flies through the air – over the top of me. I admire the grace of its aerial gallop.

And – the road to the other world. I fly, lying on my back, feet forward, head being wrenched off. Below me – towns. Large-scale and detailed at first (a spiral gallop), then – handfuls of white stone. Mountains, straits – I fly on irrepressibly; with a feeling of homesickness and final farewell. Like a feeling of flying round the Earth, passionately and hopelessly hanging on to it, and knowing that the next circuit will be in space. The same total emptiness that I so feared in life – on the swings, in the lift, on the sea, inside myself.

There was one comfort: it was all unstoppable, unchangeable, fatal. And it would get no worse. I awake with my hand lying across my breast 'from the heart' . . . Yes, of course. . . .[190]

In these last weeks before her departure, Tsvetayeva was numb. In an end of any kind, there ought to be some sort of peace, yet with premonitory dread, she feared what was waiting for her, as if she could already imagine looking back with pain towards those, like Teskovà, whom she had loved. She consoled herself only by remembering the much-loved countryside of the land to which she was returning after so long: the juniper tree, the rowanberry and the pine trees she had long missed.

Tsvetayeva and her son left Paris on 15 June 1939. While waiting for the train to Le Havre to start, she began a letter to Teskovà:

Dear Anna Antonovna!
(I am writing on my palm, that's why the childish handwriting.) This is a huge station with green windows – a frightening green garden – what doesn't grow there! At parting, Moor and I sat for a while, according to the old custom; we crossed ourselves before the empty spot where had hung the icon which has lived and travelled with me since 1918; well, we have to part with everything some time totally! This is a lesson so that later on to give up everything won't be frightening, perhaps even not strange. . . . A seventeen-year life is ending. How happy I was at that time. But the happiest period of my life –

remember this! – was Mokropsy, Vshenory; and also my
very own mountain. It's strange – yesterday, on the street
I met the hero of that mountain, [Rodzevitch] whom I
have not seen for years; he rushed at me from behind
without any explanation, he clasped his arms through
Moor's arm and mine, he walked in between us as if it
was the most natural thing . . . I have constantly been
meeting everyone. (Right now, I hear, resoundingly and
threateningly: *express de Vienne* . . . and I remember the
towers and bridges which I will never see.) They are
yelling '*En voiture, madame!*' – as if to me, taking me away
from all sorts of places of my life. There is no need to
yell – I myself know. Moor has stocked up (the train has
just started as I wrote that) with newspapers.

  We are approaching Rouen, where one time human
gratitude burned Joan of Arc (500 years later an English-
woman erected a monument to her in the same place).
We have passed Ractedale [point of no return]! – I will
await news from all of you, give my warm regards to the
whole family, I wish you all health, courage and a long
life. I dream of a meeting in your native land which is
more native to me than my own. I turn around at the
sound of it as if it were my own name. Remember I
once had a friend Sonyechka. Everyone said to me, 'Your
Sonyechka.' I am leaving in *your* necklace, in a coat with
your buttons and a belt which has *your* buckle on it! *It is
all grand and my very favourite*. I will take it all to my grave
or burn together with it. Farewell. Now everything is
already easy; now it is already faint. I embrace you and
kiss each one of you separately and all of you together. I
love you and admire you. I believe in you as in myself.[191]

The letter was posted from the station at Le Havre at 4.30 on
12 June 1939.

Part V

The Return to Russia

12
Moscow and Yelabuga
1939–1941

Tsvetayeva and Moor took a train from Le Havre to Poland and travelled to Moscow via Warsaw, where they arrived on 18 June. After Tsvetayeva had left Paris, rumours began to reach *émigrés* there that Seryozha was already dead, and someone was convinced enough to send a telegram ahead of her to warn her. The message never reached her, and it was in any case inaccurate. Both Seryozha and Alya (now pregnant by and living with a man nicknamed Mulia) were at liberty when Tsvetayeva arrived in Moscow, and for two months the whole family was reunited in a small house in the village of Bolshevo near Moscow. Seryozha was in the fairly privileged position of drawing a small salary for earlier services rendered to the Soviet state, and Alya had a job at the Society for Cultural Relations with Foreign Countries. However from the first, Seryozha was ill, and Tsvetayeva had to adjust to an increasingly enigmatic situation.

She resumed her notebook, and even the small extracts from it that have survived suggest disappointment as much as relief. Seryozha's weakness appalled her, even though she took on the harness of his support as usual, but her notes show how much she resented his lack of strength, his spiritual helplessness – *impotent* was the word she used in her notes:

To the *dacha*. Rendezvous with Seryozha, who is ill. Out for kerosense. S. buys apples. Slowly worsening heart-ache. Ordeal by telephone. Alya enigmatic, for all her

247

apparent cheerfulness. (All this is for my own, and
nobody else's, recollection. Moor will not understand it,
even if he ever reads it. Nor, indeed, *will* he read it, for
he avoids such things.) Cakes, pineapples – things are no
easier here for those. Walks with Lilya [Seryozha's sister].
My loneliness. Washing up, water and tears. The overtone
and undertone of everything is horror. Promises of a
partition [in the flat] – and the days go by. Promises of a
school for Moor – and the days go by. And the usual
wooden scenery – absence of stone, of firm foundations.
S.'s illness. Fear of his inner fear. Snippets of his life
without me; I have no time to listen; my hands full; a
strain to listen. The cellar: 100 times a day. When can I
write?[192]

Tsvetayeva's continuing loneliness, even as she was reunited
with two of those she loved most, is heart-breaking. Her sister
Anastasia was already sentenced to imprisonment in a camp,
and Moor took little interest in his mother. Nevertheless, those
two first months were relatively hopeful ones. From 27 August
1939, even that brief period of hope came to an end with
Alya's sudden arrest. Approximately a month later, Seryozha
was arrested as well.

The last happy memory Tsvetayeva had of her daughter
was seeing her in a red Czech dress, a present that Tsvetayeva
had brought with her. Four days later, Alya was forcibly taken
away. She courageously pretended to laugh off the significance
of the arrest, but the charge of espionage against Alya was
serious enough to bring her a sentence of fifteen years.
Tsvetayeva sadly noted the grimness of Alya's departure in
her journal:

I: What's the matter, Alya? Why don't you say goodbye
to anybody? She looked over her shoulder, in tears – and
shrugged.[193]

The parting with Seryozha left Tsvetayeva frantic. And it
was not easy to turn to her friends.

Tsvetayeva's meeting with Pasternak after she returned was
predictably disappointing. Perhaps this was because both of

them were exhausted by their domestic problems, though they were of a very different nature. Pasternak now had a second family and, since he had broken very painfully with his first, found the threat of any emotional disturbance terrifying – and the one thing Tsvetayeva certainly boded, after their long romance by correspondence, was emotional demand. He knew he could neither meet her need, nor risk disappointing it.

Pasternak never gave a coherent account of his first encounter with Tsvetayeva after her return to Moscow. It pained him to recall how inadequately he had behaved, and when his mistress Olga Ivinskaya teased him with the malicious suggestion 'You should have married Marina', the vehemence of his denial and his stress on the horror he felt for female hysteria clarifies his sense of failure. He afterwards blamed himself for not being willing to enter into the kind of passionate intimacy she must have been expecting. He excused it by noting that she had other friends, but truly he did not want the closeness.

In fairness, Tsvetayeva and Pasternak were, in human terms, antithetical personalities. Yevgeny, Pasternak's son, still remembers Tsvetayeva's visit to their house when he was about seventeen, and he identifies the difference between the two poets as their attitude towards ordinary, domestic life. The daily round was a burden to Tsvetayeva – not only beause she was a woman, though all the more so because of that. For Pasternak, however, domestic life was the source of endless novelty and delight.

He did want to help her, and did many things to make her situation easier. In particular, it was Pasternak who presented Tsvetayeva to the editor Victor Goltsev and ensured she had work to do immediately. She was offered the task of translating Georgian poets, work by which Pasternak had himself earned his living for many years. She was also given the work of poets writing in Yiddish using literal versions, and she learned that she could receive payment for the work without having to wait for its publication. Emotionally, Tsvetayeva may have felt rejected, but Pasternak did a good deal for her, and in some of her translations of French poetry, notably Baudelaire, her work was fine enough to give her pleasure.

Once Seryozha was arrested, however, Tsvetayeva no

longer had a place to live. For a time she stayed with Moor in a small room belonging to Seryozha's sister Elizaveta Efron, then she moved briefly to Merzlik Street. Everywhere was temporary. Pasternak made some effort to find her a place to live, and even went to see Fadeyev in Peredelkino* (Fadeyev was at that time secretary to the Writers' Union), but, as so often under pressure, Pasternak found he could only speak in an agitated, rambling manner, and never came to the point of his visit. A few evenings later, however, when Fadeyev met Tsvetayeva at Pasternak's house, the official must have understood exactly for whom Pasternak had been indirectly pleading.

Nothing came of this contact, but Tsvetayeva was sufficiently desperate to risk approaching him herself. His reply was certainly cool (without 'dear' or 'esteemed' at the opening, and with no salutation at the end). He was not altogether unhelpful, however, even though only too conscious of the 'circumstances', to which he refers obliquely in the first paragraph, that made her unacceptable to the Writers' Union.

17.1.40

Comrade Tsvetayeva!
Re your archives: I shall try to find out something, though this will not be easy in view of all the circumstances. In any case I will try to do something.

But finding a room for you in Moscow is absolutely impossible. We have a large group of good writers and poets in need of living-space. And for years we have been unable to find them a single square metre.

The only solution for you: take a room or two in Golitzino with the help of the Director of the Golitzino Rest Home (she is a member of the Local Billeting Soviet). This would cost you 200–300 roubles per month. Expensive, of course, but with your qualifications you can earn quite well just by translations – for publishers and journals. Regarding work, the Writers' Union will help you, in looking for a room in Golitzino, the Litfond

---

* A village not far from Moscow where writers were given *dachas* by the State. Pasternak himself had one there.

will also help. I have already spoken to Comrade Oskin
(Director of Litfond) and I advise you to contact him.

A. Fadeyev[194]

In her journal, Tsvetayeva reflected on her own nature,
which everyone had found almot inhumanly strong.

About myself. Everybody considers me possessed of
manly courage. I know nobody more timid than I. I fear
everything: eyes, blackness, footsteps and, most of all,
myself, my own head (if it is indeed my head that serves
me so devotedly in my notebooks, yet murders me in
real life). Nobody knows, nobody sees; it is already a year
(approximately) that my eyes have been searching for a
hook. But there are no hooks, for everywhere is electricity. No 'candelabras'. . . .

For a year I have been taking the measure of death.
Everything is ugly and terrifying. You swallow – scum;
you leap – hostility, the innate repulsiveness of water. I
don't want to confuse things (posthumously). It seems to
me that I already, posthumously, fear myself. I do not
want to die. I want not to be.

Rubbish. So long as I am needed . . . but, Lord knows,
how small I am, how incapable of anything! To live out,
to chew out, my time. The bitter absinth.[195]

Tsvetayeva had no hope of seeing her sister Anastasia, but
she felt she was still needed by her son, even though Moor
himself gave her scant evidence of this. It was for his sake that
she remained outside Moscow in order to be able to take him
to and from the local Golitzino School. She hated to leave him
there every day, to tear herself *away* from him to go to work
on translation that took up the whole day. She felt like an ox,
in harness. Her main desire on arriving in Moscow was to get
out of it again. She still had no more than a burrow, no
window, nor table. And (a terrible restriction for Tsvetayeva)
the rules forbade smoking. The first six months of 1940 were
a nightmare of loneliness and grief, in which Tsvetayeva
continued her translation of the Georgian poets even while she
moved from house to house with nowhere to call her own.

Nevertheless, she was living in a Writers' Union Club where it was possible for her and Moor to have reasonable meals. This situation did not last. In March 1940, Tsvetayeva was told by the manager of the Golitzino club that she would have to pay twice as much for her meals as other residents, and as there was no way she could afford this, she was forced to leave.

Soon Tsvetayeva's material situation had deteriorated even further than she would have believed possible. She found a poor room in Moscow where the cooking facilities were so minimal that she had to make do with only two small saucepans. There was nowhere to keep the huge mounds of literal versions from which she worked. At the same time, she knew that her own continuing freedom made her luckier than many of those she loved, who were suffocating behind stone walls.

Many old friends were dead. One of these was Osip Mandelstam, whose widow Nadezhda was living in the provinces, but no one told Madame Mandelstam that Tsvetayeva had returned. Akhmatova, however, was able to meet Tsvetayeva in 1940. She was staying in Moscow with the Ardov family when Pasternak telephoned to say that Tsvetayeva wanted to meet her.

Akhmatova's situation inside the Soviet Union had been every bit as grim as Tsvetayeva's was now – for example, Stalin had held her son hostage in prison for many years. Nevertheless, unexpectedly, in 1940 the ban against the publication of Akhmatova's poems was lifted, and a selection from her previous books with some new poems appeared in the early summer. Even though they were not the greatest poems she had written, they brought a delighted tribute from many friends including Pasternak, and queues of people tried to buy her book, the price of a second-hand copy of which had reached 150 roubles. In her handbag, Akhmatova had carried everywhere a manuscript of the cycle of poems that Tsvetayeva had written for her in 1916. She herself had written a poem to Tsvetayeva a few months before they finally met, in which she imagined the two of them walking through the wintry streets of Moscow.

In response to Pasternak's call, Akhmatova telephoned Tsvetayeva at once to arrange a meeting. The conversation was brief. When Akhmatova asked if she should come to her, Tsvetayeva answered simply: 'It would be better if I come to you.' Viktor Ardov let Tsvetayeva in, but did not have to introduce his two guests. They greeted each other without the usual platitudes, simply pressing each other's hands. Then the two poets went into the tiny room where Akhmatova usually stayed when visiting the Ardovs and remained there alone together for the best part of the day. Akhmatova never spoke fully of what they discussed, but she knew as well as anyone that the recently published selection did not contain her best work, and so she must have shown Tsvetayeva her great poems from *Requiem*. She said only that Tsvetayeva had turned out to be a perfectly normal person deeply concerned about her family's fate.

The following day, when Tsvetayeva telephoned, Akhmatova suggested that they should meet at her friend Nikolay Khardzhiyev's. They sat in his house, talking and drinking wine. Khardzhiyev well remembers the meeting. Tsvetayeva had recovered her spirits and talked brilliantly, her conversation full of Paris. Akhmatova told him later that she felt herself to be dull and cow-like in contrast, but to Khardzhiyev, Akhmatova did not appear like this at all. On the contrary, seeing her opposite the quicksilver Tsvetayeva, Khardzhiyev was struck by the contrast with Akhmatova's genuine strength. They all left Khardzhiyev's house together, and as they walked along the streets, someone stepped out of the shadows and began to follow them. Akhmatova wondered, 'Her or me?'

In spite of the deprecating comments Akhmatova made about herself, the meeting was not a disappointment to her. It confirmed her belief in a special bond between herself, Mandelstam and Tsvetayeva, and added a new and tragic dimension to her own sufferings. When she wrote of Tsvetayeva many years after her death, Akhmatova's sense of her friend's complete integrity in the face of suffering led her to call her 'Marina the martyr'. She was not misled by Tsvetayeva's display of wit, which had cost an enormous amount of nervous energy – it had been Tsvetayeva's characteristic way of paying tribute to the occasion.

It must have taken a great effort for Tsvetayeva to rouse

her flagging courage, in circumstances such as she described on 31 August 1940 in a letter to Vera Alexandrovna Mercurieva:*

> . . . My life goes very badly. My non-life. Yesterday I moved out of Ulitsa Gertsena, where we lived very well, and into a tiny temporarily vacant room on the Perzlyakovsky Pereulok. We left all our stuff. . . . It can stay until 15 September. . . . But then what???
>
> I applied to Fadeyev's deputy, Pavlenko. A charming man, in complete sympathy with me – but he can give me nothing. The Moscow writers have *not a metre* to spare. And I believe him. He offered a suburb; and when I produced my main objection – deathly boredom – at least he did not insist. Life in the suburbs is possible for a large closely knit family, where everybody helps everybody else, where all take their turn. But as it is, Moor is at school, and I am left, twenty-four hours a day, alone with my thoughts (sober, with no illusions) and feelings (insane; quasi-insane; prophetic).
>
> I applied to the Litfond. They promised to help me search for a room, but they warned me that any landlord would prefer a single man to a 'female writer with son'. No cooking, washing of clothes, etc. So I have to compete with single men!
>
> In a word, Moscow has no room for me.
>
> I have nobody to blame. Nor do I blame myself, because such has been my fate. Only – how will it end??
>
> *I have written my all.* I could, of course, have written more, but I can happily *not* write. Incidentally, I have translated nothing now for over a month. I simply do not touch a notebook. Customs, baggage, sales, gifts (something for everybody), chasing up advertisements (I have already placed four of them, and *nothing* has come of it), family, moving. . . . When will it stop?
>
> All right, so it is not only me. . . . Agreed, but my father set up the Museum of Fine Arts – the only one in the whole country. He was a founder and a collector; he

---

* A woman poet Tsvetayeva had known during the Civil War who was brave enough to risk involvement with her.

put in fourteen years of hard work. I say nothing of myself; to quote Chenier's last words: '. . . *et pourtant, il y avait quelque chose là* . . . (pointing to his forehead)'. I cannot, in all conscience, identify myself with *any* old kolkhoznik [collective farmer] or Odessite [someone from Odessa] who *also* cannot be accommodated in Moscow.

I am unable to suppress within myself the feeling of my own *right*. (Not to mention the fact that in the Rumyantsev Museum there are *three* of our libraries: that of my grandfather, Alexander Danilovich Mein; that of my mother, Maria Alexandrovna Tsvetayeva; and that of my father, Ivan Vladimirovich Tsvetayev. We have showered Moscow with gifts. And Moscow has flung me out, rejected me. Who is this Moscow, that she can be so proud to my face?

I do have friends, but they are powerless. And complete strangers begin to pity me (that embarrasses me, and sets me thinking). That is the worst thing of all, because at the slightest kind word or inflexion I dissolve into tears, like a rock under a waterfall. And Moor gets furious. He does not understand. It is not a woman crying, but a rock.

. . . My only joy – and you will laugh – is a piece of Eastern Mohammedan amber. I bought it two years ago in Paris, when it was completely dead, waxy, slime-covered. And every day, to my great joy, it comes to life, plays and shines from within. I wear it next to my skin, unseen.

Moor has started at a good school. He has just been at the parade, and tomorrow he has his first day of classes.

> . . . And if in the heart's desert,
> Deserted – so far as the eye can see,
> One pities anything – then it is the son:
> The wolf-cub, still more wolfish. . . .

(Those are old verses. Though all verses are old. There are no new ones.)

With these changes of abode, I gradually lose my sense

of reality. I am slowly being whittled away, a little like
that flock that leaves scraps of fleece on every fence. Only
my basic *negative* remains.

One more thing. I have a very cheerful nature. (Perhaps
that is not it, but there is no other word.) I used to need
very little in order to be happy. My own *table*. The health
of my family. Any weather. And freedom. That is all.
And now – such efforts to achieve this miserable happiness; it's not just cruel; it's stupid. Life should rejoice in
the happy man, should encourage him in this *rare* gift.
Because it is from the happy man that happiness flows. It
used to flow from me. It used to flow like anything. I
used to play with the accumulated burdens of others, like
an athlete with his training-weights. Freedom used to
flow from me. A person knew, deep down, that, if he
threw himself out of the window, he would fall *upwards*.
Through me people used to come to life, like the amber.
They themselves began to play. It is not my role to be
the rocks under the waterfall; rocks which *fall*, together
with the waterfall, on to (the conscience of) a person . . .
I am moved and upset by the efforts of my friends. I am
ashamed – that I am still alive.

　　It is wise old centenarians who are supposed to feel this
way. Were I ten – no, five! – years younger, part of this
burden would be removed from my *pride* by that which
we shall call, for the sake of brevity, feminine charm. (I
speak of my male friends.) But as it is, I, with my grey
hair, have absolutely no illusions; everything that people
do for me, they do *for me*, not for themselves. . . . And
that is painful. I had become so used to *giving*!

. . . My problem is that I have nothing external; all heart
and fate.

Greetings to your wonderful, quiet surroundings. I have
had no summer, but I do not regret it. The only Russian
quality in me is my conscience, and it would not have
allowed me to enjoy the air, the silence, the blue, knowing

and never for a moment forgetting that at the same instant somebody else was suffocating in the heat and the stones.

That would be an excess torture.

The summer went well. I made friends with an eighty-four-year-old nanny, who has lived in this family for sixty years. And there was a *wonderful* cat – mouse-coloured and Egyptian, long-legged; a monster, a monster, but divine. I would give my soul for such a nanny and such a cat.

Tomorrow I shall go to the Litfond ('and many, many times more') to check about a room. I don't have faith. Write to me at Merzeyakovsky Pereulok, c/o Elizaveta Yakovlevna Efron.

I am not registered here, so better not to write to me direct.

Embraces. Heartfelt thanks for remembering me. Warm greetings to Ilya Grigoryevich.

M. Ts.[196]

Tsvetayeva continued, although slowly, to work on translations. In the March number of the magazine *Thirty Days*, one of her old poems, written in 1920, was published.

SONG

Yesterday he★ still looked in my eyes, yet
    today   his looks are bent aside.   Yesterday
he sat here until the birds began, but
    today   all those larks are ravens.

Stupid creature! And you are wise, you
    live while I am stunned.
Now for the lament of women in all times:
    —My love, what was it I did to you?

And tears are   water, blood is   water,
    a woman always washes in blood and tears.
Love is a stepmother, and no mother:
    then expect no justice or mercy from her.

★ This poem cannot have been written about Seryozha.

Ships carry away the ones we love.
   Along the white road they are taken away.
And one cry stretches across the earth:
   —My love, what was it I did to you?

Yesterday he lay at my feet. He even
   compared me with the Chinese empire! Then
suddenly he let his hands fall open, and
   my life fell out like   a rusty kopeck.

A child-murderer, before some court
   I stand   loathsome and timid I am.
And yet even in Hell I shall demand:
   —My love, what was it I did to you?

I ask this chair, I ask the bed: Why?
   Why do I suffer and live in penury?
His kisses stopped. He wanted to break you.
   To kiss another girl is their reply.

He taught me to live in fire, he threw me there,
   and then abandoned me on steppes of ice.
My love, I know what you have done to me.
   —My love, what was it I did to you?

I know everything, don't argue with me!
   I can see now, I'm a lover no longer.
And now I know wherever love holds power
   Death approaches soon   like a gardener.

It is almost like shaking a tree, in time
   some ripe apple comes falling down. So
for everything, for everything   forgive me,
   my love   whatever it was I did to you.[197]

Ironically, a friend from that period of theatrical excitement,
Pavel Antokolsky, was living in Moscow, but he preferred to
see very little of Tsvetayeva. When he was interviewed thirty-
five years later, he spoke of a group of friends who sustained
her, among them Arseny Tarkovsky a poet-translator. She

was not without money, and she had work but Antokolsky remembered her as being an altogether different woman from the one he had known between 1917 and 1922. It was not just a question of a woman who had been aged through fatigue and grief. He described a reading held at Victor Goltzev's house. Tsvetayeva read in a voice unlike her own, and seemed remote from the audience. Altogether, Antokolsky's description of her suggests someone whose anxiety was preoccupying them beyond the point where ordinary human relationships were possible – as Antokolsky put it: '*Elle est autre.*' He also commented on the formal, if not overtly hostile, relationship she had with her son Moor, who customarily addressed her as '*Vous*'. Antokolsky heard him that very evening blame his mother's behaviour for their situation.

Far from her once outrageous presence, Antokolsky was struck by the subdued manner in which she read. He described it as a timid reading, not a public reading at all. He was also shocked by the change in her physical appearance. He had met her once in the intervening years in 1928 in Paris when she had sat with him in the Boulevard St Michel. Then he had found her slimmer and greyer than in her youth, but still amazingly beautiful. It must have been some time around the time of her return to Moscow that the photograph of Tsvetayeva was taken to which Bella Akhmadulina, the present-day Russian poet, alludes in the opening of her poem 'I Swear'.

I SWEAR
   by that summer snapshot taken
on someone else's porch, skewed to one
side, that looks so like a gibbet, and
points a way out of the house not into it;
where you are wearing some violent sateen dress that
cramps the muscles of your throat like armour;
and are simply sitting there, with the endurance of a
tired horse after the labour of
singing out to the end all your grief and hunger. . . .[199]

For Antokolsky, even though he admired the greatness of her poetry, Tsvetayeva remained 'a woman first and foremost'.

That Tsvetayeva could appear in public at all is perhaps more remarkable than the fact that she had been unlike her former proud self. Moving, as she had to, from place to place, she was in a state of continual panic. In jottings in the margins of her rough notebook, dated 24 January 1940, she wrote:

A new uncomfortable house – again I cannot sleep at nights. I am afraid – too much *glass* – too much solitude – night sounds and fears; a car (God knows why it's moving); a stray cat, the crackle of wood – I jump up – snuggle up close to Moor on his bed (without waking him) – and again I read . . . and again jump up and so, to daybreak.[200]

Tsvetayeva could no longer tell whether it was the work she was asked to do that bored her, or whether she had no longer anything to bring to it: 'I no longer know what is duller – my literal translation, or myself. And I have no other *self.* Without the translations I perish!'

Although many believing Communists would have been shattered in the summer of 1940 above all else by the Nazi–Soviet pact, Tsvetayeva was too weary to respond with astonishment. She was obsessed with the need to find somewhere within Moscow for herself and Moor to live. An unexpected piece of good fortune at this time was the arrival of her luggage from Paris, containing little of great value, but such things as there were she was able to sell easily. There were also some manuscripts of early poems, and Tsvetayeva prepared a selection of them for a Soviet publishing house, and even paid to have them typed out, though she had no real belief that anything would come of the project.

Now she had returned to the USSR, those patrons on whom Tsvetayeva had depended could no longer help her with gifts, and another, D. S. Mirsky, had vanished in 1937. She had to rely on friends whose lives were as much in the power of the State as was her own. And she no longer had female friends to whom she could turn with confidence, though she did write some letters to Olga Alexeyevna Mochalova (a poet friend) with whom she tried to create a relationship of the closeness she so desperately needed.

From her husband and her daughter, she heard nothing for months. Many times she stood in line in an attempt to deliver food-parcels to Seryozha in prison. In a letter (undated but probably written early 1941) to an acquaintance, Yevgeny Sormov, Tsvetayeva mentioned that his letter was the first she had received from anyone for four months. Unquestionably, this silence and fear for Alya and Seryozha were the source of that remoteness of which Antokolsky spoke. In spite of the terrible silence, Tsvetayeva wrote many letters to her daughter. Here is a moving one written in the early spring of 1941:

Moscow, spring 1941

I am forty-eight years old, and I have been writing for forty, if not for forty-two, of them. And I am, of course, a philologist by nature. Yet just now, in a tiny little dictionary – even in three of them – I discover that a *pazhit* is a pasture, not a cornfield at all, a mown and fallow field. All my life I have considered and (horrors!) possibly even written *pazhit* as a cornfield; and it is a plain meadow. But in spite of three dictionaries, I still do not believe it. *Pazhit* has the sound of the harvest, *zhatva* of harvesting *zhat*.

Yesterday on the radio some composer (one not known to me) said: 'I must write this opera very quickly, because the theatre starts work on the production on such and such a date.' I asked myself: 'How do you manage to write quickly? How can you compose quickly? Does it really depend on you?'

And then again: 'The theatre starts work on the production on such and such a date.' On the production of an unwritten, non-existent opera! The only surety is the composer's name.

Quickly! One may write without a break, without looking up from the paper – and end up with nothing to show for a full day. And one cannot even bother to sit down – and suddenly a complete quatrain is ready, having emerged during the wringing out of the shirts, or during your feverish digging into your handbag for exactly 50 kopeks, while the 20 + 20 +10 is running through your head.

Write every day, yes. I have done that all my conscious life – just in case. But from 'every day' to 'quickly' is a long way. How can he be so sure of himself? Where is his experience? I also have experience. *Rat-Catcher* was submitted to a journal which *demanded* a chapter a month. But did I ever know that I would finish before the dead-line? Did I ever know the length of a chapter, or when it would finish? Each chapter would suddenly finish itself, on the right word, and syllable.

One may fall into despair that this is a slow method, but from this despair to 'writing quickly'. . . .

Yes, yes, this is how prosperity is acquired; this is how, perhaps (let us believe this hateful wonder!) great operas are written, emerge, come into being. But with these words the dignity of the creator is lost.

No theatres, no royalties, no *necessity* will ever compel me to submit a manuscript until the last full stop has been written. And when that will be, God only knows. The God of poets.

'With God!' or 'Give, Lord . . .' – thus every work of mine has commenced right down to my most insignificant translation. It is not a prayer, if only beause it is a *demand*.

I have never begged for a rhyme from above (rhymes are *my* job), but I have begged for, demanded, strength to find it, strength to endure its tortures. And this was granted me; was served up to me. . . .

When Tsvetayeva, soon after this, heard from her daughter, she was overwhelmed with joy and pain. It was something to have evidence that Alya was still alive, to have something positive she could do to help: she could shop, she could find sugar and cocoa, she could take advice on the best way to survive in hard conditions and pass it on. At the same time, she made no effort to disguise from Alya that, although her own treatment was in no way unfair (she describes working on translations cheerfully enough), her own physical condition had deteriorated and, in appearance, she was now old.

Tsvetayeva's letter to Alya is worth quoting in its entirety.

Moscow, 12 April 1941
Saturday

Dear Alya,

At last, your first letter – in a blue envelope, dated the 4th. I stared at it from 9 A.M. to 3 P.M. when Moor came home from school. It lay on his dinner-plate, and he saw it as soon as he opened the door; and with a contented and even self-satisfied 'A-ah!' – pounced on it. He would not let me read it. Both his own letter and mine he read aloud. But even before the reading, I sent you a postcard. I couldn't wait. That was yesterday, the 11th. And on the 10th I took in a parcel and they accepted it.

I have been industriously at work finding provisions for you, Alya. I already have sugar and cocoa; I am about to have a shot at lard and cheese – the most solid I can find. I shall send you a bag of fried carrots; I dried them in the autumn on all the radiators. You can boil them. At least they are still vegetables. It is a pity, though not unnatural, that you do not eat garlic. I have a whole kilo stored up just in case. But bear in mind that raw potato is a reliable and less unpleasant method. It is effective as lemon – that I know for certain.*

I have already told you that your belongings are free. I myself was given the job of unlocking them – so we shall rescue everything. Incidentally, the moths have eaten nothing. All your things are intact – books, toys and a lot of photographs. I took for myself some kind of bark box, and I keep my beads in it. Should I, perhaps, send you the silver and turquoise bracelet for your other hand? You can wear it without taking it off; it is even difficult to take off. And perhaps one of the rings? Please answer these questions. Which blanket? (Your spare blue one got lost at Bolshov together with many others, none of them yours). I have: my colourful knitted one (big, but not heavy; warm); your father's beige plaid (small), and the dark blue Spanish shawl. I would still take the knitted one, with the shawl to follow next time (it is yours, after all). I shall also send naphthalene. The sacks are ready.

* Against diseases of vitamin deficiency

There are also two dresses – one austere, and the other more decorative; we shall adjust the sleeves. Mulia swears he will get oil of cloves for the mosquitoes. A wonderful smell – one I have worshipped since my childhood. And there will be a lot of bits and pieces for presents.

Spring is still fairly fresh here. The ice is not yet breaking up. Yesterday the cleaning lady brought me a gift of a pussy willow branch. And in the evening (I have a huge window, the width of the whole wall) I looked through it at the big yellow moon, and the moon looked back through it to me. With a fresh-skinned willow branch one feels fresh-skinned oneself – very fresh-skinned! Moor said to me just now in indignation: 'Mama, you look like an awful old village hag!' And I was very pleased that he said a 'village' one. Poor Puss! He so loves beauty and order, and our room is like the one on Boris and Gleb Street – too many things, all piled up on top of each other. His main joy is the radio, which, for some unknown reason, has started broadcasting absolutely everything. I recently heard Eva Curie from America. Alya, among my treasures (I'm writing nonsensically) I preserve your moustached gingerbread cat. Kiss Red for me – a good cat. I shall never have another cat. After that one of yours which climbed into Nikolka's cradle. I loved it madly, and it was terrible to part with it. It has remained like a nail in my heart.

I am finished my White Russian Jews. I translate every day. The main difficulty is the incoherence, imprecision and lack of motivation of the images. Everything falls to pieces. The glue and the seams show all over the place. Some of them write no rhyme or measure. It seems that after the White Russian Jews will come the Balts. I write nothing of my own. No time. A lot of housework. The cleaning lady comes once a week.

I also re-read Leskov – last winter in Golitzino. And I read Benvenuto in Goethe's translation when I was seventeen. I particularly remember the salamander and the slap.

I visited Nina a few times over the winter. She is constantly unwell, but she works, and whenever she is able, and is happy in it. I gave her a short artificial fur jacket – she really had frozen to death – and, for her birthday, one of my metal cups, from which nobody drinks except her and me.

I want to send this off now, so I shall finish. Keep strong and alert. I hope that Mulia's trip is only a matter of time. I have recently been admitted to the Grupkon of Goslitizdat – unanimously. So you see, I am trying.

Keep well. Kisses. . . .

Moor is writing to you himself.

Mama[201]

Tsvetayeva continued to write detailed letters to both Seryozha and her daughter Alya, but unfortunately only a few copies remain. In the letter above, the description of her being made a member of the branch of the Writers' Union at Goslitizdat 'unanimously' hardly indicates the way the meeting had gone. A woman had actively attacked Tsvetayeva as a former *émigré*, and a close relative of people who had been arrested. Tsvetayeva had snatched a Bakelite container, had violently thrown out all the pens and pencils, and then had taken her on in a verbal battle. Her gesture as much as her words carried the day. This was the uneasy period of the Nazi–Soviet pact, a bewildering time for believing Communists, though for Tsvetayeva, it presented no ethical problem. She had lost hope soon after her return to the Soviet Union, and was by now convinced that she was 'condemned to write as a wolf howls whatever system I live under'. By 10 June Tsvetayeva's telephone had stopped working and there was a move to a new *dacha* in the offing. However, all plans were overwhelmed by the single fact of the German invasion.

Her situation worsened at once. From being a lonely, unhappy creature with a suspect past, she was abruptly transformed into a potential spy. Her early writings in praise of Germany and German literature were scrutinized as political statements. Even her fluent knowledge of French and German seemed undesirable.

Only then, after the German invasion on 22 June 1941, did Tsvetayeva have her first and only encounter with the one friend who had been most powerfully placed in the Soviet hierarchy all that time – Ilya Ehrenburg. Ehrenburg himself described his encounter with Tsvetayeva soon after the invasion as disappointing to both of them. He said frankly:

> The meeting was a failure through my fault. My thoughts were far away, (understandably perhaps since the news was all of retreats then). Marina sensed it at once and gave our conversation the flavour of a business interview. She had come, she said, to seek my advice about translating and other matters.[202]

Once the German invasion had begun, Tsvetayeva became anxious for the fifteen-year-old Moor, who had been put in a fire-watching squad with the task of throwing fire-bombs off the roof of the high apartment building where she had rented a tiny room on the top floor. Pasternak also did fire-watching duty on the roof of the Writers' Home in Lavrushinsky, and Tsvetayeva went to see him to ask his advice about how she could help Moor. She had already formed the idea of going off to the Tartar region, where she knew several other Union writers had been evacuated. Pasternak tried to dissuade her, but he did not offer (as he well might have done) a place to stay with him at Peredelkino. This was mainly because of his own domestic situation, which was uneasy, and in any case he was always indecisive in conversation. Nevertheless, she must have been hoping for the invitation that never came.

Perhaps one of the reasons why Tsvetayeva was eager to leave Moscow was the rising suspicion of her on every side, as the Germans advanced steadily towards the city. She knew there were people who whispered, falsely, that she was hoping for their arrival. So it was that she undertook, fatefully, her own evacuation.

Pasternak saw Tsvetayeva and Moor off at River Fort on the outskirts of Moscow, from where it was possible to go by steamer to Chistopol and other towns on the river Kama. This farewell was to be their last.

> Do you think of her, geranium Yelabuga,
>   That woman of the cities long ago
> who smoked like other people cry, smoked
>   all the time, your harsh, home-grown tobacco.

This is where, dead-tired, she had to go
　begging for linen to wash. So now
let me stand here too, Marina;
　for a moment let me share your place.

An old woman, worn out with opening her
　wooden gate, said: I don't know why they
keep on coming; at my age it's torture.
　Well, I'd sell this house but who would buy it?

Yes, I remember the woman. Strict. I knew
　washing linen wasn't her job. She
never did learn how to roll her own fags, either
　so I had to do it for her. Not that rope though!

And yet that wretched hemp was
　kind to her; for the last time
she had the chance to wet her parched
　lips again with the frozen Kama.

But look at it – a nail! Not a hook. Clumsy.
　Used for the yokes of horses, too low to
reach for, still less hang from:
　it would have been as easy for her to choke!

And then that old woman, who had lived right
　through the famine, spoke to me with deference.
'And how can I get rid of this nail now?' she asked,
　touching it. 'Do you know what I could do?

Please, listen, be kind, and tell me one thing.
　How was it she came to kill herself?
You seem to have some kind of education, so
　perhaps you understand, and can help me.'

'Granny, this small room fills me with fear. All
　I really want is to fall on your shoulder and
cry with you. Remember: there is only
　murder in this world. Suicide has no existence here.'
Yevgeny Yevtushenko[203]

August 1941, Yelabuga: the flies were still alive, the river Kama still flowing. For ten days Tsvetayeva stayed as an evacuee from Moscow with the Bredelshikovs. It was a quiet, small house. Tsvetayeva shared a room with Moor. Their window looked over meadows not yet covered with Siberian snow.

She knew that her peasant hosts found her comic. They had never heard of her. All they saw were the length of her dark dress, her old brown coat and the lines of fatigue and anxiety in her face. They could not help laughing at her knitted pea-green beret, and the large apron she wore in the house, though there was something witch-like about her thin, stooping figure that made them uneasy.

Her frenetic behaviour bewildered them. She had no work permit, but every day she went out looking for work. For a day or two, a local policeman let her help with his laundry, but he was reprimanded. Yelabuga was a small town in the Tartar Autonymous Republic, and contained few wealthy people. She was unlikely to find anyone who wanted to buy her silver; nevertheless she carried it about everywhere in search of a purchaser. In the evening she was too exhausted to cook; instead she and Moor ate in the local wartime canteen.

Tsvetayeva knew that writers acceptable to the state had been evacuated to Chistopol on the other side of the river Kama, a three-day journey away, so she decided to make a last attempt to join, to beg any work, suitable or not. An earlier letter to the President of the Tartar Writers' Union, asking for work as a translator, had been ignored. Now she was willing to work in any capacity, even in the kitchens. Lydia Chukovskaya, Akhmatova's companion, absorbed the full measure of her desperation, and could not understand why fellow writers were not ashamed to see her situation. It was her judgement that Akhmatova could not have endured such humiliation. In the event, permission to work in the kitchen was refused.

In an ordinary world, she could not have been seen as presenting any threat. However, Aseev, who was in charge of allocating living space, had every reason to fear what might happen to him if he were thought to have connived at saving her. When the committee voted on the matter he abstained;

but he not only refused to arrange for her to stay, he even refused to lend her any money. After their last conversation, she sat for a long time on a bench near the river, absorbing the finality of his rejection. Then she set about returning across the river to Moor.

From this trip, she returned so bleak and weary that she did not even have the heart to clean the fish Bredelshikov had caught, still less fry it. Anastasia Ivanovna Bredelshikova did it for her; in the same spirit, she had earlier showed her how to roll home-grown cigarettes. They often smoked together, without talking much.

Tsvetayeva's silence was bitter. It was no longer possible to mistake the hostility that Moor, his face sullen, felt for her. He was a gawky boy, too big for his clothes and too strong for his age. He was unhappy because people in the street sometimes asked why he wasn't in uniform. For this, and for his separation from other boys of his own age, he blamed Tsvetayeva directly.

On Saturday, 30 August, he could be heard quarrelling violently with her. He reproached her for a lifetime of irresponsibility, which had led to the imprisonment of his father and the sentence of forced labour passed on his sister. Tsvetayeva's voice rose too but she seemed to be pleading rather than angry, and she made no attempt to rebut his charges. She continued to call him by his pet name.

That Sunday morning, all the inhabitants of Yelabuga were summoned to help in the preparation of an airstrip; everyone who turned up was given a loaf of bread. Anastasia Ivanova Bredelshikova went along with Moor, while her husband and grandson went off fishing. Tsvetayeva seemed preoccupied. She did not mind being left alone.

She was forty-nine: a lonely, hounded woman, whose spiritual stamina had been exhausted. In all her long and poverty-stricken years of exile, she had never given in. Now she no longer understood what she was struggling for. All her life she had survived because she had known that she was needed. Moor's resentment had now destroyed the whole of her remaining belief in herself.

She was not without material resources. She had over 400 roubles and, more valuably, stocks of semolina, sugar and rice. There was even the remains of a pan of cooked fish. She knew herself to be one of the greatest European poets of the century. But her inner loneliness was now complete.

No one can know with certainty what she now remembered. Her Moscow childhood, in the wooden house in the Street of the Three Ponds. Seryozha, for whom she had left the Soviet Union in 1922, and whose return there had drawn her back after him. Golden Prague, and the slums of Paris. Washing-up water and tears. Perhaps she remembered her daughter Alya in a bright-red Czech dress, in the few weeks of happiness that followed Tsvetayeva's return to Moscow. Perhaps she was haunted instead by her last glimpse of Alya, turning slowly away, with a shrug, under arrest. It was not long after that she had noted: 'I am, at the moment, dead. I do not, at the moment, exist; I do not know whether I shall exist some time in the future.'

If Stalin saw no sense in wasting resources on evacuating prisoners from the Lubianka, Seryozha would already have been shot. Tsvetayeva must have heard rumours of that possibility. And so, as she found the nail used to tether horses, and attached a hempen rope to it, she may, in thought, have been following Seryozha once again, and for the last time.

Moor did not go to his mother's funeral, and if he felt any grief for her, he showed it to no one. Akhmatova, who looked after him with great kindness after Tsvetayeva's death, noted his coldness towards his mother's memory. This is all the sadder since it may well have been for her son, to free him from the burden of her ostracism, that Tsvetayeva had taken her life when she did. If so, the gesture was wasted. Moor quickly enlisted in the army and died later in the battle for Moscow.

Seryozha was shot in the Lubianka prison. Alya, who also spent the first two years of her sentence there, lost her baby as a result of savage beatings. She was transferred in 1941 to a labour camp in the Turukhansky region, where she was sentenced to an additional ten years. She did not serve this in full, however. Pasternak (who had exchanged letters with her) and Ivinskaya took her in upon her release in 1955, after sixteen years' imprisonment and looked after her until she recovered her health. She stayed with them throughout the period when Pasternak himself came under most attack, and she later moved to a house in Tarusa, her mother's childhood home. There Alya devoted the rest of her life to arranging and preserving her mother's archives, and seeing her work into print when it became possible. She published her recollections of her mother before she died, of a heart attack, in 1975.

Anastasia spent the years 1938–40 in Siberia, and had no chance to see her sister after the latter's return to the Soviet Union. A volume of her memoirs of her sister was published in Moscow in 1971. She is at present in a Writers' Rest Home outside Moscow.

To the end of their lives, the thought of Marina's death continued to haunt all those who had known her. Pasternak mourned its arbitrary timing, for he felt, with some guilt, that if she had only been able to hold out for another month, he might have been able to find her a billet, and possibly employment, in Chistopol itself. Lydia Chukovskaya, whose fanatical service to Akhmatova sustained that poet through her last years, remembered meeting Tsvetayeva on her visit to Chistopol. She wondered aloud if Anna Akhmatova could possibly endure the severe conditions there. Tsvetayeva had bitterly observed how characteristically people assumed that she, in contrast, could bear anything. Tsvetayeva's death denied Akhmatova the chance to give Marina the poem composed in her honour, in return for so many poems dedicated to herself. She kept a photograph of Tsvetayeva, together with one of her own, because both showed them wearing the same brooch, which Tsvetayeva had given her.

When comparisons were made in literary articles between the two poets, Akhmatova was, correctly, impatient, suspecting the writers of putting them together mainly because they were women. By 1959 she felt herself free enough of the tragedy to make remarks of considerable scepticism about Tsvetayeva as she did about Pasternak, but she was never in doubt about the richness of Tsvetayeva's genius.

Notes

To avoid unnecessary repetition, I have abbreviated the details of works cited frequently after they have been mentioned for the first time, for example:
Tsvetayeva *Neizdannye pisma* ed. Gleb and Nikita Struve, (Paris, 1972) becomes *Neizdannye pisma*

1 Ariadna Efron, *Stranitsy Vospominanii* (Paris 1979), p. 17
2 Letter from Tsvetayeva to Pasternak October 1935 *Novy Mir* N4, 1969.
3 Mark Slonim, 'O Marine Tsvetayevoi' *Novy Zhurnal* New York No 1900 1970; no 103; 1971
4 Tsvetayeva, 'Art in the Light of Conscience', trans Angela Livingstone and Valentina Coe in *Modern Russian Poets on Poetry*, Ardis Press, 1974
5 Tsvetayeva, *Pisma K Anne Teskovoi* (Prague, 1969), 20 July 1926
6 'Mother and Music', *Marina Tsvetayeva, A Captive Spirit: Selected Prose* ed. and translated by J. Marin King (Ardis, 1980) p. 276.
7 From Tsvetayeva, *Evening Album*.
8 'My Pushkin', *Tsvetayeva, Selected Prose* p. 320
9 'My Pushkin', *Tsvetayeva, Selected Prose* p. 321
10 'Mother and Music', *Tsvetayeva, Selected Prose*, p. 273
11 See 'Mother and Music' *Tsvetayeva, Selected Prose*, passim.
12 Tsvetayeva to Pasternak, 25 May 1926, Tsvetayeva *Neizdannye pisma* ed Gleb and Nikita Struve, (Paris, 1972)
13 'The House at Old Pimen', *Tsvetayeva, Selected Prose*, p. 233
14 'The House at Old Pimen', *Tsvetayeva, Selected Prose* p. 228
15 'My Pushkin', *Tsvetayeva, Selected Prose*, p. 335
16 'My Pushkin', *Tsvetayeva, Selected Prose*, p. 338
17 'The Flagellant Nuns' from *Pages from Tarusa* ed Andrew Field (Boston, 1964)
18 'The Flagellant Nuns' op. cit.
19 'The House at Old Pimen', *Tsvetayeva, Selected Prose*, p. 249
20 See 'My Pushkin', *Tsvetayeva, Selected Prose*, p. 358
21 'Mother and Music', *Tsvetayeva, Selected Prose*, p. 292

22 Anastasia Tsvetayeva, *Vospominanii*, p. 109
23 'Mother and Music', *Tsvetayeva, Selected Prose*, p. 293
24 'Mother and Music', *Tsvetayeva, Selected Prose*, p. 293
25 'My Pushkin', *Tsvetayeva, Selected Prose*, p. 337
26 As quoted in Anastasia Tsvetayeva, *Vospominaniia*, p. 308
27 Anastasia Tsvetayeva, *Vospominaniia*, p. 300
28 'A Captive Spirit', *Tsvetayeva, Selected Prose*, p. 107
29 Anastasia Tsvetayeva, *Vospominaniia*, p. 357
30 Anastasia Tsvetayeva, *Vospominaniia*, p. 308
31 Gumilyov, Appolon V. (St Petersburg, 1911) As quoted in Karlinsky, *Cvetayeva, her life and art*, (Berkeley 1966)
32 'A living word about a living Man', *Tsvetayeva, Selected Prose*
33 'The opening of the Museum', *Tsvetayeva, Selected Prose*, p. 205)
34 Quoted in Karlinsky, *Marina Tsvetayeva, The woman, her world and her poetry*, (Cambridge, 1985)
35 Ariadna Efron, *Stranitsy vospominanii*, p. 29.
36 Ariadna Efron, *Stranitsy vospominanii*, p. 30
37 Ariadna Efron, *Stranitsy vospominanii*, p. 36
38 Marina Tsvetayeva, *Selected Poems*, ed and translated Elaine Feinstein 1971, 1981, 1986); *Izbrannye proizvedeniia* (Moscow/Leningrad, 1965) p. 76
39 Marina Tsvetayeva, *Selected Poems*, op cit p. 2; *Izbrannye proizvedenniia*, p. 73
40 'An otherworldly evening', *Tsvetayeva, Selected Prose*, p. 170
41 Marina Tsvetayeva, *Selected Poems*, op cit p. 1; *Izbrannye proizvedenniia*, p. 73
42 See Sophia Poliakova, *The Sunset Days of Yore: Tsvetayeva and Parnok (Zakatni oni dni: Tsvetayeva i Parnok)* (Ann Arbor, 1983)
43 *Marina Tsvetayeva, Selected Poems*, op cit p. 4; *Izbrannye proizvedenniia* p. 74-75
44 *Osip Mandelstam, Selected Poems* ed and trans James Greene (Elek, 1977)
45 Marina Tsvetayeva, *Selected Poems*, op cit p. 5; *Izbrannye proizvedenniia* op. cit. p. 72
46 Nadezhda Mandelstam, *Hope Against Hope* trans Max Hayward, (New York, 1970) p. 460
47 Marina Tsvetayeva, *Selected Poems* p. 11; *Izbrannye proizvedenniia* p. 87
48 Osip Mandelstam, *Sobaniye sochinenyiy* (Washington, New York, 1967-71)
49 Marina Tsvetayeva, *Selected Poems*, op cit p. 25
50 'Letters to Roman Gul', *Noviy Zhurnal* no. 58, 1959

51 'A living word about A Living Man', *Tsvetayeva, Selected Prose*, p. 90
52 'A Tale of Sonyechka', *Russkii Zapiski* III (1938)
53 'A Tale of Sonyechka', p. 39
54 Ibid, unpublished MS., xerox kindly supplied by the University of Basel
55 Ibid unpublished MS
56 Ibid unpublished MS
57 Ibid unpublished MS
58 Ibid unpublished MS
59 *Pisma K Anne Teskavoi*
60 'A Tale of Sonyechka', p. 43
61 'A Tale of Sonyechka', p. 44
62 'A Tale of Sonyechka', p. 52
63 'A Tale of Sonyechka', p. 59
64 'A Tale of Sonyechka', p. 60
65 'A Tale of Sonyechka', p. 61
66 Ibid, unpublished MS
67 Ibid, unpublished MS
68 *Tsvewtayeva, Izbrannye Proza v dvukh tomakh*, Russica Publishers, Inc. New York 1979: 'Dnevniki i zapiski 1917–1920' p. 65
69 Tsvetayeva, 'Dnevniki i zapiski 1917–1920' p. 31
70 Tsvetayeva, 'Dnevniki i zapiski 1917–1920' p. 32
71 Tsvetayeva, *Proza*, p. 132
72 Tsvetayeva, 'Dnevniki i zapiski 1917–1920' p. 52
73 Tsvetayeva, 'Dnevniki i zapiski 1917–1920', p. 83
74 Ariadna Efron, *Stranitsy vospominaniia*
75 Letter from Tsvetayeva to Anastasia, December 1920, *Neizdannye pisma* (Paris, 1972)
76 Pasternak attributes these sentiments to Yuri in *Dr Zhivago*
77 Letter to Anastasia, *December 1920, Neizdannye pisma* (Paris, 1972).
78 Tsvetayeva, 'Geroi Truda', p. 245
79 Tsvetayeva, Lyric 1, 'Poems for Blok', *Selected Poems* p. 18, op. cit. p. 00; *Izbrannye proizvedenniia,*. pp. 74–5
80 Tsvetayeva, Lyric 9 'Poems for Blok' p.23 *Selected Poems*, op. cit. *Izbrannye proizvedenniia*, op. cit., pp. 74–5
81 Ilya Ehrenburg, *People Years Life*, Vol. II (London)
82 Nina Berberova, *The Italics are Mine* (New York, 1969)
84 Tsvetayeva's letter to Akhmatova, 31 August 1921 (O.S.) *Neizdannye pisma* (Paris, 1972)
85 Quoted in Ariadna Efron, *Stranitsy vospominaniia* pp. 86–7.

86 Nadezhda Mandelstam, *Hope Abandoned* (London, 1974) p. 460–461

87 Ariadna Efron, *Stranitsy vospominanii* p. 75.

88 Ariadna Efron, *Stranitsy vospominanii* p. 75.

89 Ariadna Efron, *Stranitsy vospominanii* p. 79.

89 (A) Tsvetayeva, 'A Captive Spirit', *Selected Prose* p. 124

90 Ariadna Efron, *Stranitsy vospominanii* p. 91.

92 'Tsvetayeva 'A Captive Spirit', p. 131.

93 Ariadna Efron, *Stranitsy vospominanii* p. 94.

93(A) Ariadna Efron, *Stranitsy vospominanii* p. 96

94 Letter from Pasternak to Tsvetayeva, 13 June 1922 *Neizdannye pisma (Paris, 1972)*

95 Letter from Tsvetayeva to Pasternak, 29 June 1922 *Neizdannye pisma (Paris, 1972)*.

96 Letter from Tsvetayeva to Pasternak 11 February 1923, *Neizdannye pisma (Paris, 1972)* op. cit.

97 Tsvetayeva 'A Poet on Criticism' from Karlinsky and Appel *The Bitter Air of Exile*

98 *Letter from Tsvetayeva to Pasternak 29 June 1922, Neizdannye pisma (Paris, 1972)* op. cit.

99 Letter from Tsvetayeva to Pasternak 9 March 1923, *Neizdannye pisma (Paris, 1972)*.

99(A) Quoted in Ariadna Efron, *Stranitsy vospominanii* p. 132.

100 Tsvetayeva letter to Pasternak 19 November 1922 – *Neizdannye pisma (Paris, 1972)*.

101 Quoted in Nina Berberova, *The Italics are mine* (New York, 1969)

102 'Praise to the Rich,' Marina Tsvetayeva, *Selected poems*, op cit p. 28; *Izbrannye proizvedenniia* op. cit. p. 87

103 Letters to Alexander Bakhrakh, *Mosty* (Munich, 1960, vol 5; and 1961, vol 6) 20 July 1923

104 Letters to Bakhrakh, 14 July 1923

105 Letters to Bakhrakh, 25 July 1923

106 Letters to Bakhrakh, 25 July 1923

107 Letters to Bakhrakh, 17 August 1923

108 Letters to Bakhrakh, 28 August 1923

108(A) Letters to Bakhrakh, 28 August 1923

109 Letters to Bakhrakh, September 1923

110 Letters to Bakhrakh, 25 September 1923

111 Letters to Bakhrakh, 20 September 1923

112 Letters to Bakhrakh, 29 September 1923

113 Taped interview with Konstantin Rodzevitch in his apartment, 1976

114 'Poem of The Mountain' *Marina Tsvetayeva, Selected poems*, op. cit.; *Izbrannye proizvedenniia*

115 Efron's letter quoted in Ariadna Efron, *Stranitsy vospominanii* p. 167

116 Letters to Bakhrakh, January 1924

117 'Poem of the End' Marina Tsvetayeva, *Selected poems*, op. cit.; *Izbrannye proizvedenniia* op. cit. pp. 451–473

118 Quoted in Ariadna Efron, *Stranitsy vospominaniia* p. 168

119 'Poem of the End' Marina Tsvetayeva, *Selected poems*; *Izbrannye proizvedenniia* op. cit.

120 'Poem of the End' Marina Tsvetayeva, *Selected poems*; *Izbrannye proizvedenniia* op. cit.

121 Tsvetayeva to Boris Pasternak, 1923, *Neizdannye pisma (Paris, 1972)*

122 Letter to Anna Teskova, 5 December 1924, *Pisma K Anne Teskovoi (Prague, 1969)*

123 *Pisma K Anne Teskovoi, February 1925*

124 *Pisma K Anne Teskovoi, p. 10 February 1925*

125 *Pisma K Anne Teskovoi, p. 20 October 1925*

126 *Tsvetayeva to Boris Pasternak 19 July 1925, Neizdannye pisma (Paris, 1972)*

127 *Pisma K Anne Teskovoi, 10 October 1925*

128 *Pisma K Anne Teskovoi, 30 December 1925*

129 See 'The Pied Piper' Marina Tsvetayeva, *Selected poems*, op. cit.; *Izbrannye proizvedenniia* op. cit. p. 7

130 Elena Izvolskaya 'O Tsvetavoi', *Opyty* III (New York, 1954) p. 153

131 *Pisma K Anne Teskovoi, 26 May 1934*

132 *Tsvetayeva 'A Poet on Criticism'* from Karlinsky and Appel, *The Bitter Air of Exile* (University of California Press, 1977)

133 *Pisma K Anne Teskovoi, 8 June 1926*

134 *Tsvetayeva letter to Pasternak*, 10 July 1926, *Neizdannye pisma (Paris, 1972)*

135 Letter of Zinaida Gippius, quoted in Karlinsky, *Cvetayeva, 138 Mayakovsky, quoted in Tsvetyaeva to Pasternak, Neizdannye pisma 21 June 1926*

136 *Rilke, 'Elegy for Marina' written June 8, 1926*

137 *Rilke inscribed this on a copy of his French poems Vergers at the end of June, 1926*

138 Tsvetayeva to Pasternak, *Neizdannye pisma* 21 May 1926 and 29 May 1920

139 Tsvetayeva to Rilke, from *Letters, Summer, 1926* ed Yevgeny

Pasternak, Yelena Pasternak, and Konstantin M. Azadovsky (London, 1986)

140 Tsvetayeva to Pasternak, 1 January 1927 *Neizdannye pisma (Paris, 1972)* op. cit.

141 Tsvetayeva *Pisma K Anne Teskovoi, 21 February 1927*

142 Anastasia Tsvetayeva, *Vospominaniia*, p. 507

143 *Pisma K Anne Teskovoi, 12 December 1927*

144 Pisma K Anne Teskovoi, 3 January, 1928

145 *Marina Tsvetayeva, Selected poems* p. 171; Izbrannye proizvedenniia p. 262–3

146 *Pisma K Anne Teskovoi, February 1928*

147 *Slonim*

148 Letters to Georgy Ivask, *Russki Litersaturnyi archiv* ed Dmtri Chisevsky and Michael Karpovich (New York, 1956) 8 March 1935

149 Marina Tsvetayeva, *Selected poems*, op cit p. 84; *Izbrannye proizvedenniia* op. cit. p. 310–315

150 *Pisma K Anne Teskovoi*, 7 April 1929

151 *Mark Slonim, 'O Marine Tsvetayevoit*

152 *Pisma K Anne Teskavoi 21 April 1930*

153 Marina Tsvetayeva, Selected poems, op cit p. 87; *Izbrannye proizvedenniia* op. cit. p. 297–303

154 Alexander Gladkov, *Meetings with Pasternak* (London 1977)

154 *Pisma K Anne Teskovoi, 22 January 1931*

156 Karlinsky and Appel, op. cit.

157 Slonim, op. cit.

158 *Pisma K Anne Teskovoi, 31 August 1931*

159 *Slonim, op. cit.*

160 *Pisma K Anne Teskovoi, 25 February 1931*

161 *Pisma K Anne Teskovoi, 1 January 1932 t.q.*

162 'A living word about a living man', Tsvetayeva, Selected Prose.

163 *Tsvetayeva, Selected Prose*, op. cit

164 Letters to Ivask, 4 June 1934

165 *Pisma K Anne Teskovoi, 24 November 1933*

166 *Marina Tsvetayeva, Selected poems* p 83; *Izbrannye proizvedenniia.*

167 Marina Tsvetayeva, *Selected poems, op cit* p 81; *Izbrannye proizvedenniia* op. cit.

169 Letters to Ivask, 4 April 1933

171 Ariadna Efron, *Stranitsy vospominaniia* p 17

173 Olga Ivinskaya, *A Captive of Time (London 1978)*

174 *Pisma K Anne Teskovoi, 2 July 1935*

174 *Letter to Boris Pasternak Late October 1935, Novy Mir, N 4, 1969*

176 *Pisma K Anne Teskovoi, 15 February 1936*
177 *'Art in the Light of Conscience' trans Angela Livingstone, and Valentina Coe, in Modern Russian Poets on Poetry (Ardis Press, 1974)*
178 *ibid*
179 *ibid*
180 *Pisma K Anne Teskovoi, 29 May 1936*
181 *Pisma K Anne Teskovoi, 29 March 1936*
182 *Slonim op. cit.*
183 Tsvetayeva to Bunina Tsvetayeva to Bunina, 2 June 1935 Neizdannye pisma
184 Slonim
185 Slonim
186 Pisma K Anne Teskovoi, 24 September 1938. Pisma K Anne Teskovoi, 24 November 1938
   Ibid.
   Ibid.
187 Marina Tsvetayeva, Selected poems, op cit p. 99; *Izbrannye proizvedenniia* op. cit. p. 324–328
188 Marina Tsvetayeva, *Selected poems*, op cit p. 91; *Izbrannye proizvedenniia* op. cit. p. 553–558
189 Slonim op. cit.
190 *Neizdannye pisma (Paris, 1972)* p. 627–628
191 *Pisma K Anne Teskovoi, 12 June 1939*
192 *Neizdannye pisma (Paris, 1972)* p. 629
193 *Neizdannye pisma (Paris, 1972)* p. 630
194 Russian Literary TriQuarterly
195 *Neizdannye pisma (Paris, 1972)* p. 630
196 *Neizdannye pisma (Paris, 1972)* 31 August 1940
197 Marina Tsvetayeva, *Selected poems* p. 26
198 Letter to A A. Mochalova, 29 May 1940. at. *Neizdannye pisma*
199 *Novy Mir, N4 1969*
200 'I Swear', from Elaine Feinstein, Three Russian Poets, (Carcanet, 1976)
201 *Neizdannye pisma (Paris, 1972)* 12 April 1941
202 Ehrenburg, op. cit.
203 Translated from taped reading, Park Parade, Cambridge 1976

Selected Bibliography

In Russian

Ariadna Efron and Anna Saakiants, eds., *Selected Works (Izbrannaye proizvedeniia)*, Moscow-Leningrad, 1965.

Gleb and Nikita Struve, eds., *Tsvetayeva Unpublished Letters, (Neizdannye pisma)*, Paris 1972.

Ariadna Efron and Anna Saakiants, eds., excerpts from letters to various persons, published in *Novy mir,* Moscow, 1969, No. 4.

Marina Tsvetayeva, *Letters to Anna Teskova (Pisma k Anne Teskovoi)*, Prague, 1969.

Letters to Georgy Ivask in *Russian Literary Archives (Russki literaturnyi arkhiv),* Dmitry Chizhevsky and Michael Karpovich, eds., New York, 1956. 'A Tale of Sonyechka,' *Russkiii Zapiski* III (1938).

Letters to Antoly Steiger in *Opyty,* New York, 1955–7, Nos. 5, 7, and 8. Letters to Roman Gul, *Novy Zhurnal* No. 58, 1959.

Letters to Alexander Bakhrakh in *Mosty,* Munich, 1960, Vol. 5 and 1961, Vol. 6.

Ariadna Efron, *Pages from Memoirs (Stranitsy Vospominanii)* Paris, 1979.

Unpublished Works, Poetry, Drama, Prose (Neizdannye. Stikhi, teatr, proza), Paris 1976, (Contains *Juvenilia,* and 'The Tale of Sonyechka'.)

Anastasia Tsvetayeva, *Memoirs (Vospominanii)* Moscow, 1971, 1974 and 1983.

Tsvetayeva, *Proza*, (New York, 1953).

Tsvetayeva, *Izbrannaya Proza v dvuch tomakh*, Russica Publishers, Inc., New York, 1979): 'Dnevniki, zapiski, 1917–1920'.

Tsvetayeva '*Diaries of 1917–1921*', prepared for publication but only published as articles in periodicals.

Mark Slonim, *O Marine Tsvetayevoi, Novy Zhurnal*, No. 1900, 1970; No. 103; 1974.

In English

Tsvetayeva, *Selected Prose*, ed. and trans. Janet King (Ardis, 1980)

Tsvetayeva, *Selected Poems,* ed. and trans. Elaine Feinstein (OUP 1971, 1981 and Century Hutchinson 1986)

Tsvetayeva, *The Demesne of Swans,* trans. by Robin Kemball (Ardis, 1980)

Simon Karlinsky, *Marina Tsvetayeva, Her Life and Art* (Berkely, 1965)

Boris Pasternak, *Safe Conduct*

Andrew Field, *Pages from Trusa* (Boston, 1964)

Nina Berberova, *The Italics are mine* (New York, 1969)

Amanda Halght, *Akhmatova* (O.U.P. 1976)

Nadezhda Mandelstam, *Hope against Hope* (1970) *Hope Abandoned* (1977).

Henry Gifford, *Pasternak: A continued study* (C.U.P., 1977)

Alexander Gladkov, *Conversations with Pasternak*, ed. and trans. Max Hayward (London 1977)

Isaiah Berlin, *Personal Impressions* (London, 1980)

Tsvetayeva: A Pictorial Biography (Ann Arbor, 1980 with an introduction by Carl Proffer)

Olga Ivinskaya, *A Captive of Time* with notes by Max Hayward, (London 1978)

Ronald Hingley, *Nightingale Fever* (London, 1982)

Simon Karlinsky, *The Woman, the World and her Poetry*, (Cambridge, 1985).

Tsvetayeva, 'A downpour of light', trans. Donald Davie & Angela Livingstone

Tsvetayeva, '*Art in the Light of Conscience*', trans. Angela Livingstone and Valentina Coe, in *Modern Russian Poets on Poetry* (Ardis Press, 1974), pp. 147–84.

Nadezhda Mandelstam, *Hope Against Hope* (trans. Max Hayward, New York, 1979).

Tsvetayeva, 'A Poet on Criticism', from Karlinsky & Appel *The Bitter Air of Exile* (University of California Press, 1977).

Letters Summer 1926, ed. Yevgeny Pasternak, Yelena Pasternak, and Konstantin M. Azadovsky (London, 1986).

In French

Marina Tsvetayeva, *Lettre à mon frere feminin*

Lydia Tchoukovskaia, Entretiens avec Anna Akhmatova (Paris, 1980).

INDEX

Compiled by Gordon Robinson

Acmeist movement in Russian poetry, 49
Adamovich, 51
Akhmadulina, Bella, 259
Akhmatova, Anna, 15, 43, 68–9, 106, 125,
    127, 136, 210, 268, 271
  bond of love with Gumilyov, 107
  correspondence with, 108–9
  cycle of poems for her, 107, 120, 252
  loss of Gumilyov, 107, 109
  meeting on return to Moscow, 252–3
  Requiem, 253
  verse, 107
Aksyonov, 108
Aldanov, Mark, 239
Alekseyev, Professor Nikolai, 201
Aliger, Margarita, 17, 18
Anatoli, 106
Andreyevna, Anna [Czech village friend],
    174
Antokolsky, Pavel, 17, 18, 157
  relationship with, 83–4, 232, 258–9
Aragon, Louis, 217
Ardov, Viktor, 253
Aseev, 268–9

Babel, Isaak, 218
Bakhrakh, Alexander,
  correspondence, 147–53, 156
  infatuation, 149
Balmont, Elena, 104, 105
Balmont, Konstantin, 164
  friendship with, 104–5
Barbusse, Henri, 217
Barney, Natalie, Clifford, 223
Bashkirtseva, Maria, 49, 64
Bely, Andrei, 45, 46, 105, 119, 129, 134,
    138, 141, 154

break-up of marriage, 120
death, 211
friendship with, 120–2, 142
memoir of, 120, 211
praise for Marina's work, 120
return to Soviet Union, 155
support of anarchism, 48
Berberova, Nina, 106–7, 194, 203, 239
  relationship with, 144–5
Berlin, sojourn in, 117–37
  Pragerdiehle café, 118, 119, 138, 144, 147
  Russian émigrés in, 118, 135
Bernhardt, Sarah, 44, 61, 64
Blok, Alexander, 125, 142
  admiration for, 101–2
  death, 104
  poems for, 102, 103–4
  'Reverence', 103
  'The Twelve', 103
Bobrov, 109
Bolshevo, stay in, 247
Brecht, Bertolt, 217
Bredelshikova, Anastasia Ivanovna, 269
Brodsky, Josef, homage from, 15
Brussels, 202, 230
Bryusov, Valery, 49, 98
  bitter enemy, 100–1
Bunina, Vera, 212, 226–7
  correspondence, 227, 228, 229
  friendship with, 227–9
Bunin, Ivan, 176, 203
  award of Nobel Prize for Literature, 227

Catholic faith, attitude towards, 37
Chatskina, Sophia, 68
Cheka secret police, 91, 216
Chenier, 255

Chernova, Madama Kolbasina, 173
Chirikova, Liudmila, 118, 124, 174
Christopol, 266, 268, 271
Chukovskaya, Lydia, 268, 271
Churilon, Tikhon,
  Julistan, 66
  poem addressed to him, 66
  relationship with, 66
Clamart, stay at, 173, 178, 208, 209, 210,
  211, 226
Cohen, Hermann, 135
Curie, Eva, 264

Dostoevsky, Fyodor
  The Brothers Karamazov, 240
  Crime and Punishment 7, 168
Doumer, Paul, assassination of, 216
Duncan, Isadora, 113
Dunya, 82, 95

Efron, Ariadna or Alya (daughter), 62, 81,
  85, 86, 91, 93, 97, 104, 105, 109, 111,
  120, 227
  arrest, 248, 270
  arrival in Prague, 138
  birth, 59
  Communist sympathies, 219, 222, 223,
    226
  death, 18, 271
  departure from Moscow, 112–14
  education, 150–1, 164, 188
  given shelter by Pasternak, 270–1
  illnesses, 95, 163, 187–8, 189, 190
  joins Union for the Repatriation of
    Russians Abroad, 214
  letters from mother, 261–5
  life near Prague, 138–40, 143, 163–4, 165
  life with Mulia in Moscow, 247
  loyalty, 94, 139
  memoirs of mother, 15, 62, 64, 65, 68,
    109, 111, 117, 118–19, 122, 123, 143,
    150, 217, 271
  mother's attitude and influence, 62–5, 94,
    122, 163
  neglected by mother, 179, 187
  organizes Efron household, 165
  Paris exile, 170–231
  physical appearance, 100, 164, 186
  release from labour camp, 270
  work on mother's archives, 271
Efron, Elizaveta Petrovna (*née* Durnovo)
    (mother-in-law), 53
  acts of terrorism, 53–5
  death by suicide, 55, 56
  exile, 54, 55
  imprisonment, 54, 55
Efron, Elizaveta (sister-in-law), 250, 257
Efron, Georgy ('Moor') (son)

birth, 165
blames mother for situation, 259, 269
coldness towards mother's memory, 270
education, 226, 228, 251, 154, 255
illnesses, 187–8, 189, 203, 229
killed in battle for Moscow, 18, 270
mother's obsessive love, 166, 167, 168,
  179, 187
physical appearance, 187
relationship with mother deteriorates,
  222–3, 226, 230, 240, 251, 259
sympathy with Communism, 219, 223
Efron, Irina (daughter), 86, 91, 93, 94, 97
  birth, 80
  death in state orphanage, 95–6, 237
  starvation, 95
Efron, Pyotr, 61
Efron, Sergei Yakovlevich or Seryozha
    (husband), 16, 18
  arrest, 248
  arrival in Paris, 174, 175
  arrival in Prague, 109
  becomes Communist, 201, 219, 222, 223
  boyish charm, 57, 59
  change in relationship with wife, 122–3,
    135, 147
  closest years with wife, 58–9, 61
  edits university magazine, 139
  first letter from Prague, 110, 123
  involved in murder, 234, 235–6
  involvement in Eurasian Movement,
    177–8, 187, 188, 197, 201
  involvement with White cause, 80, 82, 84,
    201
  joins Union for the Repatriation of
    Russians Abroad, 214
  letters from wife, 265
  literary ambitions, 58
  loyalty to wife, 219
  marriage, 57
  meets wife, 53, 59, 230
  Pasternak's opinion of him, 218–19
  regrets his White sympathies, 158
  reunited with wife in Berlin, 122–3
  reunited with wife in Czechoslovakia, 138
  separation from his wife, 83
  sets up journal, 157, 186
  studies at Prague University, 109, 123
  shot in Lubianka Prison, 270
  sudden return to Soviet Union, 236–7
  tragic background, 54–5, 56
  tubercular illness, 53, 166–7, 170, 200,
    203, 204, 206, 207, 217, 247
  war service, 62, 67
  wife's love, 56, 61, 74, 75, 81
  wounded by wife's infidelities, 66–7, 68,
    73, 155, 156

Efron, Yakof Constantinovich (father-in-
    law), 53
  acts of terrorism, 53–5
  death, 55
Ehrenburg, Ilya, 98, 113, 123, 127, 128, 138,
    218
  break with, 142, 143, 215, 216
  discovers that Seryozha is alive, 109
  encounter with, 265–6
  First Years of Revolution, 143
  generosity to Marina, 122, 124
  Life and Death of Nicolai Kurbov, 143
  People, Years, Life, 106
  promotes Marina's work, 136
  welcomes Marina to Berlin, 118
Ehrenburg, Lyubov Mikhailovna, 130
Einstein, Albert, 34
Eurasian Movement, 177–8, 186, 188, 191,
    201, 215
  Eurasia magazine, 199, 201
  Mileposts magazine, 178

Fadeyev, A., 250–1, 254
First World War, 62
Freiburg boarding school, 38

Gabriac, Cherubina de, 210
German invasion of Russia, 265, 266
Germany, writings in praise of, 69, 265
Gide, André, 217
Gippius, Zinaida, 203
  Contemporary Notes, 181
  vitriolic critic of Marina, 181
Gladkov, Alexander, 206
Goethe, Johann Wolfgang von, 221
Gogol, Nicolai Vasiliyevich
  Dead Souls, 28
Golitzino, 250–2, 264
Golovina, Alla, 230
Goltsev, Victor, 249, 259
Goncharova, Natalya, friendship with, 200,
    207
Gorgulov, 216
Gorky, Maxim, 34, 39, 186, 187, 188, 227
  refusal to help Marina, 181
Goslitizdat Writers' Union, 265
Gronsky, Nikolai
  friendship with, 196–8
  grief at his death, 211
  arrest, 106
  execution, 107, 109
  liaison with Akhmatova, 107
Gurzuf, pilgrimage to, 52

Halpern, Salomea (formerly Princess
    Andronnikova), 18, 19, 70, 74, 238
  correspondence with, 214
  financial help from, 186, 197, 203, 209

Heine, Heinrich, 29
Holliday, Sonya
  attachment to, 86–9, 223
  death, 232
Horni Mokropsy, life at, 138, 142, 156, 163,
    243
Hugo, Victor
  'Odes to Napoleon', 44

Ilovaisky, Professor D. L., 28–9, 35, 41, 50
Ilovaisky, Nadya, 34, 36
  death, 35
  deep passion for, 35
Ilovaisky, Sergei, 34
  death, 35
  encourages Marina's writing, 29, 34
  Marina's first love, 35
intelligentsia, Communist attacks on, 106–7
Ivask, Georgy, correspondence with, 196,
    211, 215–16
Ivinskaya, Olga, 249, 270
  A Captive in Time, 219
Izvolskaya, Elena, 178, 207
  impressions of Marina, 177

Jakobson, Roman, 144
Jews, attitude towards, 90, 157

Kallin, Anna, 18
Karlinsky, Professor Simon, 14, 111, 122
Kerensky, Alexander, 79
Khardizhyev, Nickkolai, 253
Khodasevich, Vsevelod, 51, 144, 203, 229
Kirillovna nuns, story of, 31–3
Kirov, Sergei, murder of, 217
Klein, R. I., 48
Kobylinsky, Lev or Ellis, 45, 119
  first critic of Marina's work, 45
  involvement in Rumyantsev Museum
    scandal, 47, 48
  proposes marriage to Marina, 45
  support of anarchism, 48
Kogan, P. S., 127
  friendship with, 105
Koktebel, visits to, 52–3, 55, 56–7, 59, 61,
    62, 69, 79, 81, 82, 106, 209, 230
Kondakov, Nikodim, 123
Kosintseva, Liuba, 118
Kotting, Irina, 175
Kropotkin, Peter, 53
Kuzmin, Mikhail Alexeevitch, 69
Kuznetsova, Galina, 227

La Favière, summer at, 229
Lacaze, Madam, 37, 38
Lann, 99
Latest News, émigré paper, 227

publishes poetry of Marina, 198
refuses publication, 199, 211, 212, 224
Lausanne, 235
  boarding school, 37
Lavrushinsky Writers' Home, 266
Lenin, Vladimir Ilyich, 80, 113, 143
Levinson, A., 203
London visit with Mirsky, 178–9
Lunakharsky, 100

Malraux, André, 217, 218, 229–30
Mandelstam, Nadezhda, 73, 111, 252, 253
  Hope Abandoned, 70, 111
Mandelstam, Osip, 15, 18, 30, 79–80, 111
  death, 252
  dislike of Bolsheviks, 80
  poem in *Tristia*, 71–2
  poems for, 70–1, 72–3
  relationship with, 69–73, 149, 153
Mann, Heinrich, 217
Masaryk, Thomas, 124
Mayakovsky, Vladimir, 108, 125, 127, 141, 198
  criticism of, 181–2
  poems to, 204, 206
  relationship with, 198–200
  suicide of, 203–4
Meierhold, Vsevolod Emilevich, 157
Mein, Alexander Damilovich (grandfather), 29–30, 58, 255
Mercurieva, Vera Alexandrovna,
  correspondence with, 254–7
Meudon, stay at, 177, 180 196, 197, 202, 203, 206
Mirkin, 109
Mirsky, D. S. (Prince Svyatapolk-Mirksy), 19, 178, 210–11
  defence of Marina's poetry, 180
  disappearance, 260
  generosity of, 197, 209
  visits London with Marina, 178–9
Mochalova, Olga Alexeyevna, 260
Mogilevski, A., 175
Moscow
  Art Theatre, 83
  author's visits, 17–18
  battle for, 270
  departure from, 113–14
  famine of 1919, 93, 97, 98, 105
  flat in Boris and Gleb Street, 18, 58, 81–2, 86, 93, 97, 111, 143, 187
  house of childhood in the Street of the Three Ponds, 18, 24, 25, 31, 41, 57, 97, 270
  Lubianka Prison, 270
  Museum of Fine Arts, 59, 60, 105–6, 254
  Palace of the Arts, 93, 99, 101, 102, 104

Pasternak's recollections of, 33
Poets' Café, 108
Polytechnic Museum, 102
return to, 247
Rumyantsev Museum, 24, 39, 47–8, 255
Vagankov cemetery, 41
Vakhtangov Studio, 83–4, 157, 232
Vosteryakov House arts and literary group, 51
Writers' House, 106
Writers' Union, 101, 108, 250, 252
Mulia, 247, 264, 265
Munich Agreement, 237

Nabokov, Vladimir
  Speak, Memory, 144
Napoleon II, obsession with, 44, 50
Nappelbaum, Ida, 107
Nazi-Soviet Pact, 260, 265
Nervi, stay at, 35–7
New Literary Newspaper, contribution to, 207–8
Nicholas II, Tsar, 55, 60, 80
  abdication, 79
Nilender, Vladimir
  break-up with, 49
  first romance with, 45–6, 47
  proposes marriage, 45
NKVD, 201, 234, 236
  defections from, 235
Noailles, Countess de
  La Nouvelle Espérance, 68
Northern Notes, 69
  poems published in, 68
Novy Mir, 219

Old Bolsheviks, trials of, 235

Paris
  becomes a celebrity in, 175
  Congress of Writers in Defence of Culture, 217–18
  dislike of, 190
  exile in, 173–243
  Russian *émigrés* between the wars, 19, 173, 175, 177, 178, 181, 191, 195, 198, 199, 203, 204, 207, 208, 215, 229, 236, 237, 239, 247
  study at the Sorbonne, 44
  World's Fair, 232
Pasternak, Boris, 35, 215, 252
  arrival in Berlin, 129
  attacked by Communists, 271
  childhood, 34
  correspondence with, 15, 124–36, 140–3, 163, 164, 167–8, 176, 180, 182, 183–5, 216, 220–2
  Dr Zhivago, 98, 143

exhilarated by February Revolution, 97–8
gives shelter to Alya, 270–1
feeling for Marina, 176
last farewell to Marina, 266
'Lieutenant Schmidt', 180, 181
marriage, 129
meeting in Paris, 217–20
mental disturbance, 216–18
Moscow recollections, 33
mourns Marina's death, 271
My Sister, Life, 97, 131, 141, 142
praise from, 15, 125, 163, 181, 206
restrictions on, 216
reunion with, 248–9
sells books to buy bread, 97
slowly developing genius, 42
Pasternak, Leonid, 33, 34, 129, 195
Pasternak, Rosalya, 33, 129
Pasternak, Yevgenia, [or Zhenya], 129, 176, 218
Pasternak, Yevgeny, 249
Pavlenko, 254
Peredelkino, 250, 266
Parnok, Sophia
erotic involvement with, 66–8, 86, 152, 223
poem to, 67–8
rejected by, 68, 69
Peskova, Ekaterina, 39
Podvaetsky-Chabrov, 112–13, 114
Pontaillac, holiday at, 197
Poretsky, Madame, 234, 235
Potemkin mutiny, 40
Prague
arrival in, 138
Czech-Russian Society, 143
desire to return to, 16
excitement of, 16
exile in, 138–71
German occupation, 237–9
Russian *émigrés*, 144
University, 109, 124
Prokofiev, Sergei, visit from, 209
Proust, Marcel, 220
Pushkin, Alexander, 36, 37, 52, 83
death, 25, 200
Eugene Onegin, 16, 30, 42
'Feast during the Plague', 225, 231
The Gipsies, 28
Pushkin, Goncharova, 25, 200

Razin, Stenka, 79
Reinstein, assassination of, 54
Reiss, Ignace
defection from NKVD, 235
murder of, 234, 235, 236
Riga, 117

Rilke, Rainer Maria, 34, 39
correspondence with, 182–4, 220
death, 184–5, 220–1
Vergers, 182, 185
Rodzevitch, Konstantin, 18, 19, 163, 191, 200, 243–4
author's meeting with, 193–4
love affair with Marina, 152–62, 164, 193–4
marriage, 157, 180, 192–3
Rodzevitch, Moussa, 155, 157, 191, 194
Rostand, Edmond, 49, 100
L'Aiglon, 44; translation of, 44, 45, 61
Rouen, 244
Rubinstein, Nikolai, 24, 29
Rudnev, V. V., 228, 229
Russian Revolution of 1905, 35
Russian Revolution of 1917, 79–83, 86, 97–8, 104, 105, 106

St Blasien sanatorium, 39
St Gilles, summer at, 179–80
St Petersburg or Petrograd
House of the Arts, 106
massacre of the workers, 40
Peter and Paul Fortress, 54
poetry readings in, 68–9
Saker, Jacov, 68
Sand, Georges, 84
Schepkin-Kupernik, 44
Schildbach, Gertrude, 234, 235
Schiller, Johann, 221
Schmidt, Lieutenant Piotr, execution of, 40
Schumann, Robert, 221
Schwartz, Alexander Kiloayevich, 47
Schweitzer, Viktoria, 17
Scriabin, Alexander, 104, 105
Scriabina, Tatiana Fedorovna, 105
funeral of, 125, 126–8
Selected Poems of Marina Tsvetayeva, 17
Shurov, 47, 48
Slonim, Mark, 16, 131, 154, 167, 195, 198, 207, 208, 223, 229, 237u
friendship with, 144
generosity, 209
memoir, 174, 200, 201
parting with, 240–2
Solovev, 46
Sormov, Yevgeny, 261
Stalin, Josef, 215, 216, 217, 218, 219, 224, 252, 270
Steiger, Anatoly
attachment to, 230–1
correspondence with, 230–1
Steiner, Renata, 23
Suvchinsky, Peter, 177–8, 197

Suvchinsky, Vera, 18–19, 70, 178, 179, 193, 194, 197, 235–6, 237

Tarkovsky, Arseny, 258
Tarusa, country home in, 31–3, 34, 44, 271
Tchaikovsky, Peter Ilyich, 34
Teskovà, Anna, 163, 167, 202
  correspondence with, 16, 86, 135, 143, 164–5, 166, 169, 170, 174, 175, 176, 180, 190–1, 195, 198, 200, 204, 207, 208, 211, 217, 219–20, 224, 226, 231
  provides finance, 170
  visits Marina, 166
Thirty Days publishes poem, 257–8
Thurn und Taxus, Furstin von, 38–9
Tolstoy, Leo, 34, 135
  Resurrection, 34
  War and Peace, 43, 91
Traill, Vera, née Guchkova *see* Suvchinsky, Vera
Trotsky, Leon, 136, 143
Trukhachev, Andryusha, 99, 100
Trukhachev, Boris (brother-in-law), 52, 56–7, 61
  death, 98, 99
  marriage, 59
Tshebova, 150
Tsunelli, 175
Tsvetayeva, Anastasia or Asya (sister), 19, 28, 36, 37, 45, 46, 56, 61, 70, 84, 98, 112, 214, 224, 232, 251
  arrest, 248
  friendship with Gorky, 181, 186, 187
  husband's death, 98, 99
  imprisonment in Siberia, 271
  letters from Marina, 98–100
  marriage, 59
  memoir, 188, 271
  physical appearance, 27
  relationship with Marina, 34, 51
  visits Marina in Paris, 186–9
  work at father's museum, 105–6
Tsvetayev, Andrei (half-brother), 24, 28, 29, 33, 35
  becomes ward of Professor Ilovaisky, 41
Tsvetayev, Professor Ivan Vladimirovich (father), 23, 255
  awarded Order of the Guardian of Honour, 59
  death, 60
  dismissed from directorship of Rumyantsev Museum, 47–8
  illness, 57
  love for first wife, 23
  opening of his new Museum of Fine Arts, 59, 60
  parsimony, 33, 60

  relationship with Marina, 39, 44, 60
Tsvetayeva, Maria Alexandrovna (mother), 255
  antagonism to Marina, 30–1
  diary, 4307
  dominant presence, 23
  failing health, 35, 36, 37, 39, 40
  German roots, 29
  jealousy, 24, 31
  last will and testament, 41
  outstanding pianist, 24
  ridicules Marina's first poems, 28
  ruthless training of Marina at the piano, 26–7
  treatment of daughters, 26
Tsvetayeva, Marina
  asceticism of, 211
  belief in poetry, 224–5
  Berlin sojourn, 117–37
  birth of, 25
  Catholic faith, attitude towards, 37
  changed demeanour after return to Moscow, 18, 259
  childhood: adolescent revolutionary fervour, 40, 41; first poems ridiculed by mother, 28; gives up music on death of mother, 41–2; illicit compact with half-sister, 28; mother's dominant presence, 23; ruthless piano training by mother, 26–7; wild adolescence, 50
  death from suicide and funeral, 270
  education: early tuition, 27; expulsion from boarding schook, 43; Freiburg boarding school, 38; Gymnasium No. 4, Moscow, 35; Lausanne boarding school, 37; mother's influence, 23, 27; music school, 27
  essays: 'Art in the Light of Conscience', 225–6, 231; 'A Downpour of Light', 124; 'Letter to an Amazon, 223; 'Mother and Music', 228; My Jobs, 91–2; 'My Pushkin', 231; 'A Poet on Criticism', 133–6; 'Terrestrial Indications', 222
  family relationships: collapse of, 212; daughter Ariadna or Alya: attitude and influence on, 62–5, 94, 122, 163; letters to, 261–5; neglect of, 179, 187; father: 39, 44, 60; husband Sergei or Seryozha: attitude to wife's infidelities, 66–7, 68, 73, 155, 156
  change in relationship, 122–3, 135, 147; closest years, 58–9, 61; correspondence with, 110, 123, 265; love for, 56, 61, 74, 75, 81; loyalty to wife, 219; marriage, 57; meeting with, 53, 59, 230; reunions, 122–3, 138; separation from,

83; mother: antagonism of, 30–1; dominant presence of, 23; pressures to become a pianist, 26–7; ridicules first poems, 28; sense of loss at her death, 43; treatment by, 26; sister Anastasia or Asya: letters to, 98–100; relationship with, 34, 51; visit from in Paris, 186–9; son Georgy or Moor: blames mother for situation, 259, 269; deteriorating relationship, 222–3, 226, 230, 240, 251, 259; obsessive love for, 166, 167, 168, 179, 187

Fascism, horror of, 23207

faults as a mother, 64, 121–2, 179

financial circumstances and poverty, 165–6, 170, 174, 175–6, 186, 194, 203, 204, 207, 208, 209, 227–8

Germany, writings in praise of, 69, 265

homesickness, 99, 196, 213–14, 243

humanity and honesty, 17

illnesses, 188–9, 190, 194, 203, 209, 231

Jews, attitude towards, 90, 157

journal and notes, 40–1, 81, 89–90, 93, 94, 139, 242–3, 247–8, 251, 260

language, passion for playing with, 30

London visit, 178–9

loneliness, inner, 17, 238, 248, 270

love, longing for, 16, 196

love and loyalty for Soviet poets, 16, 65

memoirs, prose of Bely, 120, 211; of Voloshin, 209–10, 211; of Gronsky, 211–12

memoirs, Soviet published, 19

Moscow, years in clerical work, 91–2; departure into exile, 113–14; flat in Boris and Gleb Street, 18, 58, 81–2, 86, 93, 97, 111, 143, 187; forays into countryside for food during famine, 89–91; hardship in, 15, 83, 89–96; return to, 247; readings at arts and literature group, 51; Vakhtangov studio, 83–4, 157, 232

Napoleon II, absorption with life of, 44, 50

New Literary Newspaper, contribution to, 207–8

Northern Notes, poems published in, 68

opposition to Communist regime, 16, 143, 215–16, 224

Paris years: celebrity, 175; dislike of, 190; exile in, 173–243, quarrel with *émigré* community, 181, 198, 199, 203, 204, 207, 208, 215, 229, 236, 237, 238, 239; study at the Sorbonne, 44

physical appearance, 27, 43, 56, 61, 145, 177, 190, 210, 257, 239

poetry: *After Russia*, 191, 194–5; 'An Attempt at Jealousy', 192–3; 'The Bus', 241; Churilon, poem addressed to, 65–6; Czech notebook, poem from, 139; 'Desk', 204–6; 'The Emigrant', 134; Epitaph for Gronsky, 212; *Evening Album*, first book of poems, 45, 49–50, 100; 'Grey Hair', 142; Gumilyov execution poem, 107; 'Homesickness', 213–14; husband, poem for, 74; incestuous love theme, 101; 'Insomnia' sequence, 74; Jews, poem on, 157; *Magic Lantern*, second book of poems; 59; Mandelstam, lyrics for, 70–1, 72–3; 'New Year's Greetings' in honour of Rilke, 184; *Northern Notes*, poems published in, 68, 69; 'On a Red Steed', 120; Parnok, poem for, 67–8; *Parting*, 129; 'A Peasant', 111, 134, 135, 136, 200, 206; *Perekóp*, 203, 207; 'The Pied Piper', 167, 168, 174–5; 'Poem of the End' cycle, 154, 158–62, 176, 180; 'Poem of the Mountain', 154, 155, 158, 180; 'Poems for Blok' cycle, 102, 103–4; 'A Poet on Criticism', 208; 'Praise to the Rich', 144, 146; protest poem against German invasion of Czechoslovakia, 238–40; *Remeslo* book of poems, 128, 136; *Separation*, 120; 'Side Streets', 111; 'Song', 257–8; *Swan's Encampment*, 80, 101, 199; Tsar, poem for the, 79; 'Tsar Maiden,' 101, 105, 120; *Versts*, 120, 124

poetry readings: Brussels, 202, 230; Moscow arts and literature group, Vosteryakov House, 51; Moscow Palace of Arts, 93, 101; Moscow Polytechnic, 103; on her return to Moscow, 259; Paris, 175, 197, 229

poetry wins acceptance by new regime, 110, 164

precocity as a poet, 49

Prague years: excitement of, 16; arrival in, 138; desire to return, 16; exile in, 138–71

shortsightedness, 43, 178

spy suspect, following German invasion of Russia, 265, 266

'Florentine Nights', 124

theatre, passion for, 44, 61, 84

translation, 260, 264; French poetry, 249; Georgian poets, 249, 251; *La Nouvelle Espérance* by Countess de Noailles, 68; *L'Aiglon* by Rostand, 44, 45, 61; Mayakovsky's poems, 199–200; Pushkin's 'Feast in Praise of the Plague', 251

verse plays: *An Adventure*, 87, 174;

Casanova's End, 87; *Fortuna*, 174;
   Phoenix, 174; *Snowstorm*, 87
violence, hatred of organized, 80
Tsvetayeva, Valeria (half-sister), 24, 28, 36,
   227
   leaves home, 41
   protective role of, 31
Tsvetayeva, Varvara Dmitrievna, 23–4
Tuchkov, General, 64
Turgeneva, Asya
   break-up of marriage, 120
   Marina's adoration of, 46–7
   marries Andrei Bely, 47, 119
Turgeneva, Natasha, 46

Union for the Repatriation of Russians
   Abroad, 214, 224, 236
Usman, 89

Versailles visit, 187
Volodya, friendship with, 84–6, 88–9, 232
Vishniak, A. G. (Helikon), 138, 142–3
   passion for, 123
   publishes Marina's work in Berlin,
      118–19, 129

Voloshin, Max, 49, 56, 59, 61–2, 69, 79, 81,
   83, 98, 100, 112, 122, 157, 216
   death, 209
   Marina's memoir of, 81, 209–10, 211
   relationship with, 50–1, 52, 53
Voloshina, Pra, 52, 59, 81, 98
Vshenory, stay at, 167, 169, 170, 174, 175,
   201, 243

Weber, Dr, 39
Weber, Vera, attachment to, 39–40
White Army, 101, 152, 201
Will of Russia, The, 206, 207, 209
   contributions to, 223
Wrangel, Baroness Ludmilla Sergeyevna,
   229

Yalta, stay at, 39–40
Yelabuga, stay at, 17, 266, 268, 269
Yeshov, 232
Yevtushenko, Yevgeny, 17
   homage from, 15
   poem for Tsvetayeva, 266–7
Yurchinova, Madame, 175

Zograf-Plaksina, Madame, music school of,
   27

134279

DATE DUE